STATUTORY INSTRUMENTS

2010 No. 2955 (L.17)

FAMILY PROCEEDINGS

SENIOR COURTS OF ENGLAND AND WALES

COUNTY COURTS, ENGLAND AND WALES

MAGISTRATES' COURTS, ENGLAND AND WALES

The Family Procedure Rules 2010

Made - - - -	*13th December 2010*
Laid before Parliament	*17th December 2010*
Coming into force - -	*6th April 2011*

CONTENTS

PART 1
OVERRIDING OBJECTIVE

PART 2
APPLICATION AND INTERPRETATION OF THE RULES

PART 3

ALTERNATIVE DISPUTE RESOLUTION: THE COURT'S POWERS

PART 4

GENERAL CASE MANAGEMENT POWERS

PART 5

FORMS AND START OF PROCEEDINGS

PART 6

SERVICE

CHAPTER 1

SCOPE OF THIS PART AND INTERPRETATION

CHAPTER 2

SERVICE OF THE APPLICATION FOR A MATRIMONIAL ORDER OR CIVIL PARTNERSHIP ORDER IN THE JURISDICTION

CHAPTER 3
SERVICE OF DOCUMENTS OTHER THAN AN APPLICATION FOR A MATRIMONIAL ORDER OR CIVIL PARTNERSHIP ORDER IN THE UNITED KINGDOM

CHAPTER 4
SERVICE OUT OF THE JURISDICTION

PART 7
PROCEDURE FOR APPLICATIONS IN MATRIMONIAL AND CIVIL PARTNERSHIP PROCEEDINGS
CHAPTER 1
APPLICATION AND INTERPRETATION

CHAPTER 2
RULES ABOUT STARTING AND RESPONDING TO PROCEEDINGS

CHAPTER 3
HOW THE COURT DETERMINES MATRIMONIAL AND CIVIL PARTNERSHIP PROCEEDINGS

CHAPTER 4
COURT ORDERS

PART 8
PROCEDURE FOR MISCELLANEOUS APPLICATIONS
CHAPTER 1
PROCEDURE

CHAPTER 2
APPLICATION FOR CORRECTED GENDER RECOGNITION CERTIFICATE

CHAPTER 3
APPLICATION FOR ALTERATION OF MAINTENANCE AGREEMENT AFTER DEATH OF ONE PARTY

CHAPTER 4
APPLICATION FOR QUESTION AS TO PROPERTY TO BE DECIDED IN SUMMARY WAY

CHAPTER 5
DECLARATIONS

CHAPTER 6
APPLICATION FOR PERMISSION TO APPLY FOR A FINANCIAL REMEDY AFTER OVERSEAS PROCEEDINGS

PART 10
APPLICATIONS UNDER PART 4 OF THE FAMILY LAW ACT 1996

PART 11
APPLICATIONS UNDER PART 4A OF THE FAMILY LAW ACT 1996

PART 12
PROCEEDINGS RELATING TO CHILDREN EXCEPT PARENTAL ORDER PROCEEDINGS AND PROCEEDINGS FOR APPLICATIONS IN ADOPTION, PLACEMENT AND RELATED PROCEEDINGS
CHAPTER 1
INTERPRETATION AND APPLICATION OF THIS PART

CHAPTER 2
GENERAL RULES

CHAPTER 3
SPECIAL PROVISIONS ABOUT PUBLIC LAW PROCEEDINGS

CHAPTER 4
SPECIAL PROVISIONS ABOUT PRIVATE LAW PROCEEDINGS

CHAPTER 5
SPECIAL PROVISIONS ABOUT INHERENT JURISDICTION PROCEEDINGS

CHAPTER 6
PROCEEDINGS UNDER THE 1980 HAGUE CONVENTION, THE EUROPEAN CONVENTION, THE COUNCIL REGULATION, AND THE 1996 HAGUE CONVENTION

SECTION 1
Proceedings under the 1980 Hague Convention or the European Convention

SECTION 2
Applications relating to the Council Regulation and the 1996 Hague Convention

CHAPTER 7
COMMUNICATION OF INFORMATION: PROCEEDINGS RELATING TO CHILDREN

PART 13
PROCEEDINGS UNDER SECTION 54 OF THE HUMAN FERTILISATION AND EMBRYOLOGY ACT 2008

PART 14
PROCEDURE FOR APPLICATIONS IN ADOPTION, PLACEMENT AND RELATED PROCEEDINGS

PART 15
REPRESENTATION OF PROTECTED PARTIES

PART 16
REPRESENTATION OF CHILDREN AND REPORTS IN PROCEEDINGS INVOLVING CHILDREN
CHAPTER 1
APPLICATION OF THIS PART

CHAPTER 2
CHILD AS PARTY IN FAMILY PROCEEDINGS

CHAPTER 3
WHEN A CHILDREN'S GUARDIAN OR LITIGATION FRIEND WILL BE APPOINTED

CHAPTER 4
WHERE A CHILDREN'S GUARDIAN OR LITIGATION FRIEND IS NOT REQUIRED

CHAPTER 5
LITIGATION FRIEND

CHAPTER 6
CHILDREN'S GUARDIAN APPOINTED UNDER RULE 16.3

CHAPTER 7
CHILDREN'S GUARDIAN APPOINTED UNDER RULE 16.4

CHAPTER 8
DUTIES OF SOLICITOR ACTING FOR THE CHILD

CHAPTER 9
REPORTING OFFICER

CHAPTER 10
CHILDREN AND FAMILY REPORTER AND WELFARE OFFICER

CHAPTER 11
PARENTAL ORDER REPORTER

CHAPTER 12
SUPPLEMENTARY APPOINTMENT PROVISIONS

CHAPTER 13
OFFICERS OF THE SERVICE, WELSH FAMILY PROCEEDINGS OFFICERS AND LOCAL AUTHORITY OFFICERS: FURTHER DUTIES

CHAPTER 14
ENFORCEMENT ORDERS AND FINANCIAL COMPENSATION ORDERS: PERSONS NOTIFIED

PART 17
STATEMENTS OF TRUTH

PART 18
PROCEDURE FOR OTHER APPLICATIONS IN PROCEEDINGS

PART 19
ALTERNATIVE PROCEDURE FOR APPLICATIONS

PART 20
INTERIM REMEDIES AND SECURITY FOR COSTS
CHAPTER 1
INTERIM REMEDIES

PART 24

WITNESSES, DEPOSITIONS GENERALLY AND TAKING OF EVIDENCE IN MEMBER STATES OF THE EUROPEAN UNION

CHAPTER 1

WITNESSES AND DEPOSITIONS

CHAPTER 2

TAKING OF EVIDENCE – MEMBER STATES OF THE EUROPEAN UNION

PART 25

EXPERTS AND ASSESSORS

PART 30
APPEALS

PART 31
REGISTRATION OF ORDERS UNDER THE COUNCIL REGULATION, THE CIVIL PARTNERSHIP (JURISDICTION AND RECOGNITION OF JUDGMENTS) REGULATIONS 2005 AND UNDER THE HAGUE CONVENTION 1996

PART 32
REGISTRATION AND ENFORCEMENT OF ORDERS
CHAPTER 1
SCOPE AND INTERPRETATION OF THIS PART

CHAPTER 2
REGISTRATION ETC. OF ORDERS UNDER THE 1950 ACT
SECTION 1
Interpretation of this Chapter

SECTION 2
Registration etc of High Court and county court orders

SECTION 3
Registration etc. of Scottish and Northern Irish orders

CHAPTER 3
REGISTRATION OF MAINTENANCE ORDERS UNDER THE 1958 ACT

CHAPTER 4
REGISTRATION AND ENFORCEMENT OF CUSTODY ORDERS UNDER THE 1986 ACT

PART 33

ENFORCEMENT

CHAPTER 1

GENERAL RULES

SECTION 1

Enforcement of orders for the payment of money

SECTION 2

Committal and injunction

CHAPTER 2

COMMITTAL BY WAY OF JUDGMENT SUMMONS

CHAPTER 3

ATTACHMENT OF EARNINGS

CHAPTER 4

WARRANT OF EXECUTION

PART 34
RECIPROCAL ENFORCEMENT OF MAINTENANCE ORDERS

CHAPTER 1
ENFORCEMENT OF MAINTENANCE ORDERS UNDER THE MAINTENANCE ORDERS (FACILITIES FOR ENFORCEMENT) ACT 1920

CHAPTER 2
ENFORCEMENT OF MAINTENANCE ORDERS UNDER PART 1 OF THE 1972 ACT

SECTION 1
Reciprocal enforcement of maintenance orders under Part 1 of the 1972 Act

PART 35

MEDIATION DIRECTIVE

PART 36

TRANSITIONAL ARRANGEMENTS AND PILOT SCHEMES

36.2. Pilot schemes

GLOSSARY

The Family Procedure Rule Committee makes the following rules in exercise of the powers conferred by sections 75 and 76 of the Courts Act 2003(**a**), section 18(1) of the Maintenance Orders (Reciprocal Enforcement) Act 1972(**b**), sections 12 and 48 of the Civil Jurisdiction and Judgments Act 1982(**c**), sections 10 and 24 of the Child Abduction and Custody Act 1985(**d**), section 97(1) of the Children Act 1989(**e**), section 54(1) of the Access to Justice Act 1999(**f**), sections 52(7), 102, 109(2) and 141(1) and (3) of the Adoption and Children Act 2002(**g**), after consulting in accordance with section 79 of the Courts Act 2003(**h**).

These rules may be cited as the Family Procedure Rules 2010 and shall come into force on 6th April 2011.

PART 1

OVERRIDING OBJECTIVE

The overriding objective

1.1.—(1) These rules are a new procedural code with the overriding objective of enabling the court to deal with cases justly, having regard to any welfare issues involved.

(2) Dealing with a case justly includes, so far as is practicable—

(a) ensuring that it is dealt with expeditiously and fairly;

(b) dealing with the case in ways which are proportionate to the nature, importance and complexity of the issues;

(c) ensuring that the parties are on an equal footing;

(d) saving expense; and

(e) allotting to it an appropriate share of the court's resources, while taking into account the need to allot resources to other cases.

Application by the court of the overriding objective

1.2. The court must seek to give effect to the overriding objective when it—

(**a**) 2003 c.39. Section 75 was amended by section 15(1) and 146 of and paragraphs 308 and 338 of Schedule 4 and Part 2 of Schedule 18 to the Constitutional Reform Act 2005 (c.4). Section 76 was amended by section 12(2) of and paragraph 29 of Schedule 1 to the Constitutional Reform Act 2005 and section 261(1) of and paragraph 172 of Schedule 27 to the Civil Partnership Act 2004 (c.33) and section 62(7) of the Children Act 2004 (c.31) and section 25 of and paragraph 14 of Schedule 3 to the Children, Schools and Families Act 2010 (c.26).
(**b**) 1972 c.18. Section 18 was amended by section 109(1) and paragraphs 155(1),(2)(a) and (3) of Schedule 8 to the Courts Act 2003.
(**c**) 1982 c.27.
(**d**) 1985 c.60.
(**e**) 1989 c.41. Section 97(1) was amended by section 109(1) and paragraphs 337(1) and (2) of Schedule 8 to the Courts Act 2003 and by section 101(3) of the Adoption and Children Act 2002 (c.38).
(**f**) 1999 c.22.
(**g**) 2002 c.38. Section 102 was amended by section 40 of and paragraphs 15, 16(1), (2), (3) and (4) of Schedule 3 to the Children Act 2004. Section 141(1) and (3) were amended by section 109(1) of and paragraph 413(1) and (2) of Schedule 8 to the Courts Act 2003. Sections 102(1) to (4) and(6) to (8) and 141(1) and (3) of the Adoption and Children Act 2002 were applied with modifications for the purposes of parental orders by regulation 2 of and, Schedule 1 to the Human Fertilisation and Embryology Act (Parental Orders) Regulations 2010 (S.I.2010/985).
(**h**) Section 79 was amended by sections 15(1) and 146 of and paragraphs 308 and 341(1) of Schedule 4 and Part 2 of Schedule 18 to the Constitutional Reform Act 2005.

(a) exercises any power given to it by these rules; or

(b) interprets any rule.

Duty of the parties

1.3. The parties are required to help the court to further the overriding objective.

Court's duty to manage cases

1.4.—(1) The court must further the overriding objective by actively managing cases.

(2) Active case management includes—

(a) encouraging the parties to co-operate with each other in the conduct of the proceedings;

(b) identifying at an early stage—

(i) the issues; and

(ii) who should be a party to the proceedings;

(c) deciding promptly—

(i) which issues need full investigation and hearing and which do not; and

(ii) the procedure to be followed in the case;

(d) deciding the order in which issues are to be resolved;

(e) encouraging the parties to use an alternative dispute resolution procedure if the court considers that appropriate and facilitating the use of such procedure;

(f) helping the parties to settle the whole or part of the case;

(g) fixing timetables or otherwise controlling the progress of the case;

(h) considering whether the likely benefits of taking a particular step justify the cost of taking it;

(i) dealing with as many aspects of the case as it can on the same occasion;

(j) dealing with the case without the parties needing to attend at court;

(k) making use of technology; and

(l) giving directions to ensure that the case proceeds quickly and efficiently.

PART 2

APPLICATION AND INTERPRETATION OF THE RULES

Application of these Rules

2.1.—(1) Unless the context otherwise requires, these rules apply to family proceedings in—

(a) the High Court;

(b) a county court; and

(c) a magistrates' court.

(2) Nothing in these rules is to be construed as—

(a) purporting to apply to proceedings in a magistrates' court which are not family proceedings within the meaning of section 65 of the Magistrates' Courts Act 1980(**a**) or

(b) conferring upon a magistrate a function which a magistrate is not permitted by statute to perform.

(**a**) 1980 c.43.

The glossary

2.2.—(1) The glossary at the end of these rules is a guide to the meaning of certain legal expressions used in the rules, but is not to be taken as giving those expressions any meaning in the rules which they do not have in the law generally.

(2) Subject to paragraph (3), words in these rules which are included in the glossary are followed by ^{"GL"}.

(3) The word "service", which appears frequently in the rules, is included in the glossary but is not followed by ^{"GL"}.

Interpretation

2.3.—(1) In these rules—

"the 1973 Act" means the Matrimonial Causes Act 1973(**a**);

"the 1978 Act" means the Domestic Proceedings and Magistrates' Courts Act 1978(**b**);

"the 1980 Hague Convention" means the Convention on the Civil Aspects of International Child Abduction which was signed at The Hague on 25 October 1980;

"the 1984 Act" means the Matrimonial and Family Proceedings Act 1984(**c**);

"the 1986 Act" means the Family Law Act 1986(**d**);

"the 1989 Act" means the Children Act 1989;

"the 1990 Act" means the Human Fertilisation and Embryology Act 1990(**e**);

"the 1991 Act" means the Child Support Act 1991(**f**);

"the 1996 Act" means the Family Law Act 1996(**g**);

"the 1996 Hague Convention" means the Convention on Jurisdiction, Applicable Law, Recognition, Enforcement and Co-Operation in Respect of Parental Responsibility and Measures for the Protection of Children;

"the 2002 Act" means the Adoption and Children Act 2002;

"the 2004 Act" means the Civil Partnership Act 2004;

"the 2005 Act" means the Mental Capacity Act 2005(**h**);

"the 2008 Act" means the Human Fertilisation and Embryology Act 2008(**i**);

"adoption proceedings" means proceedings for an adoption order under the 2002 Act;

"Allocation Order" means any order made by the Lord Chancellor under Part 1 of Schedule 11 to the 1989 Act;

"alternative dispute resolution" means methods of resolving a dispute, including mediation, other than through the normal court process;

"application form" means a document in which the applicant states his intention to seek a court order other than in accordance with the Part 18 procedure;

"application notice" means a document in which the applicant states his intention to seek a court order in accordance with the Part 18 procedure;

"Assembly" means the National Assembly for Wales;

(**a**) 1973 c.18.
(**b**) 1978 c.22.
(**c**) 1984 c.42.
(**d**) 1986 c.55.
(**e**) 1990 c.37.
(**f**) 1991 c.48.
(**g**) 1996 c.27.
(**h**) 2005 c.9.
(**i**) 2008 c.22.

"bank holiday" means a bank holiday under the Banking and Financial Dealings Act 1971(**a**)
—

(a) for the purpose of service of a document within the United Kingdom, in the part of the United Kingdom where service is to take place; and

(b) for all other purposes, in England and Wales.

"business day" means any day other than—

(a) a Saturday, Sunday, Christmas Day or Good Friday; or

(b) a bank holiday;

"care order" has the meaning assigned to it by section 31(11) of the 1989 Act;

"CCR" means the County Court Rules 1981, as they appear in Schedule 2 to the CPR;

"child" means a person under the age of 18 years who is the subject of the proceedings; except that—

(a) in adoption proceedings, it also includes a person who has attained the age of 18 years before the proceedings are concluded; and

(b) in proceedings brought under the Council Regulation, the 1980 Hague Convention or the European Convention, it means a person under the age of 16 years who is the subject of the proceedings;

"child of the family" has the meaning given to it by section 105(1) of the 1989 Act;

"children and family reporter" means an officer of the Service or a Welsh family proceedings officer who has been asked to prepare a welfare report under section 7(1)(a) of the 1989(**b**) Act or section 102(3)(b) of the 2002 Act;

"children's guardian" means—

(a) in relation to a child who is the subject of and a party to specified proceedings or proceedings to which Part 14 applies, the person appointed in accordance with rule 16.3(1); and

(b) in any other case, the person appointed in accordance with rule 16.4;

"civil partnership order" means one of the orders mentioned in section 37 of the 2004 Act;

"civil partnership proceedings" means proceedings for a civil partnership order;

"civil partnership proceedings county court" means a county court so designated by the Lord Chancellor under section 36A of the 1984 Act(**c**);

"civil restraint order" means an order restraining a party—

(a) from making any further applications in current proceedings (a limited civil restraint order);

(b) from making certain applications in specified courts (an extended civil restraint order); or

(c) from making any application in specified courts (a general civil restraint order);

"Commission" means the Child Maintenance and Enforcement Commission;

"consent order" means an order in the terms applied for to which the respondent agrees;

"contact order" has the meaning assigned to it by section 8(1) of the 1989 Act;

"the Council Regulation" means Council Regulation (EC) No 2201/2003 of 27 November 2003 on jurisdiction and the recognition and enforcement of judgments in matrimonial matters and in matters of parental responsibility;

(**a**) 1971 c.80.

(**b**) Section 7(1)(a) was amended by section 74 of and paragraphs 87 and 88(a) of Schedule 7 to the Criminal Justice and Court Services Act 2000 (c.43) and section 40 of and paragraphs 5 and 6 of Schedule 3 to the Children Act 2004.

(**c**) Section 36A was amended by article 2 of and paragraphs 5, 6(1) and (2) of Schedule 1 to the Lord Chancellor (Transfer of Functions and Supplementary Provisions) (No.2) Order 2006 (S.I. 2006/1016).

"court" means, subject to any rule or other enactment which provides otherwise, the High Court, a county court or a magistrates' court;

(rule 2.5 relates to the power to perform functions of the court.)

"court of trial" means—

(a) in proceedings under the 1973 Act, a divorce county court designated by the Lord Chancellor as a court of trial pursuant to section 33(1) of the 1984 Act(**a**); or

(b) in proceedings under the 2004 Act, a civil partnership proceedings county court designated by the Lord Chancellor as a court of trial pursuant to section 36A(1)(b) of the 1984 Act; and

in proceedings under the 1973 Act pending in a divorce county court or proceedings under the 2004 Act pending in a civil partnership proceedings county court, the principal registry is treated as a court of trial having its place of sitting at the Royal Courts of Justice;

"court officer" means—

(a) in the High Court or in a county court, a member of court staff; and

(b) in a magistrates' court, the designated officer;

("designated officer" is defined in section 37(1) of the Courts Act 2003.)

"CPR" means the Civil Procedure Rules 1998;

"deputy" has the meaning given in section 16(2)(b) of the 2005 Act;

"designated county court" means a court designated as—

(a) a divorce county court;

(b) a civil partnership proceedings county court; or

(c) both a divorce county court and a civil partnership proceedings county court;

"detailed assessment proceedings" means the procedure by which the amount of costs is decided in accordance with Part 47 of the CPR;

"directions appointment" means a hearing for directions;

"district judge"—

(a) in relation to proceedings in the High Court, includes a district judge of the principal registry and in relation to proceedings in a county court, includes a district judge of the principal registry when the principal registry is treated as if it were a county court;

(b) in relation to proceedings in a district registry or a county court, means the district judge or one of the district judges of that registry or county court, as the case may be;

"district registry" means—

(a) in proceedings under the 1973 Act, any district registry having a divorce county court within its district;

(b) in proceedings under the 2004 Act, any district registry having a civil partnership proceedings county court within its district; and

(c) in any other case, any district registry having a designated county court within its district;

"divorce county court" means a county court so designated by the Lord Chancellor pursuant to section 33(1) of the 1984 Act, including the principal registry when it is treated as a divorce county court;

"the European Convention" means the European Convention on Recognition and Enforcement of Decisions concerning Custody of Children and on the Restoration of Custody of Children which was signed in Luxembourg on 20 May 1980;

(**a**) Section 33(1) was amended by section 15 of and paragraphs 171 and 172(1) and (2) of Schedule 4 to the Constitutional Reform Act 2005.

"filing", in relation to a document, means delivering it, by post or otherwise, to the court office;

"financial order" means—

(a) an avoidance of disposition order;

(b) an order for maintenance pending suit;

(c) an order for maintenance pending outcome of proceedings;

(d) an order for periodical payments or lump sum provision as mentioned in section 21(1) of the 1973 Act(**a**), except an order under section 27(6) of that Act(**b**);

(e) an order for periodical payments or lump sum provision as mentioned in paragraph 2(1) of Schedule 5 to the 2004 Act, made under Part 1 of Schedule 5 to that Act;

(f) a property adjustment order;

(g) a variation order;

(h) a pension sharing order; or

(i) a pension compensation sharing order;

("variation order", "pension compensation sharing order" and "pension sharing order" are defined in rule 9.3.)

"financial remedy" means—

(a) a financial order;

(b) an order under Schedule 1 to the 1989 Act;

(c) an order under Part 3 of the 1984 Act;

(d) an order under Schedule 7 to the 2004 Act;

(e) an order under section 27 of the 1973 Act;

(f) an order under Part 9 of Schedule 5 to the 2004 Act;

(g) an order under section 35 of the 1973 Act(**c**);

(h) an order under paragraph 69 of Schedule 5 to the 2004 Act;

(i) an order under Part 1 of the 1978 Act;

(j) an order under Schedule 6 to the 2004 Act;

(k) an order under section 10(2) of the 1973 Act(**d**); or

(l) an order under section 48(2) of the 2004 Act;

"hearing" includes a directions appointment;

"hearsay" means a statement made, otherwise than by a person while giving oral evidence in proceedings, which is tendered as evidence of the matters stated, and references to hearsay include hearsay of whatever degree;

"inherent jurisdiction" means the High Court's power to make any order or determine any issue in respect of a child, including in wardship proceedings, where it would be just and equitable to do so unless restricted by legislation or case law;

(Practice Direction 12D (Inherent Jurisdiction (including Wardship Proceedings)) provides examples of inherent jurisdiction proceedings.)

(**a**) Section 21(1) was amended by section 15 of and paragraph 2 of Schedule 2 to the Family Law Act 1996 as amended by the section 84(1) of and paragraphs 64 and 65(1) to (8) of Schedule 12 to the Welfare Reform and Pensions Act 1999 (c.30).
(**b**) Section 27(6) was amended by section 63(3) of the Domestic Proceedings and Magistrates' Courts Act 1978.
(**c**) Section 35 was amended by section 46(1) of and paragraph 13 of Schedule 1 to the Matrimonial and Family Proceedings Act 1984 and section 261(1) of and paragraph 44 of Schedule 27 to the Civil Partnership Act 2004 and section 66(1) of and paragraph 20 of Schedule 8 to the Family Law Act 1996.
(**d**) Section 10(2) has been prospectively repealed with savings by section 66(3) of and Schedule 10 to the Family Law Act 1996.

"judge", in the High Court or a county court, means, unless the context requires otherwise, a judge, district judge or a person authorised to act as such;

"jurisdiction" means, unless the context requires otherwise, England and Wales and any part of the territorial waters of the United Kingdom adjoining England and Wales;

"justices' clerk" has the meaning assigned to it by section 27(1) of the Courts Act 2003(**a**);

"legal representative" means a—

(a) barrister;

(b) solicitor;

(c) solicitor's employee;

(d) manager of a body recognised under section 9 of the Administration of Justice Act 1985(**b**); or

(e) person who, for the purposes of the Legal Services Act 2007(**c**), is an authorised person in relation to an activity which constitutes the conduct of litigation (within the meaning of the Act),

who has been instructed to act for a party in relation to proceedings;

"litigation friend" has the meaning given—

(a) in relation to a protected party, by Part 15; and

(b) in relation to a child, by Part 16;

"matrimonial cause" means proceedings for a matrimonial order;

"matrimonial order" means—

(a) a decree of divorce made under section 1 of the 1973 Act(**d**);

(b) a decree of nullity made on one of the grounds set out in sections 11 or 12 of the 1973 Act(**e**);

(c) a decree of judicial separation made under section 17 of the 1973 Act(**f**);

"note" includes a record made by mechanical means;

"officer of the Service" has the meaning given by section 11(3) of the Criminal Justice and Court Services Act 2000;

"order" includes directions of the court;

"order for maintenance pending outcome of proceedings" means an order under paragraph 38 of Schedule 5 to the 2004 Act;

"order for maintenance pending suit" means an order under section 22 of the 1973 Act(**g**);

"parental order proceedings" has the meaning assigned to it by rule 13.1;

"parental responsibility" has the meaning assigned to it by section 3 of the 1989 Act;

"placement proceedings" means proceedings for the making, varying or revoking of a placement order under the 2002 Act;

"principal registry" means the principal registry of the Family Division of the High Court;

(**a**) Section 27(1) was amended by section 15(1) of and paragraphs 308 and 326(1) and (2) of Schedule 4 to the Constitutional Reform Act 2005.

(**b**) 1985 c.61.

(**c**) 2007 c.29.

(**d**) Section 1 has been prospectively repealed by section 66(3) of and Schedule 10 to the Family Law Act 1996.

(**e**) Section 11 was amended by section 2(4) of the Marriage Act 1983 (c.32) and section 6(4) of the Marriage (Prohibited Degrees of Relationship) Act 1986 (c.16) and section 261(1) of and paragraph 40 of Schedule 27 to the Civil Partnership Act 2004 and section 12 was amended by section 148 of and paragraph 34 of Schedule 4 to the Mental Health Act 1983 (c.20) and sections 4(4) and 11 of and paragraphs 1 and 2 of Schedule 2 and paragraphs 4 and 5 of Schedule 4 to the Gender Recognition Act 2004 (c.7).

(**f**) Section 17 has been prospectively repealed by section 66(3) of and Schedule 10 to the Family Law Act 1996.

(**g**) Section 22 has been prospectively repealed by section 66(3) of and Schedule 10 to the Family Law Act 1996.

"proceedings" means, unless the context requires otherwise, family proceedings as defined in section 75(3) of the Courts Act 2003;

"professional acting in furtherance of the protection of children" includes—

(a) an officer of a local authority exercising child protection functions;

(b) a police officer who is—

(i) exercising powers under section 46 of the Act of 1989; or

(ii) serving in a child protection unit or a paedophile unit of a police force;

(c) any professional person attending a child protection conference or review in relation to a child who is the subject of the proceedings to which the information regarding the proceedings held in private relates; or

(d) an officer of the National Society for the Prevention of Cruelty to Children;

"professional legal adviser" means a—

(a) barrister;

(b) solicitor;

(c) solicitor's employee;

(d) manager of a body recognised under section 9 of the Administration of Justice Act 1985; or

(e) person who, for the purposes of the Legal Services Act 2007, is an authorised person in relation to an activity which constitutes the conduct of litigation (within the meaning of that Act),

who is providing advice to a party but is not instructed to represent that party in the proceedings;

"property adjustment order" means—

(a) in proceedings under the 1973 Act, any of the orders mentioned in section 21(2) of that Act;

(b) in proceedings under the 1984 Act, an order under section 17(1)(a)(ii) of that Act;

(c) in proceedings under Schedule 5 to the 2004 Act, any of the orders mentioned in paragraph 7(1); or

(d) in proceedings under Schedule 7 to the 2004 Act, an order for property adjustment under paragraph 9(2) or (3);

"protected party" means a party, or an intended party, who lacks capacity (within the meaning of the 2005 Act) to conduct proceedings;

"reporting officer" means an officer of the Service or a Welsh family proceedings officer appointed to witness the documents which signify a parent's or guardian's consent to the placing of the child for adoption or to the making of an adoption order or a section 84 order;

"risk assessment" has the meaning assigned to it by section 16A(3) of the 1989 Act;

"Royal Courts of Justice", in relation to matrimonial proceedings pending in a divorce county court or civil partnership proceedings pending in a civil partnership proceedings county court, means such place as may be specified in directions given by the Lord Chancellor pursuant to section 42(2)(a)(**a**) of the 1984 Act;

"RSC" means the Rules of the Supreme Court 1965 as they appear in Schedule 1 to the CPR;

"section 8 order" has the meaning assigned to it by section 8(2) of the 1989 Act;

"section 84 order" means an order made by the High Court under section 84 of the 2002 Act giving parental responsibility prior to adoption abroad;

"section 89 order" means an order made by the High Court under section 89 of the 2002 Act—

(**a**) Section 42(2)(a) was amended by section 15(1) of and paragraphs 171, 174(1) and (2) of Schedule 4 to the Constitutional Reform Act 2005.

(a) annulling a Convention adoption or Convention adoption order;

(b) providing for an overseas adoption or determination under section 91 of the 2002 Act to cease to be valid; or

(c) deciding the extent, if any, to which a determination under section 91 of the 2002 Act has been affected by a subsequent determination under that section;

"Service" has the meaning given by section 11 of the Criminal Justice and Court Services Act 2000;

"the Service Regulation" means Regulation (EC) No. 1393/2007 of the European Parliament and of the Council of 13 November 2007 on the service in the Member States of judicial and extrajudicial documents in civil or commercial matters (service of documents), and repealing Council Regulation (EC) No. 1348/2000, as amended from time to time and as applied by the Agreement made on 19 October 2005 between the European Community and the Kingdom of Denmark on the service of judicial and extrajudicial documents in civil and commercial matters;

"specified proceedings" has the meaning assigned to it by section 41(6) of the 1989 Act and rule 12.27;

"welfare officer" means a person who has been asked to prepare a report under section 7(1)(b) of the 1989 Act(**a**);

"Welsh family proceedings officer" has the meaning given by section 35(4) of the Children Act 2004.

(2) In these rules a reference to —

(a) an application for a matrimonial order or a civil partnership order is to be read as a reference to a petition for—

(i) a matrimonial order;

(ii) a decree of presumption of death and dissolution of marriage made under section 19 of the 1973 Act(**b**); or

(iii) a civil partnership order,

and includes a petition by a respondent asking for such an order;

(b) "financial order" in matrimonial proceedings is to be read as a reference to "ancillary relief";

(c) "matrimonial proceedings" is to be read as a reference to a matrimonial cause or proceedings for an application for a decree of presumption of death and dissolution of marriage made under section 19 of the 1973 Act.

(3) Where these rules apply the CPR, they apply the CPR as amended from time to time.

Modification of rules in application to serial numbers etc.

2.4. If a serial number has been assigned under rule 14.2 or the name or other contact details of a party is not being revealed in accordance with rule 29.1—

(a) any rule requiring any party to serve any document will not apply; and

(b) the court will give directions about serving any document on the other parties.

Power to perform functions conferred on the court by these rules and practice directions

2.5.—(1) Where these rules or a practice direction provide for the court to perform any function then, except where any rule or practice direction, any other enactment or any directions made by

---

(**a**)   Section 7(1)(b) was amended by section 40 of and paragraphs 5 and 6 of Schedule 3 to the Children Act 2004.

(**b**)   Section 19 was amended by section 6(4) and 17(2) of and Schedule 6 to the Domicile and Matrimonial Proceedings Act 1973 (c. 45) and subsection (4) has been prospectively repealed by section 66(1) of and paragraph 7 of Schedule 8 to the Family Law Act 1996.

the President of the Family Division under section 9 of the Courts and Legal Services Act 1990(**a**), provides otherwise, that function may be performed—

(a) in relation to proceedings in the High Court or in a district registry, by any judge or district judge of that Court including a district judge of the principal registry;

(b) in relation to proceedings in a county court, by any judge or district judge including a district judge of the principal registry when the principal registry is treated as if it were a county court; and

(c) in relation to proceedings in a magistrates' court—

(i) by any family proceedings court constituted in accordance with sections 66 and 67 of the Magistrates' Courts Act 1980(**b**); or

(ii) by a single justice of the peace who is a member of the family panel in accordance with Practice Direction 2A.

(The Justices' Clerks Rules 2005 make provision for a justices' clerk or assistant clerk to carry out certain functions of a single justice of the peace.)

(2) A deputy High Court judge and a district judge, including a district judge of the principal registry, may not try a claim for a declaration of incompatibility in accordance with section 4 of the Human Rights Act 1998(**c**).

Powers of the single justice to perform functions under the 1989 Act, the 1996 Act, the 2002 Act and the Childcare Act 2006

2.6.—(1) A single justice who is a member of the family panel may perform the functions of a magistrates' court—

(a) where an application without notice is made under sections 10, 44(1), 48(9), 50(4) and 102(1) of the 1989 Act(**d**);

(b) subject to paragraph (2), under sections 11(3) or 38(1) of the 1989 Act;

(c) under sections 4(3)(b), 4A(3)(b), 4ZA(6)(b), 7, 34(3)(b), 41, 44(9)(b) and (11)(b)(iii), 48(4), 91(15) or (17) or paragraph 11(4) of Schedule 14 of the 1989 Act;

(d) in accordance with the Allocation Order;

(e) where an application without notice is made under section 41(2) of the 2002 Act (recovery orders);

(f) where an application without notice is made for an occupation order or a non molestation order under Part 4 of the 1996 Act; or

(g) where an application is made for a warrant under section 79 of the Childcare Act 2006;

(2) A single justice of the peace may make an order under section 11(3) or 38(1) of the 1989 Act where—

(a) a previous such order has been made in the same proceedings;

(b) the terms of the order sought are the same as those of the last such order made; and

(c) a written request for such an order has been made and —

(**a**) 1990 c.41. Section 9 was amended by section 15(1) of and paragraphs 211 and 213 of Schedule 4 to the Constitutional Reform Act 2005.

(**b**) Section 66 was substituted by section 78(2) of and paragraphs 26 and 27 of Schedule 11 to the Access to Justice Act 1999 (c.22) and section 109(1) of and paragraphs 215 of Schedule 8 to the Courts Act 2003. Section 67 was substituted by section 49(1) of the Courts Act 2003 and amended by section 15(1) of and paragraphs 99, 101(1), (2), (3), (4) and (5) of the Constitutional Reform Act 2005.

(**c**) 1998 c.42. Section 4 was amended by section 40(4) of and paragraphs 66(1) and (2) of Schedule 9 to the Constitutional Reform Act 2005 and section 378(1) of and paragraph 156 of Schedule 16 to the Armed Forces Act 2006 (c.52) and section 67(1) of and paragraph 43 of Schedule 6 to the Mental Capacity Act 2005.

(**d**) Section 10 was amended by section 139(1) of and paragraphs 54 and 56(a) (b) and (c) of Schedule 3 to the Adoption and Children Act 2002 and section 77 of the Civil Partnership Act 2004 and section 36 of the Children and Young Persons Act 2008 (c. 23).

(i) the other parties and any children's guardian consent to the request and they or their legal representatives have signed the request; or

(ii) at least one of the other parties and any children's guardian consent to the request and they or their legal representatives have signed the request, and the remaining parties have not indicated that they either consent to or oppose the making of the order.

(3) The proceedings referred to in paragraph (1)(a), (c) and (d) are proceedings which are prescribed for the purposes of section 93(2)(i) of the 1989 Act.

Single justice's power to refer to a magistrates' court

2.7. Where a single justice —

(a) is performing the function of a magistrates' court in accordance with rules 2.5(1)(c)(ii) and 2.6(1) and (2); and

(b) considers, for whatever reason, that it is inappropriate to perform the function,

the single justice must refer the matter to a magistrates' court which may perform the function.

Court's discretion as to where it deals with cases

2.8. The court may deal with a case at any place that it considers appropriate.

Computation of time

2.9.—(1) This rule shows how to calculate any period of time for doing any act which is specified—

(a) by these rules;

(b) by a practice direction; or

(c) by a direction or order of the court.

(2) A period of time expressed as a number of days must be computed as clear days.

(3) In this rule "clear days" means that in computing the numbers of days—

(a) the day on which the period begins; and

(b) if the end of the period is defined by reference to an event, the day on which that event occurs,

are not included.

(4) Where the specified period is 7 days or less and includes a day which is not a business day, that day does not count.

(5) When the period specified—

(a) by these rules or a practice direction; or

(b) by any direction or order of the court,

for doing any act at the court office ends on a day on which the office is closed, that act will be in time if done on the next day on which the court office is open.

Dates for compliance to be calendar dates and to include time of day

2.10.—(1) Where the court makes an order or gives a direction which imposes a time limit for doing any act, the last date for compliance must, wherever practicable—

(a) be expressed as a calendar date; and

(b) include the time of day by which the act must be done.

(2) Where the date by which an act must be done is inserted in any document, the date must, wherever practicable, be expressed as a calendar date.

(3) Where "month" occurs in any order, direction or other document, it means a calendar month.

PART 3

ALTERNATIVE DISPUTE RESOLUTION: THE COURT'S POWERS

Scope of this Part

3.1.—(1) This Part contains the court's powers to encourage the parties to use alternative dispute resolution and to facilitate its use.

(2) The powers in this Part are subject to any powers given to the court by any other rule or practice direction or by any other enactment or any powers it may otherwise have.

Court's duty to consider alternative dispute resolution

3.2. The court must consider, at every stage in proceedings, whether alternative dispute resolution is appropriate.

When the court will adjourn proceedings or a hearing in proceedings

3.3.—(1) If the court considers that alternative dispute resolution is appropriate, the court may direct that the proceedings, or a hearing in the proceedings, be adjourned for such specified period as it considers appropriate—

(a) to enable the parties to obtain information and advice about alternative dispute resolution; and

(b) where the parties agree, to enable alternative dispute resolution to take place.

(2) The court may give directions under this rule on an application or of its own initiative.

(3) Where the court directs an adjournment under this rule, it will give directions about the timing and method by which the parties must tell the court if any of the issues in the proceedings have been resolved.

(4) If the parties do not tell the court if any of the issues have been resolved as directed under paragraph (3), the court will give such directions as to the management of the case as it considers appropriate.

(5) The court or court officer will—

(a) record the making of an order under this rule; and

(b) arrange for a copy of the order to be served as soon as practicable on the parties.

(6) Where the court proposes to exercise its powers of its own initiative, the procedure set out in rule 4.3(2) to (6) applies.

(By rule 4.1(7), any direction given under this rule may be varied or revoked.)

PART 4

GENERAL CASE MANAGEMENT POWERS

The court's general powers of management

4.1.—(1) In this Part, "statement of case" means the whole or part of, an application form or answer.

(2) The list of powers in this rule is in addition to any powers given to the court by any other rule or practice direction or by any other enactment or any powers it may otherwise have.

(3) Except where these rules provide otherwise, the court may—

(a) extend or shorten the time for compliance with any rule, practice direction or court order (even if an application for extension is made after the time for compliance has expired);

(b) make such order for disclosure and inspection, including specific disclosure of documents, as it thinks fit;

(c) adjourn or bring forward a hearing;

(d) require a party or a party's legal representative to attend the court;

(e) hold a hearing and receive evidence by telephone or by using any other method of direct oral communication;

(f) direct that part of any proceedings be dealt with as separate proceedings;

(g) stay^(GL) the whole or part of any proceedings or judgment either generally or until a specified date or event;

(h) consolidate proceedings;

(i) hear two or more applications on the same occasion;

(j) direct a separate hearing of any issue;

(k) decide the order in which issues are to be heard;

(l) exclude an issue from consideration;

(m) dismiss or give a decision on an application after a decision on a preliminary issue;

(n) direct any party to file and serve an estimate of costs; and

(o) take any other step or make any other order for the purpose of managing the case and furthering the overriding objective.

(Rule 21.1 explains what is meant by disclosure and inspection.)

(4) When the court makes an order, it may—

(a) make it subject to conditions, including a condition to pay a sum of money into court; and

(b) specify the consequence of failure to comply with the order or a condition.

(5) Where the court gives directions it will take into account whether or not a party has complied with any relevant pre-action protocol^(GL).

(6) A power of the court under these rules to make an order includes a power to vary or revoke the order.

(7) Any provision in these rules—

(a) requiring or permitting directions to be given by the court is to be taken as including provision for such directions to be varied or revoked; and

(b) requiring or permitting a date to be set is to be taken as including provision for that date to be changed or cancelled.

(8) The court may not extend the period within which a section 89 order must be made.

Court officer's power to refer to the court

4.2. Where a step is to be taken by a court officer—

(a) the court officer may consult the court before taking that step;

(b) the step may be taken by the court instead of the court officer.

Court's power to make order of its own initiative

4.3.—(1) Except where an enactment provides otherwise, the court may exercise its powers on an application or of its own initiative.

(Part 18 sets out the procedure for making an application.)

(2) Where the court proposes to make an order of its own initiative—

(a) it may give any person likely to be affected by the order an opportunity to make representations; and

(b) where it does so it must specify the time by and the manner in which the representations must be made.

(3) Where the court proposes—

(a) to make an order of its own initiative; and

(b) to hold a hearing to decide whether to make the order,

it must give each party likely to be affected by the order at least 5 days' notice of the hearing.

(4) The court may make an order of its own initiative without hearing the parties or giving them an opportunity to make representations.

(5) Where the court has made an order under paragraph (4)—

(a) a party affected by the order may apply to have it set aside$^{(GL)}$, varied or stayed$^{(GL)}$; and

(b) the order must contain a statement of the right to make such an application.

(6) An application under paragraph (5)(a) must be made—

(a) within such period as may be specified by the court; or

(b) if the court does not specify a period, within 7 days beginning with the date on which the order was served on the party making the application.

(7) If the High Court or a county court of its own initiative strikes out a statement of case or dismisses an application (including an application for permission to appeal) and it considers that the application is totally without merit—

(a) the court's order must record that fact; and

(b) the court must at the same time consider whether it is appropriate to make a civil restraint order.

Power to strike out a statement of case

4.4.—(1) Except in proceedings to which Parts 12 to 14 apply, the court may strike out$^{(GL)}$ a statement of case if it appears to the court—

(a) that the statement of case discloses no reasonable grounds for bringing or defending the application;

(b) that the statement of case is an abuse of the court's process or is otherwise likely to obstruct the just disposal of the proceedings;

(c) that there has been a failure to comply with a rule, practice direction or court order; or

(d) in relation to applications for matrimonial and civil partnership orders and answers to such applications, that the parties to the proceedings consent.

(2) When the court strikes out a statement of case it may make any consequential order it considers appropriate.

(3) Where—

(a) the court has struck out an applicant's statement of case;

(b) the applicant has been ordered to pay costs to the respondent; and

(c) before paying those costs, the applicant starts another application against the same respondent, arising out of facts which are the same or substantially the same as those relating to the application in which the statement of case was struck out,

the court may, on the application of the respondent, stay$^{(GL)}$ that other application until the costs of the first application have been paid.

(4) Paragraph (1) does not limit any other power of the court to strike out $^{(GL)}$ a statement of case.

(5) If the High Court or a county court strikes out an applicant's statement of case and it considers that the application is totally without merit—

(a) the court's order must record that fact; and

(b) the court must at the same time consider whether it is appropriate to make a civil restraint order.

Sanctions have effect unless defaulting party obtains relief

4.5.—(1) Where a party has failed to comply with a rule, practice direction or court order, any sanction for failure to comply imposed by the rule, practice direction or court order has effect unless the party in default applies for and obtains relief from the sanction.

(Rule 4.6 sets out the circumstances which the court may consider on an application to grant relief from a sanction.)

(2) Where the sanction is the payment of costs, the party in default may only obtain relief by appealing against the order for costs.

(3) Where a rule, practice direction or court order—

(a) requires a party to do something within a specified time; and

(b) specifies the consequence of failure to comply,

the time for doing the act in question may not be extended by agreement between the parties.

Relief from sanctions

4.6.—(1) On an application for relief from any sanction imposed for a failure to comply with any rule, practice direction or court order the court will consider all the circumstances including—

(a) the interests of the administration of justice;

(b) whether the application for relief has been made promptly;

(c) whether the failure to comply was intentional;

(d) whether there is a good explanation for the failure;

(e) the extent to which the party in default has complied with other rules, practice directions, court orders and any relevant pre-action protocol$^{(GL)}$;

(f) whether the failure to comply was caused by the party or the party's legal representative;

(g) whether the hearing date or the likely hearing date can still be met if relief is granted;

(h) the effect which the failure to comply had on each party; and

(i) the effect which the granting of relief would have on each party or a child whose interest the court considers relevant.

(2) An application for relief must be supported by evidence.

General power of the court to rectify matters where there has been an error of procedure

4.7. Where there has been an error of procedure such as a failure to comply with a rule or practice direction—

(a) the error does not invalidate any step taken in the proceedings unless the court so orders; and

(b) the court may make an order to remedy the error.

Power of the court to make civil restraint orders

4.8. Practice Direction 4B sets out—

(a) the circumstances in which the High Court or a county court has the power to make a civil restraint order against a party to proceedings;

(b) the procedure where a party applies for a civil restraint order against another party; and

(c) the consequences of the court making a civil restraint order.

PART 5

FORMS AND START OF PROCEEDINGS

Forms

5.1.—(1) Subject to rule 14.10(2) and (3), the forms referred to in a practice direction, shall be used in the cases to which they apply.

(2) A form may be varied by the court or a party if the variation is required by the circumstances of a particular case.

(3) A form must not be varied so as to leave out any information or guidance which the form gives to the recipient.

(4) Where these rules require a form to be sent by the court or by a party for another party to use, it must be sent without any variation except such as is required by the circumstances of the particular case.

Documents to be attached to a form

5.2. Subject to any rule or practice direction, unless the court directs otherwise, a form must have attached to it any documents which, in the form, are—

    (a) stated to be required; or

    (b) referred to.

Proceedings are started by issue of application form

5.3.—(1) Proceedings are started when a court officer issues an application at the request of the applicant.

(2) An application is issued on the date entered in the application form by the court officer.

(Rule 29.7 requires an application form to be authenticated with the stamp of the court when it is issued)

PART 6

SERVICE

CHAPTER 1

SCOPE OF THIS PART AND INTERPRETATION

Part 6 rules about service apply generally

6.1. This Part applies to the service of documents, except where—

    (a) another Part, any other enactment or a practice direction makes a different provision; or

    (b) the court directs otherwise.

Interpretation

6.2. In this Part "solicitor" includes any person who, for the purposes of the Legal Services Act 2007, is an authorised person in relation to an activity which constitutes the conduct of litigation (within the meaning of that Act).

CHAPTER 2

SERVICE OF THE APPLICATION FOR A MATRIMONIAL ORDER OR CIVIL PARTNERSHIP ORDER IN THE JURISDICTION

Interpretation

6.3. In this Chapter, unless the context otherwise requires, a reference to an application—

(a) is a reference to an application for a matrimonial or civil partnership order; and

(b) includes an application by a respondent as referred to in rule 7.4.

(Part 7 deals with applications in matrimonial or civil partnership proceedings.)

Methods of service

6.4. An application may be served by any of the following methods—

(a) personal service in accordance with rule 6.7;

(b) first class post, or other service which provides for delivery on the next business day, in accordance with Practice Direction 6A; or

(c) where rule 6.11 applies, document exchange.

Who is to serve the application

6.5.—(1) Subject to the provisions of this rule, an application may be served by—

(a) the applicant; or

(b) a court officer, if so requested by the applicant.

(2) A court officer will not serve the application if the party to be served is a child or protected party.

(3) An application must not be served personally by the applicant himself or herself.

(Rule 6.14 deals with service of the application on children and protected parties.)

Every respondent to be served

6.6. The application must be served on every respondent.

Personal service

6.7. An application is served personally on a respondent by leaving it with that respondent.

Service of application by the court

6.8.—(1) Where the application is to be served by a court officer, the applicant must give the court officer an address at which the respondent is to be served in accordance with rule 6.4.

(2) Where the court officer has sent a notification of failure of service to the applicant in accordance with rule 6.21, the applicant may request the court officer to serve the document on the respondent at an alternative address.

Service by the bailiff

6.9.—(1) An applicant may request that an application be served by a bailiff delivering a copy of the application to the respondent personally.

(2) The request must be made in accordance with Practice Direction 6A.

(3) Where the bailiff is unable to serve the application, the applicant may apply to the court for an order under rule 6.19 (service by an alternative method or at an alternative place).

(Practice Direction 6A contains provision about when a request under this rule is appropriate.)

(Rule 6.22 provides for notice of non-service by a bailiff.)

Where to serve the application – general provisions

6.10.—(1) The application must be served within the jurisdiction except as provided for by Chapter 4 of this Part (service out of the jurisdiction).

(2) The applicant must include in the application an address at which the respondent may be served.

(3) Paragraph (2) does not apply where an order made by the court under rule 6.19 (service by an alternative method or at an alternative place) specifies the place or method of service of the application.

Service of the application on a solicitor within the jurisdiction or in any EEA state

6.11.—(1) Where a solicitor acting for the respondent has notified the applicant in writing that the solicitor is instructed by the respondent to accept service of the application on behalf of the respondent at a business address within the jurisdiction, the application must be served at the business address of that solicitor.

(2) Subject to the provisions of Chapter 4 of this Part, where a solicitor acting for the respondent has notified the applicant in writing that the solicitor is instructed by the respondent to accept service of the application on behalf of the respondent at a business address within any EEA state, the application must be served at the business address of that solicitor.

("Solicitor" has the extended meaning set out in rule 6.2 and "EEA state" is defined in Schedule 1 to the Interpretation Act 1978(**a**).)

Service of the application where the respondent gives an address at which the respondent may be served

6.12. Subject to rule 6.13, the respondent may be served with the application at an address within the jurisdiction which the respondent has given for the purpose of being served with the proceedings.

Service of the application where the respondent does not give an address at which the respondent may be served

6.13.—(1) This rule applies where—

    (a) rule 6.11 (service of application on solicitor); and

    (b) rule 6.12 (respondent gives address at which respondent may be served),

do not apply and the applicant does not wish the application to be served personally under rule 6.7.

(2) Subject to paragraphs (3) to (5) the application must be served on the respondent at his usual or last known address.

(3) Where the applicant has reason to believe that the respondent no longer resides at his usual or last known address, the applicant must take reasonable steps to ascertain the current address of the respondent.

(4) Where, having taken the reasonable steps required by paragraph (3), the applicant—

    (a) ascertains the respondent's current address, the application must be served at that address; or

    (b) is unable to ascertain the respondent's current address, the applicant must consider whether there is—

(**a**) 1978 c.30.

> (i) an alternative place where; or
>
> (ii) an alternative method by which,
>
> service may be effected.

(5) If, under paragraph (4)(b), there is such a place where or a method by which service could be effected, the applicant must make an application under rule 6.19.

Service of the application on children and protected parties

6.14.—(1) Where the respondent is a child, the application form must be served on—

> (a) one of the child's parents or guardians; or
>
> (b) if there is no parent or guardian, an adult with whom the child resides or in whose care the child is.

(2) Where the respondent is a protected party, the application must be served on—

> (a) one of the following persons with authority in relation to the protected party—
>
> > (i) the attorney under a registered enduring power of attorney;
> >
> > (ii) the donee of a lasting power of attorney; or
> >
> > (iii) the deputy appointed by the Court of Protection; or
>
> (b) if there is no such person, an adult with whom the protected party resides or in whose care the protected party is.

(3) Any reference in this Chapter to a respondent or party to be served includes the person to be served with the application form on behalf of a child or protected party under paragraph (1) or (2).

(4) The court may make an order permitting an application form to be served on a child or protected party, or on a person other than the person specified in paragraph (1) or (2).

(5) An application for an order under paragraph (4) may be made without notice.

(6) The court may order that, although an application form has been sent or given to someone other than the person specified in paragraph (1) or (2), it is to be treated as if it had been properly served.

(7) Where a document is served in accordance with this rule—

> (a) it must be endorsed with the notice set out in Practice Direction 6A; and
>
> (b) the person commencing the proceedings must file a witness statement by the person on whom the application form was served stating whether—
>
> > (i) the contents of the application form; or
> >
> > (ii) the purpose and intention of the application,

were communicated to the child or protected party and, if not, why not.

(8) Paragraph (7)(b) does not apply where the Official Solicitor is, as the case may be—

> (a) the litigation friend of the protected party; or
>
> (b) the litigation friend or children's guardian of the child.

Deemed service – receipt of acknowledgment of service

6.15.—(1) Subject to paragraph (2), an application is deemed to be served if the acknowledgment of service, signed by the party served or the solicitor acting on that party's behalf, is returned to the court office.

(2) Where the signature on the acknowledgment of service purports to be that of the other party to the marriage or civil partnership, the applicant must prove that it is the signature of that party by—

> (a) giving oral evidence to that effect at the hearing; or
>
> (b) if the application is undefended, confirming it to be so in the affidavit the applicant files under rule 7.19(4).

Deemed service by post or alternative service where no acknowledgment of service filed

6.16.—(1) Subject to paragraph (2), if—

    (a) an application has been served on a respondent by post or other service which provides for delivery on the next business day;

    (b) no acknowledgment of service has been returned to the court office; and

    (c) the court is satisfied that the respondent has received the application,

the district judge may direct that the application is deemed to be served.

(2) Where—

    (a) the application alleges 2 years' separation and the respondent consents to a matrimonial or civil partnership order being granted; and

    (b) none of the other facts mentioned in section 1(2) of the 1973 Act(**a**) or section 44(5) of the 2004 Act, as the case may be, is alleged,

paragraph (1) applies only if—

    (i) the court is satisfied that the respondent has received notice of the proceedings; and

    (ii) the applicant produces a written statement, signed by the respondent, containing the respondent's consent to the grant of an order.

Proof of personal service where no acknowledgment of service filed

6.17.—(1) This rule applies where—

    (a) an application has been served on a respondent personally; and

    (b) no acknowledgment of service has been returned to the court office.

(2) The person serving the application must file a certificate of service stating the date and time of personal service.

(Practice Direction 6A makes provision for a certificate of service by a bailiff.)

(3) If the respondent served was the other party to the marriage or civil partnership, the certificate of service must show the means by which the person serving the application knows the identity of the party served.

Proof of service by the court etc.

6.18.—(1) Where a court officer serves an application by post, or other service which provides for delivery on the next business day, the court officer must note in the court records the date of—

    (a) posting; or

    (b) leaving with, delivering to or collection by the relevant service provider.

(2) A record made in accordance with paragraph (1) is evidence of the facts stated in it.

(3) This rule does not affect the operation of section 133 of the County Courts Act 1984(**b**).

(Section 133 of the County Courts Act 1984 provides that where a summons or other process issued from a county court is served by an officer of a court, service may be proved by a certificate in a prescribed form.)

(**a**)   Section 1(2) has been prospectively repealed by section 66(3) of and Schedule 10 to the Family Law Act 1996.

(**b**)   Section 133 of the County Courts Act 1984 (c.28) was amended by the Civil Procedure (Modification of Enactments) Order 1998 (S.I.1998/2940).

Service of the application by an alternative method or at an alternative place

6.19.—(1) Where it appears to the court that there is a good reason to authorise service by a method or at a place not otherwise permitted by this Part, the court may direct that service is effected by an alternative method or at an alternative place.

(2) On an application under this rule, the court may direct that steps already taken to bring the application form to the attention of the respondent by an alternative method or at an alternative place is good service.

(3) A direction under this rule must specify—

    (a) the method or place of service;

    (b) the date on which the application form is deemed served; and

    (c) the period for filing an acknowledgment of service or answer.

Power of the court to dispense with service of the application

6.20.—(1) The court may dispense with service of the application where it is impracticable to serve the application by any method provided for by this Part.

(2) An application for an order to dispense with service may be made at any time and must be supported by evidence.

(3) The court may require the applicant to attend when it decides the application.

Notification of failure of service by the court

6.21. Where—

    (a) the court serves the application by post or other service which provides for delivery on the next business day; and

    (b) the application is returned to the court,

the court will send notification to the applicant that the application has been returned.

Notice of non-service by bailiff

6.22. Where—

    (a) the bailiff is to serve an application; and

    (b) the bailiff is unable to serve it on the respondent,

the court officer will send notification to the applicant.

CHAPTER 3

SERVICE OF DOCUMENTS OTHER THAN AN APPLICATION FOR A MATRIMONIAL ORDER OR CIVIL PARTNERSHIP ORDER IN THE UNITED KINGDOM

Method of service

6.23. A document may be served by any of the following methods—

    (a) personal service, in accordance with rule 6.25;

    (b) first class post, document exchange or other service which provides for delivery on the next business day, in accordance with Practice Direction 6A;

    (c) leaving it at a place specified in rule 6.26; or

    (d) fax or other means of electronic communication in accordance with Practice Direction 6A.

(Rule 6.35 provides for the court to permit service by an alternative method or at an alternative place.)

Who is to serve

6.24.—(1) A party to proceedings will serve a document which that party has prepared, or which the court has prepared or issued on behalf of that party, except where—

(a) a rule or practice direction provides that the court will serve the document; or

(b) the court directs otherwise.

(2) Where a court officer is to serve a document, it is for the court to decide which method of service is to be used.

(3) Where the court officer is to serve a document prepared by a party, that party must provide a copy for the court and for each party to be served.

Personal service

6.25.—(1) Where required by another Part, any other enactment, a practice direction or a court order, a document must be served personally.

(2) In other cases, a document may be served personally except where the party to be served has given an address for service under rule 6.26(2)(a).

(3) A document is served personally on an individual by leaving it with that individual.

Address for service

6.26.—(1) A party to proceedings must give an address at which that party may be served with documents relating to those proceedings.

(2) Subject to paragraph (4), a party's address for service must be—

(a) the business address either within the United Kingdom or any other EEA state of a solicitor acting for the party to be served; or

(b) where there is no solicitor acting for the party to be served, an address within the United Kingdom at which the party resides or carries on business.

("EEA state" is defined in Schedule 1 to the Interpretation Act 1978.)

(3) Where there is no solicitor acting for the party to be served and the party does not have an address within the United Kingdom at which that party resides or carries on business, the party must, subject to paragraph (4), give an address for service within the United Kingdom.

(4) A party who—

(a) has been served with an application for a matrimonial or civil partnership order outside the United Kingdom; and

(b) apart from acknowledging service of the application, does not take part in the proceedings,

need not give an address for service within the United Kingdom.

(5) Any document to be served in proceedings must be sent, or transmitted to, or left at, the party's address for service unless it is to be served personally or the court orders otherwise.

(6) Where, in accordance with Practice Direction 6A, a party indicates or is deemed to have indicated that they will accept service by fax, the fax number given by that party must be at the address for service.

(7) Where a party indicates in accordance with Practice Direction 6A, that they will accept service by electronic means other than fax, the e-mail address or electronic identification given by that party will be deemed to be at the address for service.

(8) This rule does not apply where an order made by the court under rule 6.35 (service by an alternative method or at an alternative place) specifies where a document may be served.

Change of address for service

6.27. Where the address for service of a party changes, that party must give notice in writing of the change, as soon as it has taken place, to the court and every other party.

Service of an application form commencing proceedings on children and protected parties

6.28.—(1) This rule applies to the service of an application form commencing proceedings other than an application for a matrimonial or civil partnership order.

(2) An application form commencing proceedings which would otherwise be served on a child or protected party must be served—

    (a) where the respondent is a child, in accordance with rule 6.14(1); and

    (b) where the respondent is a protected party, in accordance with rule 6.14(2).

Service of other documents on or by children and protected parties where a litigation friend has been or will be appointed

6.29.—(1) This rule applies to—

    (a) a protected party; or

    (b) a child to whom the provisions of rule 16.5 and Chapter 5 of Part 16 apply (litigation friends).

(2) An application for an order appointing a litigation friend where a protected party or child has no litigation friend must be served in accordance with rule 15.8 or rule 16.13 as the case may be.

(3) Any other document which would otherwise be served on or by a child or protected party must be served on or by the litigation friend conducting the proceedings on behalf of the child or protected party.

Service on or by children where a children's guardian has been or will be appointed under rule 16.4

6.30.—(1) This rule applies to a child to whom the provisions of rule 16.4 and Chapter 7 apply.

(2) An application for an order appointing a children's guardian where a child has no children's guardian must be served in accordance with rule 16.26.

(3) Any other document which would otherwise be served on or by a child must be served on or by the children's guardian conducting the proceedings on behalf of the child.

Service on or by children where a children's guardian has been appointed under rule 16.3

6.31.—(1) This rule applies where a children's guardian has been appointed for a child in accordance with rule 16.3.

(2) Any document which would otherwise be served on the child must be served on—

    (a) the solicitor appointed by the court in accordance with section 41(3) of the 1989 Act; and

    (b) the children's guardian.

(3) Any document which would otherwise be served by the child must be served by—

    (a) the solicitor appointed by the court in accordance with section 41(3) of the 1989 Act or by the children's guardian; or

    (b) if no solicitor has been appointed as mentioned in paragraph (a), the children's guardian.

Supplementary provisions relating to service on children and protected parties

6.32.—(1) The court may direct that a document be served on a protected party or child or on some person other than a person upon whom it would be served under rules 6.28 to 6.31 above.

(2) The court may direct that, although a document has been sent or given to someone other than a person upon whom it should be served under rules 6.28 to 6.31 above, the document is to be treated as if it had been properly served.

(3) This rule and rules 6.28 to 6.31 do not apply where the court has made an order under rule 16.6 allowing a child to conduct proceedings without a children's guardian or litigation friend.

Supplementary provision relating to service on children

6.33.—(1) This rule applies to proceedings to which Part 12 applies.

(2) Where a rule requires—

    (a) a document to be served on a party;

    (b) a party to be notified of any matter; or

    (c) a party to be supplied with a copy of a document,

in addition to the persons to be served in accordance with rules 6.28 to 6.32, the persons or bodies mentioned in paragraph (3) must be served, notified or supplied with a copy of a document, as applicable, unless the court directs otherwise.

(3) The persons or bodies referred to in paragraph (2) are—

    (a) such of the following who are appointed in the proceedings—

        (i) the children's guardian (if the children's guardian is not otherwise to be served);

        (ii) the welfare officer;

        (iii) the children and family reporter;

        (iv) the officer of the Service, Welsh family proceedings officer or local authority officer acting under a duty referred to in rule 16.38; and

    (b) a local authority preparing a report under section 14A(8) or (9) of the 1989 Act.

Deemed service

6.34. A document, other than an application for a matrimonial or civil partnership order, served in accordance with these rules or a practice direction is deemed to be served on the day shown in the following table—

Method of service	Deemed day of service
First class post (or other service which provides for delivery on the next business day)	The second day after it was posted, left with, delivered to or collected by the relevant service provider, provided that day is a business day; or, if not, the next business day after that day.
Document exchange	The second day after it was left with, delivered to or collected by the relevant service provider, provided that day is a business day; or, if not, the next business day after that day.
Delivering the document to or leaving it at a permitted address.	If it is delivered to or left at the permitted address on a business day before 4.30p.m., on that day; or in any other case, on the next business day after that day.
Fax.	If the transmission of the fax is completed on a business day before 4.30p.m., on that day; or, in any other case, the next business day after the day on which it was transmitted.
Other electronic method.	If the e-mail or other electronic transmission is sent on a business day before 4.30p.m., on that day; or in any other case, on the next business day after the day on which it was sent.
Personal service	If the document is served personally before 4.30p.m. on a

	business day, on that day; or, in any other case, on the next business day after that day.

(Practice Direction 6A contains examples of how the date of deemed service is calculated.)

Service by an alternative method or at an alternative place

6.35. Rule 6.19 applies to any document in proceedings as it applies to an application for a matrimonial or civil partnership order and reference to the respondent in that rule is modified accordingly.

Power to dispense with service

6.36. The court may dispense with the service of any document which is to be served in proceedings.

Certificate of service

6.37.—(1) Where a rule, practice direction or court order requires a certificate of service, the certificate must state the details set out in the following table—

Method of service	Details to be certified
Personal service.	Date and time of personal service and method of identifying the person served.
First class post, document exchange or other service which provides for delivery on the next business day.	Date of posting, leaving with, delivering to or collection by the relevant service provider.
Delivery of document to or leaving it at a permitted place.	Date and time when the document was delivered to or left at the permitted place.
Fax.	Date and time of completion of transmission.
Other electronic method	Date and time of sending the email or other electronic transmission.
Alternative method or place permitted by court	As required by the court.

(2) An applicant who is required to file a certificate of service of an application form must do so at or before the earlier of—

(a) the first directions appointment in; or

(b) the hearing of,

the proceedings unless a rule or practice direction provides otherwise.

(Rule 17.2 requires a certificate of service to contain a statement of truth.)

Notification of outcome of service by the court

6.38. Where—

(a) a document to be served by a court officer is served by post or other service which provides for delivery on the next working day; and

(b) the document is returned to the court,

the court officer will send notification to the party who requested service that the document has been returned.

Notification of non-service by bailiff

6.39. Where—

(a) the bailiff is to serve a document; and

(b)   the bailiff is unable to serve it,

the court officer must send notification to the party who requested service.

CHAPTER 4

SERVICE OUT OF THE JURISDICTION

Scope and interpretation

6.40.—(1) This Chapter contains rules about—

(a)   service of application forms and other documents out of the jurisdiction; and

(b)   the procedure for service.

("Jurisdiction" is defined in rule 2.3.)

(2) In this Chapter—

"application form" includes an application notice;

"Commonwealth State" means a State listed in Schedule 3 to the British Nationality Act 1981(**a**); and

"the Hague Convention" means the Convention on the service abroad of judicial and extra-judicial documents in civil or commercial matters signed at the Hague on November 15, 1965.

Permission to serve not required

6.41. Any document to be served for the purposes of these rules may be served out of the jurisdiction without the permission of the court.

Period for acknowledging service or responding to application where application is served out of the jurisdiction

6.42.—(1) This rule applies where, under these rules, a party is required to file—

(a)   an acknowledgment of service; or

(b)   an answer to an application,

and sets out the time period for doing so where the application is served out of the jurisdiction.

(2) Where the applicant serves an application on a respondent in—

(a)   Scotland or Northern Ireland; or

(b)   a Member State or Hague Convention country within Europe,

the period for filing an acknowledgment of service or an answer to an application is 21 days after service of the application.

(3) Where the applicant serves an application on a respondent in a Hague Convention country outside Europe, the period for filing an acknowledgment of service or an answer to an application is 31 days after service of the application.

(4) Where the applicant serves an application on a respondent in a country not referred to in paragraphs (2) and (3), the period for filing an acknowledgment of service or an answer to an application is set out in Practice Direction 6B.

Method of service – general provisions

6.43.—(1) This rule contains general provisions about the method of service of an application for a matrimonial or civil partnership order, or other document, on a party out of the jurisdiction.

Where service is to be effected on a party in Scotland or Northern Ireland

---

(**a**)   1981 c.61.

(2) Where a party serves an application form or other document on a party in Scotland or Northern Ireland, it must be served by a method permitted by Chapter 2 (and references to "jurisdiction" in that Chapter are modified accordingly) or Chapter 3 of this Part and rule 6.26(5) applies.

Where service is to be effected on a respondent out of the United Kingdom

(3) Where the applicant wishes to serve an application form, or other document, on a respondent out of the United Kingdom, it may be served by any method—

    (a) provided for by—

        (i) rule 6.44 (service in accordance with the Service Regulation);

        (ii) rule 6.45 (service through foreign governments, judicial authorities and British Consular authorities); or

    (b) permitted by the law of the country in which it is to be served.

(4) Nothing in paragraph (3) or in any court order authorises or requires any person to do anything which is contrary to the law of the country where the application form, or other document, is to be served.

Service in accordance with the Service Regulation

6.44.—(1) This rule applies where the applicant wishes to serve the application form, or other document, in accordance with the Service Regulation.

(2) The applicant must file—

    (a) the application form or other document;

    (b) any translation; and

    (c) any other documents required by the Service Regulation.

(3) When the applicant files the documents referred to in paragraph (2), the court officer will—

    (a) seal$^{(GL)}$, or otherwise authenticate with the stamp of the court, the copy of the application form; and

    (b) forward the documents to the Senior Master of the Queen's Bench Division.

(The Service Regulation is annexed to Practice Direction 6B.)

(Article 20(1) of the Service Regulation provides that the Regulation prevails over other provisions contained in any other agreement or arrangement concluded by Member States.)

Service through foreign governments, judicial authorities and British Consular authorities

6.45.—(1) Where the applicant wishes to serve an application form, or other document, on a respondent in any country which is a party to the Hague Convention, it may be served—

    (a) through the authority designated under the Hague Convention in respect of that country; or

    (b) if the law of that country permits—

        (i) through the judicial authorities of that country; or

        (ii) through a British Consular authority in that country.

(2) Where the applicant wishes to serve an application form, or other document, on a respondent in any country which is not a party to the Hague Convention, it may be served, if the law of that country so permits—

    (a) through the government of that country, where that government is willing to serve it; or

    (b) through a British Consular authority in that country.

(3) Where the applicant wishes to serve an application form, or other document, in—

    (a) any Commonwealth State which is not a party to the Hague Convention;

    (b) the Isle of Man or the Channel Islands; or

(c) any British Overseas Territory,

the methods of service permitted by paragraphs (1)(b) and (2) are not available and the applicant or the applicant's agent must effect service on a respondent in accordance with rule 6.43 unless Practice Direction 6B provides otherwise.

(4) This rule does not apply where service is to be effected in accordance with the Service Regulation.

(A list of British overseas territories is reproduced in Practice Direction 6B.)

Procedure where service is to be through foreign governments, judicial authorities and British Consular authorities

6.46.—(1) This rule applies where the applicant wishes to serve an application form, or other document, under rule 6.45(1) or (2).

(2) Where this rule applies, the applicant must file—

(a) a request for service of the application form, or other document, by specifying one or more of the methods in rule6.45(1) or (2);

(b) a copy of the application form or other document;

(c) any other documents or copies of documents required by Practice Direction 6B; and

(d) any translation required under rule 6.47.

(3) When the applicant files the documents specified in paragraph (2), the court officer will—

(a) seal$^{(GL)}$, or otherwise authenticate with the stamp of the court, the copy of the application form or other document; and

(b) forward the documents to the Senior Master of the Queen's Bench Division.

(4) The Senior Master will send documents forwarded under this rule—

(a) where the application form, or other document, is being served through the authority designated under the Hague Convention, to that authority; or

(b) in any other case, to the Foreign and Commonwealth Office with a request that it arranges for the application form or other document to be served.

(5) An official certificate which—

(a) states that the method requested under paragraph (2)(a) has been performed and the date of such performance;

(b) states, where more than one method is requested under paragraph (2)(a), which method was used; and

(c) is made by—

(i) a British Consular authority in the country where the method requested under paragraph (2)(a) was performed;

(ii) the government or judicial authorities in that country; or

(iii) the authority designated in respect of that country under the Hague Convention,

is evidence of the facts stated in the certificate.

(6) A document purporting to be an official certificate under paragraph (5) is to be treated as such a certificate, unless it is proved not to be.

Translation of application form or other document

6.47.—(1) Except where paragraphs (4) and (5) apply, every copy of the application form, or other document, filed under rule 6.45 (service through foreign governments, judicial authorities and British Consular authorities) must be accompanied by a translation of the application form or other document.

(2) The translation must be—

(a) in the official language of the country in which it is to be served; or

(b) if there is more than one official language of that country, in any official language which is appropriate to the place in the country where the application form or other document is to be served.

(3) Every translation filed under this rule must be accompanied by a statement by the person making it that it is a correct translation, and the statement must include that person's name, address and qualifications for making the translation.

(4) The applicant is not required to file a translation of the application form, or other document, filed under rule 6.45 where it is to be served in a country of which English is an official language.

(5) The applicant is not required to file a translation of the application form or other document filed under rule 6.45 where—

(a) the person on whom the document is to be served is able to read and understand English; and

(b) service of the document is to be effected directly on that person.

(This rule does not apply to service in accordance with the Service Regulation which contains its own provisions about the translation of documents.)

Undertaking to be responsible for expenses of the Foreign and Commonwealth Office

6.48. Every request for service filed under rule 6.46 (procedure where service is to be through foreign governments, judicial authorities etc.) must contain an undertaking by the person making the request—

(a) to be responsible for all expenses incurred by the Foreign and Commonwealth Office or foreign judicial authority; and

(b) to pay those expenses to the Foreign and Commonwealth Office or foreign judicial authority on being informed of the amount.

PART 7

PROCEDURE FOR APPLICATIONS IN MATRIMONIAL AND CIVIL PARTNERSHIP PROCEEDINGS

CHAPTER 1

APPLICATION AND INTERPRETATION

Application and interpretation

7.1.—(1) The rules in this Part apply to matrimonial and civil partnership proceedings.

(2) The rules in this Part do not apply to magistrates' courts.

(3) In this Part—

"defended case" means matrimonial proceedings or civil partnership proceedings in which—

(a) an answer has been filed opposing the grant of a matrimonial or civil partnership order on the application, and has not been struck out; or

(b) the respondent has filed an application for a matrimonial or civil partnership order in accordance with rule 7.14 and neither party's application has been disposed of; or

(c) rule 7.12(11) applies, notice has been given of intention to rebut and that notice has not been withdrawn,

and in which no matrimonial or civil partnership order has been made; and

"undefended case" means matrimonial proceedings or civil partnership proceedings other than a defended case.

(4) In this Part—

    (a) a reference to a conditional order is a reference to a civil partnership order (other than a separation order) which has not been made final; and

    (b) a reference to a final order is a reference to a conditional order which has been made final.

District Registries

7.2. A reference in this Part to a registry for a place at which sittings of the High Court in matrimonial or civil partnership proceedings are authorised is a reference—

    (a) to the district registry for that place;

    (b) where the place has no district registry, such district registry as the Lord Chancellor may designate for the purpose; or

    (c) if the place is not situated within the district of any district registry, the principal registry.

Principal Registry

7.3.—(1) A provision of this Part which refers to—

    (a) proceedings being started or heard in a divorce county court or a civil partnership proceedings county court; or

    (b) the transfer of proceedings to or from such a court,

includes a reference to the principal registry when treated as such a court.

(2) Proceedings to which this Part applies which were started in the principal registry or have been transferred to it as if it were a county court are treated as pending—

    (a) if the proceedings are matrimonial proceedings, in a divorce county court; and

    (b) if the proceedings are civil partnership proceedings, in a civil partnership proceedings county court.

References to respondents

7.4.—(1) Where a respondent makes an application for a matrimonial order or a civil partnership order, unless the context otherwise requires, the rules in this Part shall apply with necessary modifications as if the reference to a respondent is a reference to the applicant in the other party's application for a matrimonial order or a civil partnership order.

(2) Where a respondent makes an application for a matrimonial order, unless the context otherwise requires, the rules in this Part shall apply with necessary modifications as if the reference to a co-respondent is a reference to a party cited in the respondent's application for a matrimonial order.

CHAPTER 2

RULES ABOUT STARTING AND RESPONDING TO PROCEEDINGS

Starting proceedings

7.5.—(1) Matrimonial proceedings may be started in any divorce county court.

(2) Civil partnership proceedings may be started in any civil partnership proceedings county court.

Statement of reconciliation

7.6. Where the applicant is legally represented, the legal representative must, unless the court directs otherwise, complete and file with the application a statement in the form for this purpose referred to in Practice Direction 5A, certifying whether the legal representative has discussed with the applicant the possibility of a reconciliation and given the applicant the names and addresses of persons qualified to help effect a reconciliation.

Limitation on applications in respect of same marriage or civil partnership

7.7.—(1) Subject to paragraph (2), a person may not make more than one application for a matrimonial or civil partnership order in respect of the same marriage or civil partnership unless—

(a) the first application has been dismissed or finally determined; or

(b) the court gives permission.

(2) Where a person—

(a) has, within one year of the date of the marriage or civil partnership, made an application for, as the case may be, a decree of judicial separation or an order for separation; and

(b) then, after that one-year period has passed, wishes to apply for a decree of divorce or a dissolution order on the same facts as those mentioned in the first application,

that person does not need the court's permission to make the application referred to in sub-paragraph (b).

Service of application

7.8.—(1) After an application for a matrimonial or civil partnership order has been issued by the court, a copy of it must be served on the respondent and on any co-respondent.

(Rule 6.5 provides for who may serve an application for a matrimonial or civil partnership order.)

(2) When the application is served on a respondent it must be accompanied by—

(a) a form for acknowledging service;

(b) a notice of proceedings; and

(c) where applicable, a copy of the statement of arrangements for children.

Withdrawal of application before service

7.9. An application for a matrimonial or civil partnership order may be withdrawn at any time before it has been served by giving notice in writing to the court where the proceedings were started.

Who the parties are

7.10.—(1) The parties to matrimonial proceedings or civil partnership proceedings are—

(a) the parties to the marriage or civil partnership concerned; and

(b) any other person who is to be a party in accordance with a provision of the rules in this Part.

(2) Subject to paragraph (3), where an application for a matrimonial order or an answer to such an application alleges that the other party to the marriage has committed adultery with a named person, that named person is to be the co-respondent.

(3) The named person referred to in paragraph (2) is not to be a co-respondent where—

(a) the court so directs;

(b) that person has died; or

(c) unless the court directs otherwise—

(i) that person is under 16 years of age; or

(ii) the other party to the marriage is alleged in the application or answer to have committed rape on the named person.

(4) Where an application for a matrimonial or civil partnership order or an answer alleges that the other party to the marriage or civil partnership has had an improper association with a named person, the court may direct that the named person is to be a party to the application, unless the named person has died.

(5) An application for directions under paragraph (3)(a) or (c) may be made without notice if the acknowledgment of service indicates that no party intends to defend the case.

Nullity: Interim and full gender recognition certificates

7.11.—(1) Where the application is for—

(a) nullity of marriage under section 12(g) of, or paragraph 11(1)(e) of Schedule 1 to, the 1973 Act(**a**); or

(b) an order of nullity of civil partnership under section 50(1)(d) of the 2004 Act,

the court officer must send to the Secretary of State a notice in writing that the application has been made.

(2) Where a copy of an interim gender recognition certificate has been filed with the application, that certificate must be attached to the notice.

(3) Where no copy of an interim gender recognition certificate has been filed the notice must also state—

(a) in matrimonial proceedings—

(i) the names of the parties to the marriage and the date and place of the marriage, and

(ii) the last address at which the parties to the marriage lived together as husband and wife;

(b) in civil partnership proceedings—

(i) the names of the parties to the civil partnership and the date on, and the place at which, the civil partnership was formed, and

(ii) the last address at which the parties to the civil partnership lived together as civil partners of each other; and

(c) in either case, such further particulars as the court officer considers appropriate.

(4) Where—

(a) the application is for a decree of nullity of marriage under section 12(h) of the 1973 Act(**b**) or for an order of nullity of civil partnership under section 50(1)(e) of the 2004 Act; and

(b) a full gender recognition certificate has been issued to the respondent,

the applicant must file a copy of that full certificate with the application unless the court, on an application made without notice, directs otherwise.

What the respondent and co-respondent should do on receiving the application

7.12.—(1) The respondent, and any co-respondent, must file an acknowledgment of service within 7 days beginning with the date on which the application for a matrimonial or civil partnership order was served.

(2) This rule is subject to rule 6.42 (which specifies how the period for filing an acknowledgment of service is calculated where the application is served out of the jurisdiction).

(3) The acknowledgment of service must—

(**a**) Section 12(g) was inserted by section 4(4) of and paragraph 2 of Schedule 2 to the Gender Recognition Act 2004.

(**b**) Section 12(h) was inserted by section 11 of and paragraphs 4 and 5 of Schedule 4 to the Gender Recognition Act 2004.

(a) subject to paragraph (4), be signed by the respondent or the respondent's legal representative or, as the case may be, the co respondent or the co respondent's legal representative;

(b) include the respondent's or, as the case may be, the co respondent's address for service; and

(c) where it is filed by the respondent, indicate whether or not the respondent intends to defend the case.

(4) Where paragraph (5) or (6) applies, the respondent must sign the acknowledgment of service personally.

(5) This paragraph applies where—

(a) the application for a matrimonial order alleges that the respondent has committed adultery; and

(b) the respondent admits the adultery.

(6) This paragraph applies where—

(a) the application for a matrimonial or civil partnership order alleges that the parties to the marriage or civil partnership concerned have been separated for more than 2 years; and

(b) the respondent consents to the making of the matrimonial or civil partnership order.

(7) Where the respondent does not agree with the proposals set out in the applicant's statement of arrangements for children, the respondent may file a statement of arrangements for children under section 41(1) of the 1973(a) Act or section 63(1) of the 2004 Act.

(8) A respondent who wishes to defend the case must file and serve an answer within 21 days beginning with the date by which the acknowledgment of service is required to be filed.

(9) An answer is not required where the respondent does not object to the making of the matrimonial or civil partnership order but objects to paying the costs of the application or to the applicant's statement of arrangements for children.

(10) A respondent may file an answer even if the intention to do so was not indicated in the acknowledgment of service.

(11) Where the application is for nullity of marriage under section 12(d) of the 1973 Act or for nullity of civil partnership under section 50(1)(b) of the 2004 Act and the respondent files an answer containing no more than a simple denial of the facts stated in the application, the respondent must, if intending to rebut the matters stated in the application, give notice to the court of that intention when filing the answer.

(12) A respondent to an application for a matrimonial or civil partnership order alleging 2 years' separation and the respondent's consent may—

(a) indicate consent to the making of the matrimonial or civil partnership order in writing at any time after service of the application, whether in the acknowledgment of service or otherwise;

(b) indicate lack of consent to the making of that order, or withdraw any such consent already given, by giving notice to the court.

(13) Where a respondent gives a notice under paragraph (12)(b) and no other relevant fact is alleged, the proceedings must be stayed(GL), and notice of the stay(GL) given to the parties by the court officer.

(14) In this rule, a "relevant fact" is—

(a) in matrimonial proceedings, one of the facts mentioned in section (1)(2) of the 1973 Act; and

(b) in civil partnership proceedings, one of the facts mentioned in section 44(5) of the 2004 Act.

(a)   Section 41(1) has been prospectively repealed by section 66(3) of and Schedule 10 to the Family Law Act 1996.

(The form of the answer is referred to in Practice Direction 5A.)

Amendments to the application and the answer

7.13.—(1) Unless paragraph (2) applies—

(a) a party making an application for a matrimonial or civil partnership order may amend the application at any time before an answer to it has been filed;

(b) a party who has filed an answer may amend the answer.

(2) No amendment to an application for a matrimonial or civil partnership order or to an answer may be made under paragraph (1) if an application under rule 7.19(1) has been made in relation to the marriage or civil partnership concerned.

(3) Where an amendment is made under paragraph (1)—

(a) if the document amended is the application—

(i) it must be served in accordance with rule 7.8 (service of application); and

(ii) rule 7.12 (what the respondent and co respondent should do) applies;

(b) rule 7.10 (parties) applies; and

(c) any person who becomes a co-respondent to the proceedings in accordance with rule 7.10 as a consequence of such an amendment must be served with the documents required to be served on a co-respondent with an application for a matrimonial or civil partnership order.

(4) Paragraphs (1) and (2) do not apply if the amendment is made—

(a) with the written consent of all the other parties; or

(b) with the permission of the court.

(5) Where the court gives permission for a party to amend that party's application for a matrimonial or civil partnership order or answer it may give directions as to—

(a) the service of the amended application or answer and any accompanying documents;

(b) the joining of any additional parties in accordance with rule 7.10; and

(c) the extent to which rule 7.12 must be complied with in respect of any amended application.

(6) The court may direct that any person cease to be a party if, in consequence of any amendment made under this rule, that person—

(a) no longer falls within rule 7.10(2) or (4); or

(b) falls within rule 7.10(4) but it is no longer desirable for that person to be a party to the proceedings.

How the respondent can make an application

7.14.—(1) A respondent who wishes to make an application for a matrimonial or civil partnership order must make the application for that order within 21 days beginning with the date by which the respondent's acknowledgment of service is required to be filed, unless the court gives permission to make the application after that time has passed.

(2) Where the respondent makes an application under this rule, that application is to be treated as an application in the same proceedings for the purposes of this Part.

Further information about the contents of the application and the answer

7.15.—(1) The court may at any time order a party—

(a) to clarify any matter which is in dispute in the proceedings; or

(b) to give additional information in relation to any such matter, whether or not the matter is contained or referred to in the application for a matrimonial or civil partnership order or in the answer.

(2) Paragraph (1) is subject to any rule of law to the contrary.

(3) Where the court makes an order under paragraph (1), the party against whom it is made must—

(a) file the reply to the order made under paragraph (1); and

(b) serve a copy of it on each of the other parties,

within the time specified by the court.

(4) The court may direct that information provided by a party to another party (whether given voluntarily or following an order made under paragraph (1)) must not be used for any purpose except for the proceedings in which it is given.

CHAPTER 3

HOW THE COURT DETERMINES MATRIMONIAL AND CIVIL PARTNERSHIP PROCEEDINGS

General rule – hearing to be in public

7.16.—(1) The general rule is that a hearing to which this Part applies is to be in public.

(2) The requirement for a hearing to be in public does not require the court to make special arrangements for accommodating members of the public.

(3) A hearing, or any part of it, may be in private if—

(a) publicity would defeat the object of the hearing;

(b) it involves matters relating to national security;

(c) it involves confidential information (including information relating to personal financial matters) and publicity would damage that confidentiality;

(d) a private hearing is necessary to protect the interests of any child or protected party;

(e) it is a hearing of an application made without notice and it would be unjust to any respondent for there to be a public hearing; or

(f) the court considers this to be necessary, in the interests of justice.

(4) A hearing of an application for rescission of an order by consent under rule 7.28 is, unless the court directs otherwise, to be in private.

(5) The court may order that the identity of any party or witness must not be disclosed if it considers non-disclosure necessary in order to protect the interests of that party or witness.

Exercise of jurisdiction in cases heard at place other than the court in which the case is proceeding

7.17. Where a defended case is to be heard at a place other than the court in which it is proceeding, a judge of that other court may exercise all the powers that would be exercisable by a judge of the court in which the case is proceeding.

Notice of hearing

7.18. The court officer will give notice to the parties—

(a) of the date, time and place of every hearing which is to take place in a case to which they are a party; and

(b) in the case of a hearing following a direction under rule 7.20(2)(a), of the fact that, unless the person wishes or the court requires, the person need not attend.

Applications for a decree nisi or a conditional order

7.19.—(1) An application may be made to the court for it to consider the making of a decree nisi, a conditional order, a decree of judicial separation or a separation order in the proceedings—

    (a) at any time after the time for filing the acknowledgment of service has expired, provided that no party has filed an acknowledgment of service indicating an intention to defend the case; and

    (b) in any other case, at any time after the time for filing an answer to every application for a matrimonial or civil partnership order made in the proceedings has expired.

(2) An application under paragraph (1) may be made—

    (a) in a case within paragraph (1)(a), by the applicant; and

    (b) in any other case, by either party to the marriage or civil partnership in question.

(3) An application under this rule must, if the information which was required to be provided by the application form is no longer correct, be accompanied by a statement setting out particulars of the change.

(4) If neither party has filed an answer opposing the making of a decree nisi, a conditional order, a decree of judicial separation or a separation order on the other's application, then an application under this rule must be accompanied by an affidavit—

    (a) stating whether there have been any changes in the information given in the application or in any statement of arrangements for children;

    (b) confirming that, subject to any changes stated, the contents of the application and any statement of arrangements for children are true; and

    (c) where the acknowledgment of service has been signed by the other party, confirming that party's signature on the acknowledgment of service.

What the court will do on an application for a decree nisi, a conditional order, a decree of judicial separation or a separation order

7.20.—(1) This rule applies where an application is made under rule 7.19.

(2) If at the relevant time the case is an undefended case, the court must—

    (a) if satisfied that the applicant is entitled to—

        (i) in matrimonial proceedings, a decree nisi or a decree of judicial separation (as the case may be); or

        (ii) in civil partnership proceedings, a conditional order or a separation order (as the case may be),

so certify and direct that the application be listed before a district judge for the making of the decree or order at the next available date;

    (b) if not so satisfied, direct—

        (i) that any party to the proceedings provide such further information, or take such other steps, as the court may specify; or

        (ii) that the case be listed for a case management hearing.

(3) If the applicant has applied for costs, the court may, on making a direction under paragraph (2)(a)—

    (a) if satisfied that the applicant is entitled to an order for costs, so certify; or

    (b) if not so satisfied, make no direction about costs.

(4) If at the relevant time the case is a defended case, the court must direct that the case be listed for a case management hearing.

(5) The court may, when giving a direction under paragraph (2)(b), direct that the further information provided be verified by an affidavit.

(6) The court must not give directions under this rule unless at the relevant time it is satisfied—

(a) that a copy of each application for a matrimonial or civil partnership order or answer (including any amended application or answer) has been properly served on each party on whom it is required to be served; and

(b) that —

(i) in matrimonial proceedings, the application for a decree nisi or a decree of judicial separation; or

(ii) in civil partnership proceedings, the application for a conditional order or separation order,

was made at a time permitted by rule 7.19(1).

(7) In this rule, "the relevant time" means the time at which the court is considering an application made under rule 7.19(1).

Further provisions about costs

7.21.—(1) Subject to paragraph (2), any party to matrimonial or civil partnership proceedings may be heard on any question as to costs at the hearing of the proceedings.

(2) In the case of a hearing following a direction under rule 7.20(2)(a), a party will not be heard unless that party has, not less than 2 days before the hearing, served on every other party written notice of that party's intention to attend the hearing and apply for, or oppose the making of, an order for costs.

What the court must do for the case management hearing

7.22.—(1) This rule applies to a case in which the court has directed a case management hearing under rule 7.20.

(2) Where a hearing has been directed under rule 7.20(4) the court must—

(a) decide where the hearing in the case should take place;

(b) set a timetable for the filing and service of evidence;

(c) make such order for the disclosure and inspection of documents as it considers appropriate; and

(d) give directions as to the conduct of the final hearing and the attendance of witnesses.

(Rule 21.1 explains what is meant by disclosure and inspection.)

(3) Where a hearing has been directed under rule 7.20(2)(b)(ii), the court must—

(a) consider what further evidence is required properly to dispose of the proceedings and give directions about the filing and service of such evidence;

(b) consider whether any further information is required about the arrangements for the children of the family and give directions about the filing and service of such information;

(c) give directions for the further conduct of the proceedings, including—

(i) giving a direction that on compliance with any directions under sub-paragraph (a) or (b) a further application may be made under rule 7.19(1) for the proceedings to be dealt with under rule 7.20(2)(a); or

(ii) giving a direction that the case is not suitable for determination under that rule.

(4) Where the court gives a direction under paragraph (3)(c)(ii), it may also give directions under paragraph (2) or direct that the case be listed for a further hearing at which such directions will be given.

(5) Any party to proceedings which are not being dealt with under rule 7.20(2)(a) may apply to the court for further directions at any time.

(Part 3 sets out the court's powers to encourage the parties to use alternative dispute resolution and Part 4 sets out the court's general case management powers.)

Where proceedings under this Part may be heard

7.23. A case, other than one dealt with under rule 7.20(2)(a), may be heard, where it is proceeding in the court set out in column 1 of the following table—

  (a) in matrimonial proceedings, at the place referred to in column 2;

  (b) in civil partnership proceedings, at the place referred to in column 3.

	Matrimonial Proceedings	*Civil Partnership Proceedings*
A county court.	Any divorce county court designated as a court of trial.	Any civil partnership proceedings county court designated as a court of trial.
The principal registry when proceedings are treated as pending in a county court.	The Royal Courts of Justice.	The Royal Courts of Justice.
The High Court (including the principal registry other than when proceedings are treated as pending in a county court.).	a) The Royal Courts of Justice. b) Any court at which sittings of the High Court in matrimonial proceedings are authorised.	a) The Royal Courts of Justice. b) Any court at which sittings of the High Court in civil partnership proceedings are authorised.

The circumstances in which proceedings may be transferred between courts

7.24.—(1) A court may transfer the hearing of a case which is due to be heard in one court to another court of the same type at which hearings of those proceedings are permitted under rule 7.23.

(2) A court in which matrimonial or civil partnership proceedings are pending may order them, or an application made in the course of them—

  (a) if the proceedings are pending in the High Court, to be transferred from the registry in which they are pending to another district registry;

  (b) if the proceedings are matrimonial proceedings pending in a divorce county court, to be transferred from that county court to another divorce county court; and

  (c) if the proceedings are civil partnership proceedings pending in a civil partnership proceedings county court, to be transferred from that county court to another civil partnership proceedings county court.

(3) An order transferring the hearing of an application must not be made under paragraph (2) unless it would be more convenient than transferring the proceedings themselves.

(4) No transfer may be made under this rule or under section 38 or 39 of the 1984 Act(**a**) (transfers between High Court and a county court) unless—

  (a) the parties consent to the transfer;

  (b) the court has held a hearing to determine whether a transfer should be ordered; or

  (c) the court has transferred a case without a hearing where neither party has, within 14 days of being notified in writing of the court's intention to make such an order, requested a hearing to determine whether a transfer should be ordered.

(5) Proceedings—

  (a) which are transferred from the High Court to a divorce county court or a civil partnership proceedings county court and are to continue after the transfer in the

---

(**a**) Section 38 was amended by article 3 of the Civil Partnership (Family Proceedings and Housing Consequential Amendments) Order 2005 (S.I. 2005/3336) and section 108(5) of and paragraph 51 of Schedule 13 to the Children Act 1989 and section 261(1) of and paragraphs 93 and 94 of Schedule 27 to the Civil Partnership Act 2004.

principal registry are to be treated as pending in a divorce or civil partnership proceedings county court (as the case may be); and

(b) which are transferred from a divorce county court or a civil partnership proceedings county court to the High Court and are to continue after the transfer in the principal registry are no longer to be treated as pending in a divorce or civil partnership proceedings county court (as the case may be).

(6) Proceedings transferred from a divorce county court or a civil partnership proceedings county court to the High Court are to proceed in the registry nearest to the court from which they were transferred unless—

(a) the order transferring the proceedings directs otherwise; or

(b) the court subsequently orders.

The procedure for complying with section 41 of 1973 Act or section 63 of 2004 Act

7.25.—(1) Before the court—

(a) gives a direction under rule 7.20(2)(a); or

(b) makes—

(i) in matrimonial proceedings, a decree nisi or decree of judicial separation; or

(ii) in civil partnership proceedings, a conditional order or a separation order,

it must consider the matters set out in paragraph (2).

(2) The matters referred to in paragraph (1) are—

(a) whether there are any children of the family to whom section 41(1) of the 1973 Act or section 63(1) of the 2004 Act (as the case may be) applies; and

(b) if there are such children, and no application is pending in relation to them under Part 1 or 2 of the 1989 Act, the matters set out in section 41(1)(b) of the 1973 Act or in section 63(1)(b) of the 2004 Act (as the case may be).

(3) Where the court is satisfied that—

(a) there are no children of the family to whom—

(i) in matrimonial proceedings, section 41 of the 1973 Act applies; and

(ii) in civil partnership proceedings, section 63 of the 2004 Act applies; or

(b) there are such children but the court need not exercise its powers under the 1989 Act or its power to give a relevant direction with respect to any of them,

it must give a certificate to that effect.

(4) Where the court does not issue a certificate under paragraph (3) it may direct that—

(a) the parties, or any of them, must file further evidence relating to the arrangements for the children and may direct what specific matters must be dealt with in that evidence;

(b) a welfare report on the children, or any of them, be prepared;

(c) the parties, or any of them, attend a hearing for the court to consider the matter.

(5) Where the court makes a direction under paragraph (4) or a relevant direction, it must state in writing—

(a) its reasons for doing so; and

(b) in the case of a relevant direction, the exceptional circumstances which make it desirable in the interests of the child that the court should make such a direction.

(6) Nothing in this rule affects the court's power to make an order under the 1989 Act or a relevant direction.

(7) The court officer must send the parties—

(a) a copy of any certificate given under paragraph (3);

(b) a copy of any direction made under paragraph (4);

(c) a copy of any relevant direction; and

(d) a copy of any statement under paragraph (5).

(8) In this rule—

"parties" means a party to the marriage or civil partnership concerned and any person who appears to the court to have the care of any child of the family; and

"relevant direction" means—

(a) in matrimonial proceedings, a direction under section 41(2) of the 1973 Act;

(b) in civil partnership proceedings, a direction under section 63(2) of the 2004 Act.

Medical examinations in proceedings for nullity of marriage

7.26.—(1) Where the application is for a decree of nullity of marriage on the ground of incapacity to consummate or wilful refusal to do so, the court must determine whether medical examiners should be appointed to examine the parties or either of them.

(2) The court must only appoint medical examiners under paragraph (1) where it considers that it is necessary for the proper disposal of the case.

(3) The person to be examined must, in the presence of the medical examiner, sign a statement identifying that person as the party to whom the order for examination applies.

(4) The medical examiner must certify on the same statement that it was signed in his or her presence by the person who has been examined.

(5) The person who carries out the examination must prepare a report and file it with the court by the date directed by the court.

(6) Either party is entitled to see a copy of a report filed under paragraph (5).

Stay of proceedings

7.27.—(1) Where—

(a) the court is considering an application in accordance with rule 7.20 or gives directions under rule 7.22;

(b) it appears to the court that there are proceedings continuing in any country outside England and Wales which are in respect of the marriage or civil partnership in question or which are capable of affecting its validity or subsistence; and

(c) the court considers that the question whether the proceedings should be stayed$^{(GL)}$ under paragraph 9 of Schedule 1 to the Domicile and Matrimonial Proceedings Act 1973(**a**) or, for civil partnership proceedings, under rules made under sections 75 and 76 of the Courts Act 2003,

the court must give directions for the hearing of that question.

(2) Where at any time after the making of an application under this Part it appears to the court in matrimonial proceedings that, under Articles 16 to 19 of the Council Regulation, the court does not have jurisdiction to hear the application and is or may be required to stay$^{(GL)}$ the proceedings, the court will—

(a) stay$^{(GL)}$ the proceedings; and

(b) fix a date for a hearing to determine the questions of jurisdiction and whether there should be a further stay$^{(GL)}$ or other order.

(3) The court must give reasons for its decision under Articles 16 to 19 of the Council Regulation and, where it makes a finding of fact, state such finding of fact.

(**a**) Paragraph 9 of Schedule 1 was amended by section 19(5) of and paragraphs 7(1), (2), (3), (4) and (5) of Schedule 3 to the Family Law Act 1996 and regulation 4 of the European Communities (Matrimonial Jurisdiction and Judgments) Regulations 2001(S.I. 2001/310).

(4) An order under Article 17 of the Council Regulation that the court has no jurisdiction over the proceedings will be recorded by the court or the court officer in writing.

(5) The court may, if all parties agree, deal with any question about the jurisdiction of the court without a hearing.

CHAPTER 4

COURT ORDERS

The circumstances in which an order may be set aside (rescission)

7.28.—(1) The court must not hear an application by a respondent for—

(a) the rescission of a decree of divorce under section 10(1) of the 1973 Act;

(b) the rescission of a dissolution order under section 48(1) of the 2004 Act,

less than 14 days after service of the application.

(2) Either party to the marriage concerned may apply—

(a) after the decree nisi has been made but before it has been made absolute; or

(b) after a decree of judicial separation has been made

for the rescission of the decree on the grounds that the parties are reconciled and both consent to the rescission.

(3) Either party to the civil partnership concerned may apply—

(a) after a conditional order has been made but before it has been made final; or

(b) after a separation order has been made,

for the rescission of the order on the grounds that the parties are reconciled and both consent to the rescission.

Applications under section 10(2) of 1973 Act or section 48(2) of 2004 Act

7.29. Where the court makes—

(a) in the case of divorce, a decree absolute following an application under section 10(2) of the 1973 Act; or

(b) in the case of dissolution, a final order following an application under section 48(2) of the 2004 Act,

it must make a written record of the reasons for deciding to make that decree absolute or final order.

Orders under section 10A(2) of the 1973 Act

7.30.—(1) Where the court has made an order under section 10A(2) of the 1973 Act, the declaration referred to in that section must—

(a) be made and signed by both parties to the marriage concerned;

(b) give particulars of the proceedings in which the order was obtained;

(c) confirm that the steps required to dissolve the marriage in accordance with the religious usages appropriate to the parties have been taken;

(d) be accompanied by—

(i) a certificate from a relevant religious authority that all such steps have been taken; or

(ii) such other documents showing the relevant steps have been taken as the court may direct; and

(iii) be filed at the court either before or together with an application to make the decree nisi absolute,

under rule 7.32 or 7.33.

(2) Where the certificate referred to in paragraph (1)(d)(i) is not in English it must be accompanied by a translation of that certificate into English, certified by a notary public or authenticated by statement of truth.

(3) The court may direct that the declaration need not be accompanied by the material mentioned in paragraph (1)(d).

(4) In this rule a religious authority is "relevant" if the party who made the application for the order under section 10A(2) of the 1973 Act considers that authority competent to confirm that the steps referred to in paragraph (1)(c) have been taken.

Applications to prevent decrees nisi being made absolute or conditional orders being made final

7.31.—(1) This rule applies to an application under section 8 or 9 of the 1973 Act(**a**) or under section 39 or 40 of the 2004 Act to prevent —

(a) in the case of divorce or nullity of marriage, a decree nisi being made absolute; or

(b) in the case of dissolution or nullity of civil partnership, a conditional order being made final.

(2) An application to which this rule applies must be made using the Part 18 procedure, subject to paragraphs (3) to (6) of this rule.

(3) The person making an application to which this rule applies must within 28 days of filing the application apply to the court to give directions for the hearing of the application.

(4) Where the person making an application to which this rule applies does not apply for directions under paragraph (3), then the person in whose favour the decree nisi or conditional order (as the case may be) was made may do so.

(5) Rule 7.22(2) applies to an application to which this rule applies as it applies to an application for a matrimonial or civil partnership order.

(6) Where an application to which this rule applies is made by the Queen's Proctor—

(a) the Queen's Proctor may give written notice, to the court and to the party in whose favour the decree nisi or conditional order (as the case may be) was made, of the Queen's Proctor's intention to make an application to prevent the decree nisi being made absolute or the conditional order being made final; and

(b) where the Queen's Proctor does so the application under paragraph (1) must be made within 21 days beginning with the date on which the notice is given.

Making decrees nisi absolute or conditional orders final by giving notice

7.32.—(1) Unless rule 7.33 applies—

(a) in matrimonial proceedings, a spouse in whose favour a decree nisi has been made may give notice to the court that he or she wishes the decree nisi to be made absolute; or

(b) in civil partnership proceedings, a civil partner in whose favour a conditional order has been made may give notice to the court that he or she wishes the conditional order to be made final.

(2) Subject to paragraphs (3) and (4), where the court receives a notice under paragraph (1) it will make the decree nisi absolute or the conditional order final (as the case may be) if it is satisfied that—

(a) no application for rescission of the decree nisi or the conditional order is pending;

(b) no appeal against the making of the decree nisi or the conditional order is pending;

(**a**) Section 8 was amended by section 66(1) and (3) of and paragraph 5 of Schedule 8 to the Family Law Act 1996 and section 9 was prospectively repealed by section 66(3) of and Schedule 10 to the Family Law Act 1996.

(c) no order has been made by the court extending the time for bringing an appeal of the kind mentioned in sub-paragraph (b), or if such an order has been made, that the time so extended has expired;

(d) no application for an order of the kind mentioned in sub-paragraph (c) is pending;

(e) no application to prevent the decree nisi being made absolute or the conditional order being made final is pending;

(f) the court has complied with section 41(1) of the 1973 Act or section 63(1) of the 2004 Act, as the case may be, and has not given any direction under subsection (2) of either of those sections;

(g) the provisions of section 10(2) to (4) of the 1973 Act or section 48(2) to (4) of the 2004 Act do not apply or have been complied with;

(h) any order under section 10A(2) of the 1973 Act has been complied with; and

(i) where the decree nisi was made on the ground in section 12(g) of, or paragraph 11(1)(e) of Schedule 1 to, the 1973 Act, or the conditional order was made under section 50(1)(d) of the 2004 Act—

(i) there is not pending a reference under section 8(5) of the Gender Recognition Act 2004 in respect of the application on which the interim gender recognition certificate to which the application relates was granted;

(ii) that interim certificate has not been revoked under section 8(6)(b) of that Act; and

(iii) no appeal is pending against an order under section 8(6)(a) of that Act.

(3) Where the notice is received more than 12 months after the making of the decree nisi or the conditional order, it must be accompanied by an explanation in writing stating—

(a) why the application has not been made earlier;

(b) whether the applicant and respondent have lived together since the decree nisi or the conditional order was made, and, if so, between what dates;

(c) if the applicant is female, whether she has given birth to a child since the decree nisi or the conditional order was made and whether it is alleged that the child is or may be a child of the family;

(d) if the respondent is female, whether the applicant has reason to believe that she has given birth to a child since the decree nisi or the conditional order was made and whether it is alleged that the child is or may be a child of the family.

(4) Where paragraph (3) applies, the court may—

(a) require the applicant to file an affidavit verifying the explanation; and

(b) make such order on the application as it thinks fit, but where it orders the decree nisi to be made absolute or the conditional order to be made final that order is not to take effect until the court is satisfied that none of the matters mentioned in paragraph (2)(a) to (i) applies.

Applications to make decrees nisi absolute or conditional orders final

7.33.—(1) An application must be made—

(a) in matrimonial proceedings, for the decree nisi to be made absolute; or

(b) in civil partnership proceedings, for the conditional order to be made final,

where the conditions set out in paragraph (2) apply.

(2) The conditions referred to in paragraph (1) are—

(a) the Queen's Proctor gives notice to the court under rule 7.31(6)(a) and has not withdrawn that notice;

(b) there are other circumstances which ought to be brought to the attention of the court before the application is granted; or

(c) the application is made—

    (i) in matrimonial proceedings, by the spouse against whom the decree nisi was made; or

    (ii) in civil partnership proceedings, by the civil partner against whom the conditional order was made.

(3) An application under this rule to which paragraph (2)(a) applies must be—

    (a) made to a judge, but not a district judge; and

    (b) served on the Queen's Proctor.

(4) Where the court orders—

    (a) in matrimonial proceedings, a decree to be made absolute under this rule; or

    (b) in civil partnership proceedings, a conditional order to be made final under this rule,

that order is not to take effect until the court is satisfied about the matters mentioned in rule 7.32(2)(a) to (i) .

What the court officer must do when a decree nisi is made absolute

7.34. In matrimonial proceedings, where a decree nisi is made absolute the court officer must—

    (a) endorse that fact on the decree nisi together with the precise time at which the decree was made absolute; and

    (b) send a certificate that a decree nisi has been made absolute to the applicant, the respondent, any co-respondent and any other party.

What the court officer must do when a conditional order is made final

7.35. Where a conditional order is made final the court officer must—

    (a) endorse that fact on the conditional order together with the precise time at which the order was made final; and

    (b) send the final order to the applicant, the respondent and any other party.

Records of decrees absolute and final orders

7.36.—(1) A central index of decrees absolute and final orders must be kept under the control of the principal registry.

(2) Any person, on payment of the prescribed fee, may require a search to be made of that index and to be provided with a certificate showing the results of that search.

(3) Any person who requests it must, on payment of the prescribed fee, be issued with a copy of the decree absolute or final order.

PART 8

PROCEDURE FOR MISCELLANEOUS APPLICATIONS

CHAPTER 1

PROCEDURE

Procedure

8.1. Subject to rules 8.13 and 8.24, applications to which this Part applies must be made in accordance with the Part 19 procedure.

CHAPTER 2

APPLICATION FOR CORRECTED GENDER RECOGNITION CERTIFICATE

Scope of this Chapter

8.2. The rules in this Chapter apply to an application under section 6(1) of the Gender Recognition Act 2004 for the correction of a full gender recognition certificate issued under section 5(1) or 5A(1) of that Act(**a**).

Where to start proceedings

8.3. The application must be made to the court which issued the original certificate unless the court directs otherwise.

Who the parties are

8.4. Where the applicant is—

 (a) the person to whom the original certificate was issued, the Secretary of State must be a respondent;

 (b) the Secretary of State, the person to whom the original certificate was issued must be a respondent.

Delivery of copy certificate to Secretary of State

8.5. Where the court issues a corrected full gender recognition certificate, a court officer must send a copy of the corrected certificate to the Secretary of State.

CHAPTER 3

APPLICATION FOR ALTERATION OF MAINTENANCE AGREEMENT AFTER DEATH OF ONE PARTY

Scope of this Chapter

8.6. The rules in this Chapter apply to an application under section 36 of the 1973 Act(**b**) or paragraph 73 of Schedule 5 to the 2004 Act to alter a maintenance agreement after the death of one of the parties.

Where to start proceedings

8.7.—(1) The application may be made in the High Court or a county court.

(2) Where the application is made in a county court it must be made in the divorce county court or civil partnership proceedings county court for the district in which—

 (a) the deceased resided at the time of death; or

 (b) if the deceased did not reside in England and Wales at the time of death—

  (i) the respondent or one of the respondents resides or carries on business; or

  (ii) where the respondent is the personal representative of the deceased, the deceased's estate is situated; or

 (c) if neither (a) nor (b) applies—

  (i) the applicant resides or carries on business; or

(**a**) Section 5A(1) was inserted by section 250(1) and (4) of the Civil Partnership Act 2004.
(**b**) Section 36 was amended by section 26(1) of the Inheritance (Provision for Family and Dependants) Act 1975 (c.63).

(ii) where the applicant is the personal representative of the deceased, the deceased's estate is situated.

Who the parties are

8.8.—(1) Where the applicant is—

    (a) the surviving party to the agreement, the personal representative of the deceased must be a respondent;

    (b) the personal representative of the deceased, the surviving party to the agreement must be a respondent.

(2) The court may at any time direct that—

    (a) any person be made a party to proceedings; or

    (b) a party be removed.

Representative parties

8.9.—(1) The court may, before or after the application has been filed at court, make an order appointing a person to represent any other person or persons in the application where the person or persons to be represented—

    (a) are unborn;

    (b) cannot be found;

    (c) cannot easily be ascertained; or

    (d) are a class of persons who have the same interest in an application and—

        (i) one or more members of that class are within sub-paragraphs (a), (b) or (c); or

        (ii) to appoint a representative would further the overriding objective.

(2) An application for an order under paragraph (1) may be made by—

    (a) any person who seeks to be appointed under the order; or

    (b) any party to the application.

(3) An application for an order under paragraph (1) must be served on—

    (a) all parties to the application to alter the maintenance agreement, if that application has been filed at court;

    (b) the person sought to be appointed, if that person is not the applicant or a party to the application; and

    (c) any other person as directed by the court.

(4) The court's approval is required to settle proceedings in which a party is acting as a representative.

(5) The court may approve a settlement where it is satisfied that the settlement is for the benefit of all the represented persons.

(6) Unless the court directs otherwise, any order made on an application in which a party is acting as a representative—

    (a) is binding on all persons represented in the proceedings; and

    (b) may only be enforced by or against a person who is not a party with the permission of the court.

(7) An application may be brought by or against trustees, executors or administrators without adding as parties any persons who have a beneficial interest in the trust or estate and any order made on the application is binding on the beneficiaries unless the court orders otherwise.

Acknowledgment of service

8.10.—(1) A respondent who is a personal representative of the deceased must file with the acknowledgment of service a statement setting out—

(a) full particulars of the value of the deceased's estate for probate after providing for the discharge of the funeral, testamentary and administration expenses, debts and liabilities (including inheritance tax and interest); and

(b) the people (including names, addresses and details of any persons under disability) or classes of people beneficially interested in the estate and the value of their interests so far as ascertained.

(2) The respondent must file the acknowledgment of service and any statement required under this rule within 28 days beginning with the date on which the application is served.

Hearings may be in private

8.11. The court may decide to hear any application to which this Chapter applies in private.

CHAPTER 4

APPLICATION FOR QUESTION AS TO PROPERTY TO BE DECIDED IN SUMMARY WAY

Scope of this Chapter

8.12. The rules in this Chapter apply to an application under section 17 of the Married Women's Property Act 1882(**a**) or section 66 of the 2004 Act.

Procedure

8.13. Where an application for an order under section 17 of the Married Women's Property Act 1882(**b**) or section 66 of the 2004 Act is made in any proceedings for a financial order, the application must be made in accordance with the Part 18 procedure.

Where to start proceedings

8.14.—(1) The application may be made in the High Court or a county court.

(2) Where the application is made in a county court it must be made in the court—

(a) in which any matrimonial proceedings or civil partnership proceedings have been started or are intended to be started by the applicant or the respondent; or

(b) in the absence of any such proceedings, for the district in which the applicant or respondent resides.

(3) The application may be made to the principal registry as if it were a county court if—

(a) any matrimonial proceedings or civil partnership proceedings have been started there or are intended to be started there by the applicant or the respondent; and

(b) those proceedings are or will be treated as pending in a divorce county court or civil partnership proceedings county court.

Mortgagees as parties

8.15.—(1) Where particulars of a mortgage are provided with the application—

(a) the applicant must serve a copy of the application on the mortgagee; and

---

(**a**) 1882 c.75.
(**b**) Section 17 was amended by the Statute Law (Repeals) Act 1969 (c.52) and section 43 of the Matrimonial and Family Proceedings Act 1984.

(b) the mortgagee may, within 14 days beginning with the date on which the application was received, file an acknowledgment of service and be heard on the application.

(2) The court must direct that a mortgagee be made a party to the proceedings where the mortgagee requests to be one.

Injunctions

8.16.—(1) The court may grant an injunction^(GL) only if the injunction^(GL) is ancillary or incidental to the assistance sought by the applicant.

(2) Applications for injunctive relief must be made in accordance with the procedure in rule 20.4 (how to apply for an interim remedy) and the provisions of rule 20.5 (interim injunction^(GL) to cease if application is stayed^(GL)) apply.

Application of other rules

8.17. Rule 9.24 applies where the court has made an order for sale under section 17 of the Married Women's Property Act 1882 or section 66 of the 2004 Act.

CHAPTER 5

DECLARATIONS

Scope of this Chapter

8.18. The rules in this Chapter apply to applications made in accordance with—

    (a) section 55 of the 1986 Act (declarations as to marital status) and section 58 of the 2004 Act (declarations as to civil partnership status);

    (b) section 55A of the 1986 Act(**a**) (declarations of parentage);

    (c) section 56(1)(b) and (2) of the 1986 Act(**b**) (declarations of legitimacy or legitimation); and

    (d) section 57 of the 1986 Act(**c**) (declarations as to adoptions effected overseas).

Where to start proceedings

8.19. The application may be made in the High Court or a county court and applications under section 55A of the 1986 Act may also be made in a magistrates' court.

Who the parties are

8.20.—(1) In relation to the proceedings set out in column 1 of the following table, column 2 sets out who the respondents to those proceedings will be.

Proceedings	*Respondent*
Applications for declarations as to marital or civil partnership status.	The other party to the marriage or civil partnership in question or, where the applicant is a third party, both parties to the marriage or civil partnership.
Applications for declarations of parentage.	The person whose parentage is in issue or any person who is or is alleged to be the parent of the person whose parentage is in issue.

(**a**) Section 55A was inserted by section 83(1) and (2) of the Child Support, Pensions and Social Security Act 2000 (c. 19).

(**b**) Section 56(1) was amended by section 83(5) of and paragraphs 3 and 5(a) of Schedule 8 to the Child Support, Pensions and Social Security Act 2000.

(**c**) Section 57 was amended by section 139(1) of and paragraphs 46, and 49(a) and (b) of Schedule 3 to the Adoption and Children Act 2002 (c.38) and section 83(5) of and paragraphs 3 and 6 of Schedule 8 to the Child Support, Pensions and Social Security Act 2000.

| Applications for declarations of legitimacy or legitimation. | The applicant's father and mother or the survivor of them. |
| Applications for declarations as to adoption effected overseas. | The person(s) whom the applicant is claiming are or are not the applicant's adoptive parents. |

(2) The applicant must include in his application particulars of every person whose interest may be affected by the proceedings and his relationship to the applicant.

(3) The acknowledgment of service filed under rule 19.5 must give details of any other persons the respondent considers should be made a party to the application or be given notice of the application.

(4) Upon receipt of the acknowledgment of service, the court must give directions as to any other persons who should be made a respondent to the application or be given notice of the proceedings.

(5) A person given notice of proceedings under paragraph (4) may, within 21 days beginning with the date on which the notice was served, apply to be joined as a party.

(6) No directions may be given as to the future management of the case under rule 19.9 until the expiry of the notice period in paragraph (5).

The role of the Attorney General

8.21.—(1) The applicant must, except in the case of an application for a declaration of parentage, send a copy of the application and all accompanying documents to the Attorney General at least one month before making the application.

(2) The Attorney General may, when deciding whether to intervene in the proceedings, inspect any document filed at court relating to any family proceedings mentioned in the declaration proceedings.

(3) If the court is notified that the Attorney General wishes to intervene in the proceedings, a court officer must send the Attorney General a copy of any subsequent documents filed at court.

(4) The court must, when giving directions under rule 8.20(4), consider whether to ask the Attorney General to argue any question relating to the proceedings.

(5) If the court makes a request to the Attorney General under paragraph (4) and the Attorney General agrees to that request, the Attorney General must serve a summary of the argument on all parties to the proceedings.

Declarations of parentage

8.22.—(1) If the applicant or the person whose parentage or parenthood is in issue, is known by a name other than that which appears in that person's birth certificate, that other name must also be stated in any order and declaration of parentage.

(2) A court officer must send a copy of a declaration of parentage and the application to the Registrar General within 21 days beginning with the date on which the declaration was made.

CHAPTER 6

APPLICATION FOR PERMISSION TO APPLY FOR A FINANCIAL REMEDY AFTER OVERSEAS PROCEEDINGS

Scope of this Chapter

8.23. Subject to rule 9.26(6), the rules in this Chapter apply to an application for permission to apply for a financial remedy under section 13 of the 1984 Act and paragraph 4 of Schedule 7 to the 2004 Act.

(Rule 9.26(6) enables the application for permission to apply for a financial remedy under section 13 of the 1984 Act or paragraph 4 of Schedule 7 to the 2004 Act to be heard at the same time as the application for a financial remedy under Part 3 of the 1984 Act or Schedule 7 to the 2004 Act where that application is an application for a consent order.)

Where and how to start proceedings

8.24.—(1) Subject to paragraph (2), the application must be made in the principal registry.

(2) Where rule 9.26(6) applies, the application must be made in the court hearing the application for a financial remedy.

(Rule 9.5(2) specifies the court where the application for the consent order should be filed.)

(3) The application must be made in accordance with the Part 18 procedure.

Application to be made without notice

8.25.—(1) The court may grant an application made without notice if it appears to the court that there are good reasons for not giving notice.

(2) If the applicant makes an application without giving notice, the applicant must state the reasons why notice has not been given.

Notification of hearing date

8.26. The court officer must—

    (a) fix a date, time and place for the hearing of the application by a judge, but not a district judge; and

    (b) give notice of the date of the hearing to the applicant.

Hearings to be in private unless the court directs otherwise

8.27. An application under this Chapter must be heard in private unless the court directs otherwise.

Direction that application be dealt with by a district judge of the principal registry

8.28. If the application is granted, the judge may direct that the application for a financial remedy under Part 3 of the 1984 Act or Schedule 7 to the 2004 Act may be heard by a district judge of the principal registry.

CHAPTER 7

APPLICATION FOR THE TRANSFER OF A TENANCY UNDER SECTION 53 OF, AND SCHEDULE 7 TO, THE 1996 ACT

Scope of this Chapter

8.29. This Chapter applies to an application for the transfer of a tenancy under section 53 of, and Schedule 7 to, the 1996 Act.

Where to start proceedings

8.30.—(1) Subject to paragraph (2), the application may be made in the High Court or a county court.

(2) The application must be made to the court in which any divorce, judicial separation, nullity or civil partnership proceedings are pending between the parties.

Service of the application

8.31.—(1) The court will serve a copy of the application on—

    (a) the respondent; and

(b) the landlord (as defined by paragraph 1 of Schedule 7 to the 1996 Act(**a**)),

unless the court directs that the applicant must do so.

(2) Where service is effected by the applicant, the applicant must file a certificate of service.

Who the parties are

8.32. The court will direct that a landlord be made a party to the proceedings where the landlord requests to be one.

Orders for disclosure

8.33. Any party may apply to the court under rule 21.2 for an order that any person must attend an appointment before the court and produce any documents that are specified or described in the order.

Injunctions

8.34.—(1) The court may grant an injunction[GL] only if the injunction[GL] is ancillary or incidental to the assistance sought by the applicant.

(2) Applications for injunctive relief must be made in accordance with the procedure in rule 20.4 (how to apply for an interim remedy) and the provisions of rule 20.5 (interim injunction[GL] to cease if application is stayed[GL]) apply accordingly.

CHAPTER 8

APPLICATIONS FOR ORDERS PREVENTING AVOIDANCE UNDER SECTION 32L OF THE CHILD SUPPORT ACT 1991

Scope of this Chapter

8.35. Subject to rule 8.40, the rules in this Chapter apply to applications made under section 32L (1) and (2) of the 1991 Act(**b**).

Interpretation

8.36. In this Chapter—

"child support maintenance" has the meaning assigned to it in section 3(6) of the 1991 Act(**c**);

"reviewable disposition" has the meaning assigned to it in section 32L(5) of the 1991 Act.

Where to start proceedings

8.37.—(1) The application must be made to the High Court and be filed in—

(a) the principal registry ; or

(b) any district registry.

(2) The application may be heard by a judge but not a district judge except —

(a) a district judge of the principal registry of the Family Division; or

(b) a district judge in a district registry who is directed by a judge to hear the application.

(**a**) Paragraph 1 of Schedule 7 to the Family Law Act 1996 was amended by section 82 of and paragraphs 16(1) and (2) of Schedule 9 to the Civil Partnership Act 2004 and article 2 of and paragraph 10(b)(i) of the Schedule to the Housing Act 1996 (Consequential Amendments) Order 1997 (S.I. 1997/74).

(**b**) Section 32L was inserted by section 24 of the Child Maintenance and Other Payments Act 2008 (c.6).

(**c**) Section 3(6) was amended by section 1(2) of the Child Support, Pensions and Social Security Act 2000.

(Section 32L(10)(a) of the 1991 Act defines "court" for the purposes of section 32L as being the High Court only.)

Who the parties are

8.38.—(1) The applicant to the proceedings is the Commission and the respondent is the person who has failed to pay child support maintenance.

(2) The court may at any time direct that —

    (a) any person be made a party to proceedings; or

    (b) a party be removed from the proceedings.

Service of the application

8.39.—(1) The applicant must serve the application and a copy of the applicant's written evidence on—

    (a) any respondent;

    (b) the person in whose favour the reviewable disposition is alleged to have been made; and

    (c) such other persons as the court directs.

(2) Where an application includes an application relating to land, the applicant must serve a copy of the application on any —

    (a) mortgagee;

    (b) trustee of a trust of land or settlement; and

    (c) other person who has an interest in the land,

of whom particulars are given in the application.

(3) Any person served under paragraph (2) may make a request to the court in writing, within 14 days beginning with the date of service of the application, for a copy of the applicant's written evidence.

(4) Any person who —

    (a) is served with copies of the application and the applicant's written evidence under paragraph (1); or

    (b) receives a copy of the applicant's written evidence following a request under paragraph (3),

may, within 14 days beginning with the date of service or receipt, file a statement in answer.

(5) A statement in answer filed under paragraph (4) must be verified by a statement of truth.

Applications without notice

8.40.—(1) This rule applies to an application under section 32L(1) of the 1991 Act.

(2) The court may grant an application made without notice if it appears to the court that there are good reasons for not giving notice.

(3) If the applicant makes an application without giving notice, the evidence in support of the application must state the reasons why notice has not been given.

(4) If the court grants an application under paragraph (2)—

    (a) the order must include a provision allowing any respondent to apply to the court for an order to be reconsidered as soon as just and convenient at a full hearing; and

    (b) the applicant must, as soon as reasonably practicable, serve upon each respondent a copy of the order and a copy of the written evidence in support of the application.

CHAPTER 9

APPLICATION FOR CONSENT TO MARRIAGE OF A CHILD OR TO REGISTRATION OF CIVIL PARTNERSHIP OF A CHILD

Scope of this Chapter

8.41. The rules in this Chapter apply to an application under—

  (a) section 3 of the Marriage Act 1949(**a**); or

  (b) paragraph 3, 4 or 10 of Schedule 2 to the 2004 Act.

Child acting without a children's guardian

8.42. The child may bring an application without a children's guardian, unless the court directs otherwise.

Who the respondents are

8.43. Where an application follows a refusal to give consent to—

  (a) the marriage of a child; or

  (b) a child registering as the civil partner of another person,

every person who has refused consent will be a respondent to the application.

PART 9

APPLICATIONS FOR A FINANCIAL REMEDY

CHAPTER 1

APPLICATION AND INTERPRETATION

Application

9.1. The rules in this Part apply to an application for a financial remedy.

("Financial remedy" and "financial order" are defined in rule 2.3)

Application of Magistrates' Courts Rules 1981

9.2. Unless the context otherwise requires, and subject to the rules in this Part, the following rules of the Magistrates' Courts Rules 1981(**b**) apply to proceedings in a magistrates' court which are family proceedings under section 65 of the Magistrates' Courts Act 1980—

  (a) rule 39(6) (method of making periodical payments);

  (b) rule 41 (revocation etc. of orders for periodical payments);

  (c) rule 43 (service of copy of order);

  (d) rule 44 (remission of sums due under order);

  (e) rule 45 (duty of designated officer to notify subsequent marriage or formation of civil partnership of person entitled to payments under a maintenance order);

  (f) rule 48 (to whom payments are to be made);

  (g) rule 49 (duty of designated officer to give receipt);

(**a**) 1949 c.76.
(**b**) S.I. 1981/552.

(h) rule 51 (application for further time);

(i) rule 62 (particulars relating to payment of lump sum under a magistrates' courts maintenance order etc. to be entered in register);

(j) rule 66 (register of convictions, etc.);

(k) rule 67 (proof of service, handwriting, etc.);

(l) rule 68 (proof of proceedings); and

(m) rule 69 (proof that magistrates' court maintenance orders, etc, have not been revoked, etc.).

Interpretation

9.3.—(1) In this Part—

"avoidance of disposition order" means—

(a) in proceedings under the 1973 Act, an order under section 37(2)(b) or (c) of that Act;

(b) in proceedings under the 1984 Act, an order under section 23(2)(b) or 23(3) of that Act(**a**);

(c) in proceedings under Schedule 5 to the 2004 Act, an order under paragraph 74(3) or (4); or

(d) in proceedings under Schedule 7 to the 2004 Act, an order under paragraph 15(3) or (4);

"the Board" means the Board of the Pension Protection Fund;

"FDR appointment" means a Financial Dispute Resolution appointment in accordance with rule 9.17;

"order preventing a disposition" means—

(a) in proceedings under the 1973 Act, an order under section 37(2)(a) of that Act;

(b) in proceedings under the 1984 Act, an order under section 23(2)(a) of that Act;

(c) in proceedings under Schedule 5 to the 2004 Act, an order under paragraph 74(2); or

(d) in proceedings under Schedule 7 to the 2004 Act, an order under paragraph 15(2);

"pension arrangement" means—

(a) an occupational pension scheme;

(b) a personal pension scheme;

(c) shareable state scheme rights;

(d) a retirement annuity contract;

(e) an annuity or insurance policy purchased, or transferred, for the purpose of giving effect to rights under an occupational pension scheme or a personal pension scheme; and

(f) an annuity purchased, or entered into, for the purpose of discharging liability in respect of a pension credit under section 29(1)(b) of the Welfare Reform and Pensions Act 1999 or under corresponding Northern Ireland legislation;

"pension attachment order" means—

(a) in proceedings under the 1973 Act, an order making provision under section 25B or 25C of that Act(**b**);

(**a**) Sections 23(2) (a) and (b) and 23(3) have been prospectively substituted with savings by section 15 of and paragraph 4 of Schedule 2 to the Family Law Act 1996.

(**b**) Section 25B was inserted by section 166(1) of the Pensions Act 1995 (c.26) and amended by section 21 of and paragraphs 1(1),(2),(4),(5)(a),(5)(b), (6),(7)(a),(7)(b), (8)(a), (8)(b), (8)(c) and (9) of the Welfare Reform and Pensions Act 1999 (c.30) and subsections (8) and (9) were inserted by section 16(3) of the Family Law Act 1996 and the section was modified by regulations 2 and 4(1) and (2)(b) of the Divorce etc (Pension Protection Fund) Regulations 2006 (S.I. 2006/1932). Section 25C was inserted by section 166(1) of the Pensions Act 1995 and amended by section 66(1) of and paragraph 11 of Schedule 8 to the Family Law Act 1996 and also amended by section 21 of and paragraphs 2(1), (2), (3)(a)(i) and (ii), (3)(b), (4)(a), (4)(b) and (5) of Schedule 4 to the Welfare Reform and Pensions Act 1999.

(b) in proceedings under the 1984 Act, an order under section 17(1)(a)(i) of that Act making provision equivalent to an order referred to in paragraph (a);

(c) in proceedings under Schedule 5 to the 2004 Act, an order making provision under paragraph 25 or paragraph 26; or

(d) in proceedings under Schedule 7 to the 2004 Act, an order under paragraph 9(2)(**a**) or (3) making provision equivalent to an order referred to in paragraph (c);

"pension compensation attachment order" means—

(a) in proceedings under the 1973 Act, an order making provision under section 25F of that Act;(**b**)

(b) in proceedings under the 1984 Act, an order under section 17(1)(a)(i) of that Act(**c**) making provision equivalent to an order referred in to paragraph (a);

(c) in proceedings under Schedule 5 to the 2004 Act, an order under paragraph 34A; and

(d) in proceedings under Schedule 7 to the 2004 Act, an order under paragraph 9(2) or (3) making provision equivalent to an order referred to in paragraph (c);

"pension compensation sharing order" means—

(a) in proceedings under the 1973 Act, an order under section 24E of that Act(**d**);

(b) in proceedings under the 1984 Act, an order under section 17(1)(c) of that Act;

(c) in proceedings under Schedule 5 to the 2004 Act, an order under paragraph 19A ; and

(d) in proceedings under Schedule 7 to the 2004 Act, an order under paragraph 9(2) or (3)(**e**) making provision equivalent to an order referred to in paragraph (c);

"pension sharing order" means—

(a) in proceedings under the 1973 Act, an order making provision under section 24B of that Act(**f**);

(b) in proceedings under the 1984 Act, an order under section 17(1)(b) of that Act;

(c) in proceedings under Schedule 5 to the 2004 Act, an order under paragraph 15; or

(d) in proceedings under Schedule 7 to the 2004 Act, an order under paragraph 9(2) or (3) making provision equivalent to an order referred to in paragraph (c);

"pension scheme" means, unless the context otherwise requires, a scheme for which the Board has assumed responsibility in accordance with Chapter 3 of Part 2 of the Pensions Act 2004 (pension protection) or any provision in force in Northern Ireland corresponding to that Chapter;

"PPF compensation" has the meaning given to it—

(a) in proceedings under the 1973 Act, by section 21C of the 1973 Act(**g**);

(b) in proceedings under the 1984 Act, by section 18(7) of the 1984 Act; and

(c) in proceedings under the 2004 Act, by paragraph 19F of Schedule 5 to the 2004 Act;

"relevant valuation" means a valuation of pension rights or benefits as at a date not more than 12 months earlier than the date fixed for the first appointment which has been furnished or requested for the purposes of any of the following provisions—

(**a**) Paragraph 9(2) of Schedule 7 to the Civil Partnership Act 2004 was amended by section 120 of and paragraphs 14, 20(1), 20(2)(a) and (b) of the Pensions Act 2008 (c. 30).

(**b**) Section 25F was inserted by section 120 of and paragraphs 1 and 7 of Schedule 6 to the Pensions Act 2008.

(**c**) Section 17(1)(a)(i) was amended by section 66(1) of and paragraph 32(2) of Schedule 8 to the Family Law Act 1996 as amended by section 84(1) of and paragraphs 66(1) and (14) of Schedule 12 to the Welfare Reform and Pensions Act 1999.

(**d**) Section 24E was inserted by section 120 of and paragraphs 1 and 3 of Schedule 6 to the Pensions Act 2008.

(**e**) Paragraphs 9(2) and (3) of Schedule 7 to the Civil Partnership Act 2004 were amended by section 120 of and paragraphs 14 and 20(2)(b) of Schedule 6 to the Pensions Act 2008.

(**f**) Section 24B was inserted by section 19 of and paragraphs 1 and 4 of Schedule 3 to the Welfare Reform and Pensions Act 1999.

(**g**) Section 21C was inserted by section 120 of and paragraphs 1 and 2 of Schedule 6 to the Pensions Act 2008.

(a) the Pensions on Divorce etc (Provision of Information) Regulations 2000(**a**);

(b) regulation 5 of and Schedule 2 to the Occupational Pension Schemes (Disclosure of Information) Regulations 1996(**b**) and regulation 11 of and Schedule 1 to the Occupational Pension Schemes (Transfer Value) Regulations 1996(**c**);

(c) section 93A or 94(1)(a) or (aa) of the Pension Schemes Act 1993(**d**);

(d) section 94(1)(b) of the Pension Schemes Act 1993 or paragraph 2(a) (or, where applicable, 2(b)) of Schedule 2 to the Personal Pension Schemes (Disclosure of Information) Regulations 1987(**e**);

(e) the Dissolution etc. (Pensions) Regulations 2005(**f**);

"variation order" means—

(a) in proceedings under the 1973 Act, an order under section 31 of that Act; or

(b) in proceedings under the 2004 Act, an order under Part 11 of Schedule 5 to that Act.

(2) References in this Part to a county court are to be construed, in relation to proceedings for a financial order, as references to a divorce county court or a civil partnership proceedings county court, as the case may be.

CHAPTER 2

PROCEDURE FOR APPLICATIONS

When an Application for a financial order may be made

9.4. An application for a financial order may be made—

(a) in an application for a matrimonial or civil partnership order; or

(b) at any time after an application for a matrimonial or civil partnership order has been made.

Where to start proceedings

9.5.—(1) An application for a financial remedy must be filed—

(a) if there are proceedings for a matrimonial order or a civil partnership order which are proceeding in a designated county court, in that court; or

(b) if there are proceedings for a matrimonial order or a civil partnership order which are proceeding in the High Court, in the registry in which those proceedings are taking place.

(2) In any other case, in relation to the application set out in column 1 of the following table, column 2 sets out where the application must be filed.

(**a**) S.I. 2000/1048.

(**b**) S.I. 1996/1655.

(**c**) S.I. 1996/1847 Regulation 11 was amended by regulations 5(b), 5(c), 5(d)(i) and (ii), 5(e), 5(f) and 5(g) of the Occupational Pension Scheme (Transfer Values) (Amendment) Regulations 2008 (S.I. 2008/1050) and regulations 4(a)(ii) and 4(b) of the Occupational Pension Scheme (Winding Up and Transfer Values) (Amendment) Regulations 2005 (S.I. 2005/72) and regulation 8 of the Occupational, Personal and Stakeholder Pensions (Miscellaneous Amendment) Regulations 2009 (S.I. 2009/615 and Schedule 1 was amended by regulations 7(a)(ii), (iii), (iv)(aa), (iv)(bb) and 7(b) of Occupational Pension Scheme (Transfer Values) (Amendment) Regulations 2008.

(**d**) 1993 c.48 Section 93A was inserted by section 153 of the Pensions Act 1965 (c.26) and section 94(1)(a) and (aa) were amended by section 154(1) and (2) of the Pensions Act 1995.

(**e**) S.I. 1987/1110.

(**f**) S.I. 2005/2920.

Provision under which application is made	Court where application must be filed
Section 27 of the 1973 Act(**a**).	Divorce county court.
Part 9 of Schedule 5 to the 2004 Act.	Civil partnership proceedings county court.
Part 3 of the 1984 Act.	Principal Registry or, in relation to an application for a consent order, a divorce county court.
Schedule 7 to the 2004 Act.	Principal Registry or, in relation to an application for a consent order, a civil partnership proceedings county court.
Section 35 of the 1973 Act(**b**).	High Court, a divorce county court or a magistrates' court.
Paragraph 69 of Schedule 5 to the 2004 Act.	High Court, a civil partnership proceedings county court or a magistrates' court.
Schedule 1 to the 1989 Act.	High Court, designated county court or a magistrates' court.
Part 1 of the 1978 Act.	magistrates' court.
Schedule 6 to the 2004 Act.	magistrates' court.

(3) An application for a financial remedy under Part 3 of the 1984 Act or Schedule 7 to the 2004 Act which is proceeding in the High Court must be heard by a judge, but not a district judge, of that court unless a direction has been made that the application may be heard by a district judge of the principal registry.

(Rule 8.28 enables a judge to direct that an application for a financial remedy under Part 3 of the 1984 Act or Schedule 7 to the 2004 Act may be heard by a district judge of the principal registry.)

Application for an order preventing a disposition

9.6.—(1) The Part 18 procedure applies to an application for an order preventing a disposition.

(2) An application for an order preventing a disposition may be made without notice to the respondent.

("Order preventing a disposition" is defined in rule 9.3.)

Application for interim orders

9.7.—(1) A party may apply at any stage of the proceedings for—

    (a) an order for maintenance pending suit;

    (b) an order for maintenance pending outcome of proceedings;

    (c) an order for interim periodical payments;

    (d) an interim variation order; or

    (e) any other form of interim order.

(2) The Part 18 procedure applies to an application for an interim order.

(**a**) Section 27 was amended by sections 4 and 46(1) of and paragraph 13 of Schedule 1 to the Matrimonial and Family Proceedings Act 1984 and section 63(1), (2), (3), (4) and (5) as substituted by section 33(1) of and paragraph 52 of Schedule 2 to the Family Law Reform Act 1987 (c.42) and section 89(2)(b) and Schedule 3 to the Domestic Proceedings and Magistrates' Courts Act 1978 and section 66(1) of and paragraph 13(2), (3), and (4) of Schedule 8 to the Family Law Act 1996 and section 6(1) of the Domicile and Matrimonial Proceedings Act 1973.

(**b**) Section 35 was amended by section 46(1) of and paragraph 13 of Schedule 1 to the Matrimonial and Family Proceedings Act 1984 and by section 109(1) of and paragraph 169 of Schedule 8 to the Courts Act 2003 and section 261(1) of and paragraph 44 of Schedule 27 to the Civil Partnership Act 2004 and section 66(1) of and paragraph 20 of Schedule 8 to the Family Law Act 1996.

(3) Where a party makes an application before filing a financial statement, the written evidence in support must—

    (a) explain why the order is necessary; and

    (b) give up to date information about that party's financial circumstances.

(4) Unless the respondent has filed a financial statement, the respondent must, at least 7 days before the court is to deal with the application, file a statement of his means and serve a copy on the applicant.

(5) An application for an order mentioned in paragraph (1)(e) may be made without notice.

Application for periodical payments order at same rate as an order for maintenance pending suit

  9.8.—(1) This rule applies where there are matrimonial proceedings and—

    (a) a decree nisi of divorce or nullity of marriage has been made;

    (b) at or after the date of the decree nisi an order for maintenance pending suit is in force; and

    (c) the spouse in whose favour the decree nisi was made has made an application for an order for periodical payments.

(2) The spouse in whose favour the decree nisi was made may apply, using the Part 18 procedure, for an order providing for payments at the same rate as those provided for by the order for maintenance pending suit.

Application for periodical payments order at same rate as an order for maintenance pending outcome of proceedings

  9.9.—(1) This rule applies where there are civil partnership proceedings and—

    (a) a conditional order of dissolution or nullity of civil partnership has been made;

    (b) at or after the date of the conditional order an order for maintenance pending outcome of proceedings is in force;

    (c) the civil partner in whose favour the conditional order was made has made an application for an order for periodical payments.

(2) The civil partner in whose favour the conditional order was made may apply, using the Part 18 procedure, for an order providing for payments at the same rate as those provided for by, the order for maintenance pending the outcome of proceedings.

CHAPTER 3

APPLICATIONS FOR FINANCIAL REMEDIES FOR CHILDREN

Application by parent, guardian etc for financial remedy in respect of children

  9.10.—(1) The following people may apply for a financial remedy in respect of a child—

    (a) a parent, guardian or special guardian of any child of the family;

    (b) any person in whose favour a residence order has been made with respect to a child of the family, and any applicant for such an order;

    (c) any other person who is entitled to apply for a residence order with respect to a child;

    (d) a local authority, where an order has been made under section 31(1)(a) of the 1989 Act placing a child in its care;

    (e) the Official Solicitor, if appointed the children's guardian of a child of the family under rule 16.24; and

    (f) a child of the family who has been given permission to apply for a financial remedy.

(2) In this rule "residence order" has the meaning given to it by section 8(1) of the 1989 Act.

Children to be separately represented on certain applications

9.11.—(1) Where an application for a financial remedy includes an application for an order for a variation of settlement, the court must, unless it is satisfied that the proposed variation does not adversely affect the rights or interests of any child concerned, direct that the child be separately represented on the application.

(2) On any other application for a financial remedy the court may direct that the child be separately represented on the application.

(3) Where a direction is made under paragraph (1) or (2), the court may if the person to be appointed so consents, appoint—

(a) a person other than the Official Solicitor; or

(b) the Official Solicitor,

to be a children's guardian and rule 16.24(5) and (6) and rules 16.25 to 16.28 apply as appropriate to such an appointment.

CHAPTER 4

PROCEDURE IN THE HIGH COURT AND COUNTY COURT AFTER FILING AN APPLICATION

Duties of the court and the applicant upon issuing an application

9.12.—(1) When an application under this Part is issued in the High Court or in a county court—

(a) the court will fix a first appointment not less than 12 weeks and not more than 16 weeks after the date of the filing of the application; and

(b) subject to paragraph (2), within 4 days beginning with the date on which the application was filed, a court officer will—

(i) serve a copy of the application on the respondent; and

(ii) give notice of the date of the first appointment to the applicant and the respondent.

(2) Where the applicant wishes to serve a copy of the application on the respondent and on filing the application so notifies the court—

(a) paragraph (1)(b) does not apply;

(b) a court officer will return to the applicant the copy of the application and the notice of the date of the first appointment; and

(c) the applicant must,—

(i) within 4 days beginning with the date on which the copy of the application is received from the court, serve the copy of the application and notice of the date of the first appointment on the respondent; and

(ii) file a certificate of service at or before the first appointment.

(Rule 6.37 sets out what must be included in a certificate of service.)

(3) The date fixed under paragraph (1), or for any subsequent appointment, must not be cancelled except with the court's permission and, if cancelled, the court must immediately fix a new date.

Service of application on mortgagees, trustees etc

9.13.—(1) Where an application for a financial remedy includes an application for an order for a variation of settlement, the applicant must serve copies of the application on—

(a) the trustees of the settlement;

(b) the settlor if living; and

(c) such other persons as the court directs.

(2) In the case of an application for an avoidance of disposition order, the applicant must serve copies of the application on the person in whose favour the disposition is alleged to have been made.

(3) Where an application for a financial remedy includes an application relating to land, the applicant must serve a copy of the application on any mortgagee of whom particulars are given in the application.

(4) Any person served under paragraphs (1), (2) or (3) may make a request to the court in writing, within 14 days beginning with the date of service of the application, for a copy of the applicant's financial statement or any relevant part of that statement.

(5) Any person who—

    (a)   is served with copies of the application in accordance with paragraphs (1), (2) or (3); or

    (b)   receives a copy of a financial statement, or a relevant part of that statement, following an application made under paragraph (4),

may within 14 days beginning with the date of service or receipt file a statement in answer.

(6) Where a copy of an application is served under paragraphs (1), (2) or (3), the applicant must file a certificate of service at or before the first appointment.

(7) A statement in answer filed under paragraph (5) must be verified by a statement of truth.

Procedure before the first appointment

9.14.—(1) Not less than 35 days before the first appointment both parties must simultaneously exchange with each other and file with the court a financial statement in the form referred to in Practice Direction 5A.

(2) The financial statement must—

    (a)   be verified by an affidavit; and

    (b)   accompanied by the following documents only—

        (i)   any documents required by the financial statement;

        (ii)   any other documents necessary to explain or clarify any of the information contained in the financial statement; and

        (iii)   any documents provided to the party producing the financial statement by a person responsible for a pension arrangement, either following a request under rule 9.30 or as part of a relevant valuation; and

        (iv)   any notification or other document referred to in rule 9.37(2), (4) or (5) which has been received by the party producing the financial statement.

(3) Where a party was unavoidably prevented from sending any document required by the financial statement, that party must at the earliest opportunity—

    (a)   serve a copy of that document on the other party; and

    (b)   file a copy of that document with the court, together with a written explanation of the failure to send it with the financial statement.

(4) No disclosure or inspection of documents may be requested or given between the filing of the application for a financial remedy and the first appointment, except—

    (a)   copies sent with the financial statement, or in accordance with paragraph (3); or

    (b)   in accordance with paragraphs (5) and (6).

(Rule 21.1 explains what is meant by disclosure and inspection.)

(5) Not less than 14 days before the hearing of the first appointment, each party must file with the court and serve on the other party—

    (a)   a concise statement of the issues between the parties;

    (b)   a chronology;

(c) a questionnaire setting out by reference to the concise statement of issues any further information and documents requested from the other party or a statement that no information and documents are required; and

(d) a notice stating whether that party will be in a position at the first appointment to proceed on that occasion to a FDR appointment.

(6) Not less than 14 days before the hearing of the first appointment, the applicant must file with the court and serve on the respondent confirmation—

(a) of the names of all persons served in accordance with rule 9.13(1) to (3); and

(b) that there are no other persons who must be served in accordance with those paragraphs.

Duties of the court at the first appointment

9.15.—(1) The first appointment must be conducted with the objective of defining the issues and saving costs.

(2) At the first appointment the court must determine—

(a) the extent to which any questions seeking information under rule 9.14(5)(c) must be answered; and

(b) what documents requested under rule 9.14(5)(c) must be produced,

and give directions for the production of such further documents as may be necessary.

(3) The court must give directions where appropriate about—

(a) the valuation of assets (including the joint instruction of joint experts);

(b) obtaining and exchanging expert evidence, if required;

(c) the evidence to be adduced by each party; and

(d) further chronologies or schedules to be filed by each party.

(4) If the court decides that a referral to a FDR appointment is appropriate it must direct that the case be referred to a FDR appointment.

(5) If the court decides that a referral to a FDR appointment is not appropriate it must direct one or more of the following—

(a) that a further directions appointment be fixed;

(b) that an appointment be fixed for the making of an interim order;

(c) that the case be fixed for a final hearing and, where that direction is given, the court must determine the judicial level at which the case should be heard.

(By rule 3.3 the court may also direct that the case be adjourned if it considers that alternative dispute resolution is appropriate.)

(6) In considering whether to make a costs order under rule 28.3(5), the court must have particular regard to the extent to which each party has complied with the requirement to send documents with the financial statement and the explanation given for any failure to comply.

(7) The court may—

(a) where an application for an interim order has been listed for consideration at the first appointment, make an interim order;

(b) having regard to the contents of the notice filed by the parties under rule 9.14(5)(d), treat the appointment (or part of it) as a FDR appointment to which rule 9.17 applies;

(c) in a case where a pension sharing order or a pension attachment order is requested, direct any party with pension rights to file and serve a Pension Inquiry Form, completed in full or in part as the court may direct; and

(d) in a case where a pension compensation sharing order or a pension compensation attachment order is requested, direct any party with PPF compensation rights to file and serve a Pension Protection Fund Inquiry Form, completed in full or in part as the court may direct.

(8) Both parties must personally attend the first appointment unless the court directs otherwise.

After the first appointment

9.16.—(1) Between the first appointment and the FDR appointment, a party is not entitled to the production of any further documents except—

(a)   in accordance with directions given under rule 9.15(2); or

(b)   with the permission of the court.

(2) At any stage—

(a)   a party may apply for further directions or a FDR appointment;

(b)   the court may give further directions or direct that parties attend a FDR appointment.

The FDR appointment

9.17.—(1) The FDR appointment must be treated as a meeting held for the purposes of discussion and negotiation.

(2) The judge hearing the FDR appointment must have no further involvement with the application, other than to conduct any further FDR appointment or to make a consent order or a further directions order.

(3) Not less than 7 days before the FDR appointment, the applicant must file with the court details of all offers and proposals, and responses to them.

(4) Paragraph (3) includes any offers, proposals or responses made wholly or partly without prejudice$^{(GL)}$, but paragraph (3) does not make any material admissible as evidence if, but for that paragraph, it would not be admissible.

(5) At the conclusion of the FDR appointment, any documents filed under paragraph (3), and any filed documents referring to them, must, at the request of the party who filed them, be returned to that party and not retained on the court file.

(6) Parties attending the FDR appointment must use their best endeavours to reach agreement on matters in issue between them.

(7) The FDR appointment may be adjourned from time to time.

(8) At the conclusion of the FDR appointment, the court may make an appropriate consent order.

(9) If the court does not make an appropriate consent order as mentioned in paragraph (8), the court must give directions for the future course of the proceedings including, where appropriate—

(a)   the filing of evidence, including up to date information; and

(b)   fixing a final hearing date.

(10) Both parties must personally attend the FDR appointment unless the court directs otherwise.

CHAPTER 5

PROCEDURE IN THE MAGISTRATES' COURT AFTER FILING AN APPLICATION

Duties of the court and the applicant upon filing an application

9.18.—(1) When an application for an order under this Part is issued in a magistrates' court—

(a)   the court will fix a first hearing date not less than 4 weeks and not more than 8 weeks after the date of the filing of the application; and

(b)   subject to paragraph (2), within 4 days beginning with the date on which the application was filed, a court officer will—

(i)   serve a copy of the application on the respondent;

(ii)   give notice of the date of the first hearing to the applicant and the respondent; and

(iii)   send a blank financial statement to both the applicant and the respondent.

(2) Where the applicant wishes to serve a copy of the application on the respondent and, on filing the application, so notifies the court—

    (a) paragraph (1)(b) does not apply;

    (b) a court officer will return to the applicant the copy of the application and the notice of the date of the first hearing; and

    (c) the applicant must—

        (i) within 4 days beginning with the date on which the copy of the application is received from the court, serve the copy of the application and notice of the date of the first hearing on the respondent;

        (ii) send a blank financial statement to the respondent; and

        (iii) file a certificate of service at or before the first hearing.

(3) The date fixed under paragraph (1), or for any other subsequent hearing or appointment must not be cancelled except with the court's permission and, if cancelled, the court must immediately fix a new date.

Procedure before the first hearing

9.19.—(1) Not more than 14 days after the date of the issue of the application both parties must simultaneously exchange with each other and file with the court a financial statement referred to in Practice Direction 5A.

(2) The financial statement must—

    (a) be verified by an affidavit; and

    (b) contain the following documents only—

        (i) any documents required by the financial statement; and

        (ii) any other documents necessary to explain or clarify any of the information contained in the financial statement.

(3) Where a party was unavoidably prevented from sending any document required by the financial statement, that party must at the earliest opportunity—

    (a) serve a copy of that document on the other party; and

    (b) file a copy of that document with the court, together with a statement explaining the failure to send it with the financial statement.

(4) No disclosure or inspection of documents may be requested or given between the filing of the application for a financial remedy and the first hearing except copies sent with the financial statement or in accordance with paragraph (3).

(Rule 21.1 explains what is meant by disclosure and inspection.)

Power of the court to direct filing of evidence and set dates for further hearings

9.20. Unless the court is able to determine the application at the first hearing the court may direct that further evidence be filed and set a date for a directions hearing or appointment or final hearing.

Who the respondent is on an application under section 20 or section 20A of the 1978 Act(a) or Part 6 of Schedule 6 to the 2004 Act

9.21. In relation to proceedings set out in column 1 of the following table, column 2 sets out who the respondents to those proceedings will be.

(a)   Section 20A was inserted by section 33(1) of and paragraph 69 of Schedule 2 to the Family Law Reform Act 1987 and substituted by section 108(5) of and paragraph 39 of Schedule 13 to the Children Act 1989.

Proceedings	Respondent
Application under section 20 of the 1978 Act, except an application for variation of an order.	The other party to the marriage; and where the order to which the application relates requires periodical payments to be made to, or in respect of, a child who is 16 years of age or over, that child.
Application under paragraphs 30 to 34 of Schedule 6 to the 2004 Act, except an application for variation of an order.	The other party to the civil partnership; and where the order to which the application relates requires periodical payments to be made to, or in respect of, a child who is 16 years of age or over, that child.
Application for the revival of an order under section 20A of the 1978 Act or paragraph 40 of Schedule 6 to the 2004 Act.	The parties to the proceedings leading to the order which it is sought to have revived.

Proceedings by or against a person outside England and Wales for orders under section 20 of the 1978 Act or paragraphs 30 to 34 of Schedule 6 to the 2004 Act other than proceedings for variation of orders

9.22.—(1) Subject to the provisions of this rule, the jurisdiction conferred on a court by virtue of section 20 of the 1978 Act or paragraphs 30 to 34 of Schedule 6 to the 2004 Act is exercisable when proceedings are brought by or against a person residing outside England and Wales.

(2) Subject to paragraph (3), where the court is satisfied that the respondent has been outside England and Wales for the whole of the period beginning one month before the making of the application and ending with the date of the hearing, it may proceed with the application provided that—

    (a) the applicant provided the court with an address for service of the application and written notice of the hearing on the respondent; or

    (b) the court is satisfied that the respondent has been made aware of the application and of the time and place appointed for the hearing otherwise than by service of the application upon the respondent by the court; and

    (c) it is reasonable in all the circumstances to proceed in the absence of the respondent.

(3) The court must not make the order for which the application is made unless it is satisfied that—

    (a) during the period of 6 months immediately preceding the making of the application the respondent was continuously outside England and Wales, or was not in England and Wales on more than 30 days; and

    (b) having regard to any communication to the court in writing purporting to be from the respondent, it is reasonable in all the circumstances to do so.

(4) This rule does not apply in relation to proceedings to vary an order for periodical payments.

(Rules made under section 144 of the Magistrates' Courts Act 1980 make provision in respect of proceedings by or against a person outside England and Wales for variation of orders under section 20 of the 1978 Act or paragraphs 30 to 34 of Schedule 6 to the 2004 Act.)

Duty to make entries in the court's register

9.23.—(1) Where the designated officer for the court receives notice of any direction made in the High Court or a county court under section 28 of the 1978 Act(**a**) by virtue of which an order

---

(**a**)   Section 28 was inserted with savings by section 66(1) of and paragraph 28(2) and (3) of Schedule 8 to the Family Law Act 1996 and subsection (2) was repealed by Schedule 10 to that Act.

made by the court under that Act or the 2004 Act ceases to have effect, particulars of the direction must be entered in the court's register.

(2) Where—

    (a)   in proceedings under the 1978 Act, the hearing of an application under section 2 of that Act(**a**) is adjourned after the court has decided that it is satisfied of any ground mentioned in section 1(**b**); or

    (b)   in proceedings under the 2004 Act, the hearing of an application under Part 1 of Schedule 6 to that Act is adjourned after the court has decided that it is satisfied of any ground mentioned in paragraph 1,

and the parties to the proceedings agree to the resumption of the hearing in accordance with section 31 of the 1978 Act by a court which includes justices who were not sitting when the hearing began, particulars of the agreement must be entered into the court's register.

CHAPTER 6

GENERAL PROCEDURE

Power to order delivery up of possession etc.

9.24.—(1) This rule applies where the court has made an order under—

    (a)   section 24A of the 1973 Act(**c**);

    (b)   section 17(2) of the 1984 Act;

    (c)   Part 3 of Schedule 5 to the 2004 Act; or

    (d)   paragraph 9(4) of Schedule 7 to the 2004 Act.

(2) When the court makes an order mentioned in paragraph (1), it may order any party to deliver up to the purchaser or any other person—

    (a)   possession of the land, including any interest in, or right over, land;

    (b)   receipt of rents or profits relating to it; or

    (c)   both.

Where proceedings may be heard

9.25.—(1) Paragraph (2) applies to an application—

    (a)   for a financial order;

    (b)   under Part 3 of the 1984 Act; or

    (c)   under Schedule 7 to the 2004 Act.

(2) An application mentioned in paragraph (1) must be heard—

    (a)   where the case is proceeding in the county court, at any court of trial; and

    (b)   where the case is proceeding in the High Court—

        (i)   at the Royal Courts of Justice; or

        (ii)   in matrimonial or civil partnership proceedings, any court at which sittings of the High Court are authorised.

(3) An application for an order under—

(**a**)   Section 2 was amended by sections 15(1) and 146 of and paragraphs 96(1), (2) and (3) of Schedule 4 to and Part 2 of Schedule 18 to the Constitutional Reform Act 2005.

(**b**)   Section 1 was amended by section 46(1) of and paragraph (c) of Schedule 1 to the Matrimonial and Family Proceedings Act 1984 and prospectively repealed with savings by sections 18(1) and 66(3) of and Schedule 10 to the Family Law Act 1996.

(**c**)   Section 24A was inserted by section 7 of the Matrimonial Homes and Property Act 1981 (c.24) and subsection 6 was inserted by section 46(1) of and Schedule 1 to that Act and the section was amended by section 66(1) and 66(3) of and paragraph 8 of Schedule 8 to and Schedule 10 to the Family Law Act 1996 and by section 261(1) of and paragraph 42 of Schedule 27 to the Civil Partnership Act 2004.

(a) section 27 of the 1973 Act(**a**); or

(b) Part 9 of Schedule 5 to the 2004 Act,

must be heard in a court of trial or in the High Court.

(4) A court may transfer a case to another court exercising the same jurisdiction, either of its own initiative or on the application of one of the parties, if—

(a) the parties consent to the transfer;

(b) the court has held a hearing to determine whether a transfer should be ordered; or

(c) paragraph (5) applies.

(5) A court may transfer a case without a hearing if—

(a) the court has notified the parties in writing that it intends to order a transfer; and

(b) neither party has, within 14 days of the notification being sent, requested a hearing to determine whether a transfer should be ordered.

Applications for consent orders for financial remedy

9.26.—(1) Subject to paragraph (5) and to rule 35.2, in relation to an application for a consent order—

(a) the applicant must file two copies of a draft of the order in the terms sought, one of which must be endorsed with a statement signed by the respondent to the application signifying agreement; and

(b) each party must file with the court and serve on the other party, a statement of information in the form referred to in Practice Direction 5A.

(2) Where each party's statement of information is contained in one form, it must be signed by both the applicant and respondent to certify that they have read the contents of the other party's statement.

(3) Where each party's statement of information is in a separate form, the form of each party must be signed by the other party to certify that they have read the contents of the statement contained in that form.

(4) Unless the court directs otherwise, the applicant and the respondent need not attend the hearing of an application for a consent order.

(5) Where all or any of the parties attend the hearing of an application for a financial remedy the court may—

(a) dispense with the filing of a statement of information; and

(b) give directions for the information which would otherwise be required to be given in such a statement in such a manner as it thinks fit.

(6) In relation to an application for a consent order under Part 3 of the 1984 Act or Schedule 7 to the 2004 Act, the application for permission to make the application may be heard at the same time as the application for a financial remedy if evidence of the respondent's consent to the order is filed with the application.

(The following rules contain provision in relation to applications for consent orders - rule 9.32 (pension sharing order), rule 9.34 (pension attachment order), rule 9.41 (pension compensation sharing orders) and rule 9.43 (pension compensation attachment orders.)

(**a**) Section 27 was amended by sections 4 and 46(1) and paragraph 13 of Schedule 1 to the Matrimonial and Family Proceedings Act 1984 and sections 63(1), (2), (3) (4) and (5) and 89(2)(b) of and Schedule 3 to the Domestic Proceedings and Magistrates' Courts Act 1978 and sections 33(1) and 66(1) and paragraph 52 of Schedule 2 and paragraphs 13(2), (3) and (4) of Schedule 8 to the Family Law Act 1996 and section 6(1) of the Domicile and Matrimonial Proceedings Act 1973.

CHAPTER 7

ESTIMATES OF COSTS

Estimates of Costs

9.27.—(1) Subject to paragraph (2), at every hearing or appointment each party must produce to the court an estimate of the costs incurred by that party up to the date of that hearing or appointment.

(2) Not less than 14 days before the date fixed for the final hearing of an application for a financial remedy, each party ("the filing party") must (unless the court directs otherwise) file with the court and serve on each other party a statement giving full particulars of all costs in respect of the proceedings which the filing party has incurred or expects to incur, to enable the court to take account of the parties' liabilities for costs when deciding what order (if any) to make for a financial remedy.

(3) This rule does not apply to magistrates' courts.

(Rule 28.3 makes provision for orders for costs in financial remedy proceedings.)

Duty to make open proposals

9.28.—(1) Not less than 14 days before the date fixed for the final hearing of an application for a financial remedy, the applicant must (unless the court directs otherwise) file with the court and serve on the respondent an open statement which sets out concise details, including the amounts involved, of the orders which the applicant proposes to ask the court to make.

(2) Not more than 7 days after service of a statement under paragraph (1), the respondent must file with the court and serve on the applicant an open statement which sets out concise details, including the amounts involved, of the orders which the respondent proposes to ask the court to make.

CHAPTER 8

PENSIONS

Application and interpretation of this Chapter

9.29.—(1) This Chapter applies

    (a) where an application for a financial remedy has been made; and

    (b) the applicant or respondent is the party with pension rights.

(2) In this Chapter—

    (a) in proceedings under the 1973 Act and the 1984 Act, all words and phrases defined in sections 25D(3) and (4) of the 1973 Act(**a**) have the meaning assigned by those subsections;

    (b) in proceedings under the 2004 Act—

        (i) all words and phrases defined in paragraphs 16(4) to (5) and 29 of Schedule 5 to that Act have the meanings assigned by those paragraphs; and

        (ii) "the party with pension rights" has the meaning given to "civil partner with pension rights" by paragraph 29 of Schedule 5 to the 2004 Act;

    (c) all words and phrases defined in section 46 of the Welfare Reform and Pensions Act 1999(**b**) have the meanings assigned by that section.

(**a**) Section 25D(3) and (4) was amended by sections 21 and 84(1) of and paragraphs 3(1) and (5) of Schedule 4 to and paragraphs 64 and 66(1) and (4) of Schedule 12 to the Welfare Reform and Pensions Act 1999 and section 66(1) of and Schedule 8 to the Family Law Act 1996.

(**b**) Section 46 was amended by section 320 of and Part 1 of Schedule 13 to the Pensions Act 2004 (c.35) and articles 15(1) and (4) of the Taxation of Pension Schemes (Consequential Amendments) Order 2006 (S.I. 2006/745).

What the party with pension rights must do when the court fixes a first appointment

9.30.—(1) Where the court fixes a first appointment as required by rule 9.12(1)(a) the party with pension rights must request the person responsible for each pension arrangement under which the party has or is likely to have benefits to provide the information referred to in regulation 2(2) of the Pensions on Divorce etc (Provision of Information) Regulations 2000.

(The information referred to in regulation 2 of the Pensions on Divorce etc (Provision of Information) Regulations 2000 relates to the valuation of pension rights or benefits.)

(2) The party with pension rights must comply with paragraph (1) within 7 days beginning with the date on which that party receives notification of the date of the first appointment.

(3) Within 7 days beginning with the date on which the party with pension rights receives the information under paragraph (1) that party must send a copy of it to the other party, together with the name and address of the person responsible for each pension arrangement.

(4) A request under paragraph (1) need not be made where the party with pension rights is in possession of, or has requested, a relevant valuation of the pension rights or benefits accrued under the pension arrangement in question.

Applications for pension sharing orders

9.31. Where an application for a financial remedy includes an application for a pension sharing order, or where a request for such an order is added to an existing application for a financial remedy, the applicant must serve a copy of the application on the person responsible for the pension arrangement concerned.

Applications for consent orders for pension sharing

9.32.—(1) This rule applies where—

   (a)   the parties have agreed on the terms of an order and the agreement includes a pension sharing order;

   (b)   service has not been effected under rule 9.31; and

   (c)   the information referred to in paragraph (2) has not otherwise been provided.

(2) The party with pension rights must—

   (a)   request the person responsible for the pension arrangement concerned to provide the information set out in Section C of the Pension Inquiry Form; and

   (b)   on receipt, send a copy of the information referred to in sub-paragraph (a) to the other party.

Applications for pension attachment orders

9.33.—(1) Where an application for a financial remedy includes an application for a pension attachment order, or where a request for such an order is added to an existing application for a financial remedy, the applicant must serve a copy of the application on the person responsible for the pension arrangement concerned and must at the same time send—

   (a)   an address to which any notice which the person responsible is required to serve on the applicant is to be sent;

   (b)   an address to which any payment which the person responsible is required to make to the applicant is to be sent; and

   (c)   where the address in sub-paragraph (b) is that of a bank, a building society or the Department of National Savings, sufficient details to enable the payment to be made into the account of the applicant.

(2) A person responsible for a pension arrangement who receives a copy of the application under paragraph (1) may, within 21 days beginning with the date of service of the application, request the

party with the pension rights to provide that person with the information disclosed in the financial statement relating to the party's pension rights or benefits under that arrangement.

(3) If the person responsible for a pension arrangement makes a request under paragraph (2), the party with the pension rights must provide that person with a copy of the section of that party's financial statement that relates to that party's pension rights or benefits under that arrangement.

(4) The party with the pension rights must comply with paragraph (3)—

    (a) within the time limited for filing the financial statement by rule 9.14(1); or

    (b) within 21 days beginning with the date on which the person responsible for the pension arrangement makes the request,

whichever is the later.

(5) A person responsible for a pension arrangement who receives a copy of the section of a financial statement as required pursuant to paragraph (4) may, within 21 days beginning with the date on which that person receives it, send to the court, the applicant and the respondent a statement in answer.

(6) A person responsible for a pension arrangement who files a statement in answer pursuant to paragraph (5) will be entitled to be represented at the first appointment, or such other hearing as the court may direct, and the court must within 4 days, beginning with the date on which that person files the statement in answer, give the person notice of the date of the first appointment or other hearing as the case may be.

Applications for consent orders for pension attachment

9.34.—(1) This rule applies where service has not been effected under rule 9.33(1).

(2) Where the parties have agreed on the terms of an order and the agreement includes a pension attachment order, then they must serve on the person responsible for the pension arrangement concerned—

    (a) a copy of the application for a consent order;

    (b) a draft of the proposed order, complying with rule 9.35; and

    (c) the particulars set out in rule 9.33(1).

(3) No consent order that includes a pension attachment order must be made unless either—

    (a) the person responsible for the pension arrangement has not made any objection within 21 days beginning with the date on which the application for a consent order was served on that person; or

    (b) the court has considered any such objection, and for the purpose of considering any objection the court may make such direction as it sees fit for the person responsible to attend before it or to furnish written details of the objection.

Pension sharing orders or pension attachment orders

9.35. An order for a financial remedy, whether by consent or not, which includes a pension sharing order or a pension attachment order, must—

    (a) in the body of the order, state that there is to be provision by way of pension sharing or pension attachment in accordance with the annex or annexes to the order; and

    (b) be accompanied by a pension sharing annex or a pension attachment annex as the case may require, and if provision is made in relation to more than one pension arrangement there must be one annex for each pension arrangement.

Duty of the court upon making a pension sharing order or a pension attachment order

9.36.—(1) A court which varies or discharges a pension sharing order or a pension attachment order, must send, or direct one of the parties to send—

    (a) to the person responsible for the pension arrangement concerned; or

(b) where the Board has assumed responsibility for the pension scheme or part of it, the Board;

the documents referred to in paragraph (4).

(2) A court which makes a pension sharing order or pension attachment order, must send, or direct one of the parties to send to the person responsible for the pension arrangement concerned, the documents referred to in paragraph (4).

(3) Where the Board has assumed responsibility for the pension scheme or part of it after the making of a pension sharing order or attachment order but before the documents have been sent to the person responsible for the pension arrangement in accordance with paragraph (2), the court which makes the pension sharing order or the pension attachment order, must send, or direct one of the parties to send to the Board the documents referred to in paragraph (4).

(4) The documents to be sent in accordance with paragraph (1) to (3) are—

(a) in the case of—

(i) proceedings under the 1973 Act, a copy of the decree of judicial separation;

(ii) proceedings under Schedule 5 to the 2004 Act, a copy of the separation order;

(iii) proceedings under Part 3 of the 1984 Act, a copy of the document of divorce, annulment or legal separation;

(iv) proceedings under Schedule 7 to the 2004 Act, a copy of the document of dissolution, annulment or legal separation;

(b) in the case of divorce or nullity of marriage, a copy of the decree absolute under rule 7.31 or 7.32; or

(c) in the case of dissolution or nullity of civil partnership, a copy of the order making the conditional order final under rule 7.31 or 7.32; and

(d) a copy of the pension sharing order or the pension attachment order, or as the case may be of the order varying or discharging that order, including any annex to that order relating to that pension arrangement but no other annex to that order.

(5) The documents referred to in paragraph (1) must be sent—

(a) in proceedings under the 1973 Act and the 1984 Act, within 7 days beginning with the date on which—

(i) the relevant pension sharing or pension attachment order is made; or

(ii) the decree absolute of divorce or nullity or decree of judicial separation is made,

whichever is the later; and

(b) in proceedings under the 2004 Act, within 7 days beginning with the date on which—

(i) the relevant pension sharing or pension attachment order is made; or

(ii) the final order of dissolution or nullity or separation order is made,

whichever is the later.

Procedure where Pension Protection Fund becomes involved with the pension scheme

9.37.—(1) This rule applies where—

(a) rules 9.30 to 9.34 or 9.36 apply; and

(b) the party with the pension rights ("the member") receives or has received notification in compliance with the Pension Protection Fund (Provision of Information) Regulations 2005 ("the 2005 Regulations")(**a**)—

(i) from the trustees or managers of a pension scheme, that there is an assessment period in relation to that scheme; or

---

(**a**) S.I. 2005/674.

(ii) from the Board that it has assumed responsibility for the pension scheme or part of it.

(2) If the trustees or managers of the pension scheme notify or have notified the member that there is an assessment period in relation to that scheme, the member must send to the other party, all the information which the Board is required from time to time to provide to the member under the 2005 Regulations including—

(a) a copy of the notification; and

(b) a copy of the valuation summary,

in accordance with paragraph (3).

(3) The member must send the information or any part of it referred to in paragraph (2)—

(a) if available, when the member sends the information received under rule 9.30(1); or

(b) otherwise, within 7 days of receipt.

(4) If the Board notifies the member that it has assumed responsibility for the pension scheme, or part of it, the member must—

(a) send a copy of the notification to the other party within 7 days of receipt; and

(b) comply with paragraph (5).

(5) Where paragraph (4) applies, the member must—

(a) within 7 days of receipt of the notification, request the Board in writing to provide a forecast of the member's compensation entitlement as described in the 2005 Regulations; and

(b) send a copy of the forecast of the member's compensation entitlement to the other party within 7 days of receipt.

(6) In this rule—

(a) "assessment period" means an assessment period within the meaning of Part 2 of the Pensions Act 2004; and

(b) "valuation summary" has the meaning assigned to it by the 2005 Regulations.

CHAPTER 9

PENSION PROTECTION FUND COMPENSATION

Application and interpretation of this Chapter

9.38.—(1) This Chapter applies—

(a) where an application for a financial remedy has been made; and

(b) the applicant or respondent is, the party with compensation rights.

(2) In this Chapter "party with compensation rights" —

(a) in proceedings under the 1973 Act and the 1984 Act, has the meaning given to it by section 25G(5) of the 1973 Act;

(b) in proceedings under the 2004 Act, has the meaning given to "civil partner with compensation rights" by paragraph 37(1) of Schedule 5 to the 2004 Act(**a**).

What the party with compensation rights must do when the court fixes a first appointment

9.39.—(1) Where the court fixes a first appointment as required by rule 9.12(1)(a) the party with compensation rights must request the Board to provide the information about the valuation of entitlement to PPF compensation referred to in regulations made by the Secretary of State under section 118 of the Pensions Act 2008.

(**a**) Paragraph 37(1) was amended by section 120 of and paragraph 14, 16(1), (5)(a)(b) and 17(10) of Schedule 6 to the Pensions Act 2008.

(2) The party with compensation rights must comply with paragraph (1) within 7 days beginning with the date on which that party receives notification of the date of the first appointment.

(3) Within 7 days beginning with the date on which the party with compensation rights receives the information under paragraph (1) that party must send a copy of it to the other party, together with the name and address of the trustees or managers responsible for each pension scheme.

(4) Where the rights to PPF Compensation are derived from rights under more than one pension scheme, the party with compensation rights must comply with this rule in relation to each entitlement.

Applications for pension compensation sharing orders

9.40. Where an application for a financial remedy includes an application for a pension compensation sharing order or where a request for such an order is added to an existing application for a financial remedy, the applicant must serve a copy of the application on the Board.

Applications for consent orders for pension compensation sharing

9.41.—(1) This rule applies where—

    (a) the parties have agreed on the terms of an order and the agreement includes a pension compensation sharing order;

    (b) service has not been effected under rule 9.40; and

    (c) the information referred to in paragraph (2) has not otherwise been provided.

(2) The party with compensation rights must—

    (a) request the Board to provide the information set out in Section C of the Pension Protection Fund Inquiry Form; and

    (b) on receipt, send a copy of the information referred to in sub-paragraph (a) to the other party.

Applications for pension compensation attachment orders

9.42. Where an application for a financial remedy includes an application for a pension compensation attachment order or where a request for such an order is added to an existing application for a financial remedy, the applicant must serve a copy of the application on the Board and must at the same time send—

    (a) an address to which any notice which the Board is required to serve on the applicant is to be sent;

    (b) an address to which any payment which the Board is required to make to the applicant is to be sent; and

    (c) where the address in sub-paragraph (b) is that of a bank, a building society or the Department of National Savings, sufficient details to enable the payment to be made into the account of the applicant.

Applications for consent orders for pension compensation attachment

9.43.—(1) This rule applies where service has not been effected under rule 9.42.

(2) Where the parties have agreed on the terms of an order and the agreement includes a pension compensation attachment order, then they must serve on the Board—

    (a) a copy of the application for a consent order;

    (b) a draft of the proposed order, complying with rule 9.44; and

    (c) the particulars set out in rule 9.42.

Pension compensation sharing orders or pension compensation attachment orders

9.44. An order for a financial remedy, whether by consent or not, which includes a pension compensation sharing order or a pension compensation attachment order, must—

(a) in the body of the order, state that there is to be provision by way of pension compensation sharing or pension compensation attachment in accordance with the annex or annexes to the order; and

(b) be accompanied by a pension compensation sharing annex or a pension compensation attachment annex as the case may require, and if provision is made in relation to entitlement to PPF compensation that derives from rights under more than one pension scheme there must be one annex for each such entitlement.

Duty of the court upon making a pension compensation sharing order or a pension compensation attachment order

9.45.—(1) A court which makes, varies or discharges a pension compensation sharing order or a pension compensation attachment order, must send, or direct one of the parties to send, to the Board—

(a) in the case of—

(i) proceedings under Part 3 of the 1984 Act, a copy of the document of divorce, annulment or legal separation;

(ii) proceedings under Schedule 7 to the 2004 Act, a copy of the document of dissolution, annulment or legal separation;

(b) in the case of —

(i) divorce or nullity of marriage, a copy of the decree absolute under rule 7.32 or 7.33;

(ii) dissolution or nullity of civil partnership, a copy of the order making the conditional order final under rule 7.32 or 7.33;

(c) in the case of separation—

(i) in the matrimonial proceedings, a copy of the decree of judicial separation;

(ii) in civil partnership proceedings, a copy of the separation order; and

(d) a copy of the pension compensation sharing order or the pension compensation attachment order, or as the case may be of the order varying or discharging that order, including any annex to that order relating to that PPF compensation but no other annex to that order.

(2) The documents referred to in paragraph (1) must be sent—

(a) in proceedings under the 1973 Act and the 1984 Act, within 7 days beginning with the date on which—

(i) the relevant pension compensation sharing or pension compensation attachment order is made; or

(ii) the decree absolute of divorce or nullity or the decree of judicial separation is made,

whichever is the later; and

(b) in proceedings under the 2004 Act, within 7 days beginning with the date on which—

(i) the relevant pension compensation sharing or pension compensation attachment order is made; or

(ii) the final order of dissolution or nullity or separation order is made,

whichever is the later.

PART 10

APPLICATIONS UNDER PART 4 OF THE FAMILY LAW ACT 1996

Scope and interpretation of this Part

10.1. The rules in this Part apply to proceedings under Part 4 of the 1996 Act.

Applications for an occupation order or a non-molestation order

10.2.—(1) An application for an occupation order or a non-molestation order must be supported by a witness statement.

(2) Subject to paragraph (3), an application for an occupation order or a non-molestation order may be made without notice.

(3) An application for an occupation order or a non-molestation order may, in a magistrates' court, be made with the permission of the court without notice in which case the applicant must file the application at the time when the application is made or as directed by the court.

(4) Where an application is made without notice, the witness statement in support of the application must state the reasons why notice has not been given.

(Section 45 of the 1996 Act sets out the criteria for making an order without notice.)

Service of the application

10.3.—(1) In an application made on notice, the applicant must serve—

    (a) a copy of the application together with any statement in support; and

    (b) notice of any hearing or directions appointment set by the court,

on the respondent personally—

        (i) not less than 2 days before the hearing; or

        (ii) within such period as the court may direct.

(2) Where the applicant is acting in person, the applicant may request the court officer to serve the application on the respondent.

(3) In an application for an occupation order under section 33, 35 or 36 of the 1996 Act(**a**), the applicant must serve on the mortgagee and any landlord of the dwelling-house in question—

    (a) a copy of the application; and

    (b) notice of the right to make representations in writing or orally at any hearing.

(4) The applicant must file a certificate of service after serving the application.

(Rule 6.23 makes provision for the different methods of serving a document and rule 6.35 provides for the court to authorise service by an alternative method.)

Transfer of pending proceedings to another court

10.4. Subject to any enactment, where an application for an occupation order or a non-molestation order is pending, the court may transfer the proceedings to another court of its own initiative or on the application of either party.

(**a**) Section 33 was amended by section 82 of and paragraphs 4(1), (2), (3), (7), (4)(a) and (b), (5) and 6(a) to (e) of Schedule 9 to the Civil Partnership Act 2004. Section 35 was amended by section 82 of and paragraphs 6(1) to 6(10) of Schedule 9 to that Act. Section 36 was amended by sections 2(2) and 58(1) of and paragraphs 34(1) to (3) of Schedule 10 to the Domestic Violence, Crime and Victims Act 2004 (c.28) and section 82 of and paragraph 7 of Schedule 9 to the Civil Partnership Act 2004.

Privacy

10.5. In the High Court and a county court, any hearing relating to an application for an occupation order or a non-molestation order will be in private unless the court directs otherwise.

Service of an order

10.6.—(1) The applicant must, as soon as reasonably practicable, serve on the respondent personally—

    (a) a copy of the order; and

    (b) where the order is made without notice—

        (i) a copy of the application together with any statement supporting it; and

        (ii) in a magistrates' court, a copy of the record of the reasons for a decision.

(Rule 27.2(8) makes provision for the court officer to supply a copy of the reasons for the court's decision to the persons referred to in rule 27.2(9).)

(2) The court must serve the documents listed in paragraph (1) if—

    (a) an applicant, acting in person, so requests; or

    (b) the court made the order of its own initiative.

(3) In an application for an occupation order under section 33, 35 or 36 of the 1996 Act, the applicant must serve a copy of any order made on the mortgagee and any landlord of the dwelling-house in question.

Representations made by a mortgagee or landlord

10.7. The court may direct that a hearing be held in order to consider any representations made by a mortgagee or a landlord.

Applications to vary, extend or discharge an order

10.8. Rules 10.5 to 10.7 apply to applications to vary, extend or discharge an order.

Orders containing provisions to which a power of arrest is attached

10.9. Where the court makes an occupation order containing one or more provisions to which a power of arrest is attached ("relevant provisions")—

    (a) each relevant provision must be set out in a separate paragraph in the order; and

    (b) a paragraph containing a relevant provision must not include a provision of the order to which the power of arrest is not attached.

Service of an order on the officer for the time being in charge of a police station

10.10.—(1) Where the court makes—

    (a) an occupation order to which a power of arrest is attached; or

    (b) a non-molestation order,

a copy of the order must be delivered to the officer for the time being in charge of—

        (i) the police station for the applicant's address; or

        (ii) such other police station as the court may specify.

(2) A copy of the order delivered under paragraph (1) must be accompanied by a statement showing that the respondent has been served with the order or informed of its terms (whether by being present when the order was made or by telephone or otherwise).

(3) The documentation referred to in paragraphs (1) and (2) must be delivered by—

(a) the applicant; or

(b) the court officer, where the order was served following a request under rule 10.6(2).

(4) Paragraph (5) applies where an order is made varying or discharging—

(a) a provision of an occupation order to which a power of arrest is attached; or

(b) a provision of a non-molestation order.

(5) The court officer must—

(a) immediately inform—

(i) the officer who received a copy of the order under paragraph (1); and

(ii) if the applicant's address has changed, the officer for the time being in charge of the police station for the new address; and

(b) deliver a copy of the order referred to in paragraph (4)(a) or (b) and the order referred to in paragraph (1) to any officer so informed.

Proceedings following arrest in a county court or the High Court

10.11.—(1) This rule applies where a person is arrested pursuant to—

(a) a power of arrest attached to a provision of an occupation order; or

(b) a warrant of arrest issued on an application under section 47(8) of the 1996 Act(**a**).

(2) The court before which a person is brought following arrest may—

(a) determine whether the facts, and the circumstances which led to the arrest, amounted to disobedience of the order; or

(b) adjourn the proceedings.

(3) Where the proceedings are adjourned and the arrested person is released—

(a) unless the court directs otherwise, the matter must be dealt with within 14 days beginning with the date of arrest; and

(b) the arrested person must be given not less than 2 days' notice of the hearing.

(4) An application notice seeking the committal for contempt of court of the arrested person may be issued if the arrested person is not dealt with within the period mentioned in paragraph (3)(a).

(The powers of a county court and the High Court to remand in custody or on bail are contained in section 47 of and Schedule 5 to the Family Law Act 1996(**b**).)

(For proceedings following arrest in a magistrates' court see rules made under section 144 of the Magistrates' Courts Act 1980.)

Enforcement of an order in a county court

10.12. Rule 1 of Order 29 of the CCR (enforcement of judgment to do or abstain from doing any act) has effect as if, for paragraph (3), there were substituted the following—

"(3) At the time when the order is drawn up, the court officer will—

(a) where the order made is (or includes) a non-molestation order; or

(b) where the order made is an occupation order and the court so directs,

issue a copy of the order, indorsed with or incorporating a notice as to the consequences of disobedience, for service in accordance with paragraph (2).".

(**a**) Section 47(8) was amended by section 58(1) to and paragraphs 38(1) and (5) of Schedule 10 to the Domestic Violence, Crime and Victims Act 2004.

(**b**) Section 47 was amended by section 58(1) and (2) of and paragraphs 38(1) to (5) of Schedule 10 to and Schedule 11 to the Domestic Violence, Crime and Victims Act 2004.

(For enforcement of an order generally in a county court or the High Court see Part 33. For enforcement of an order in a magistrates' court see rules made under section 144 of the Magistrates' Courts Act 1980.)

Enforcement of an undertaking in a county court

10.13.—(1) This rule applies to applications for the enforcement of undertakings by committal order in a county court.

(2) Rule 1A of Order 29 of the CCR (undertaking given by party) applies with the necessary modifications, where an application is made in a county court to commit a person for breach of an undertaking.

(For enforcement of an undertaking in a magistrates' court see rules made under section 144 of the Magistrates' Courts Act 1980.)

Power to adjourn the hearing for consideration of the penalty

10.14. The High Court or a county court may adjourn the hearing for consideration of the penalty to be imposed for any contempt of court found proved and such a hearing may be restored if the respondent does not comply with any conditions specified by the court.

(Rules made under section 144 of the Magistrates' Courts Act 1980 contain an equivalent power for magistrates' courts.)

Hospital orders or guardianship orders under the Mental Health Act 1983

10.15.—(1) Where the High Court or a county court makes a hospital order under the Mental Health Act 1983 the court officer must—

    (a) send to the hospital any information which will be of assistance in dealing with the patient; and

    (b) inform the applicant when the respondent is being transferred to hospital.

(2) Where the High Court or a county court makes a guardianship order under the Mental Health Act 1983, the court officer must send any information which will be of assistance in dealing with the patient to—

    (a) the patient's guardian; and

    (b) where the guardian is a person other than the local services authority, the local services authority.

(Section 51 of the 1996 Act(**a**) provides a magistrates' court with a power to make a hospital order or a guardianship order under the Mental Health Act 1983 and attention is drawn to rules made under section 144 of the Magistrates' Courts Act 1980.)

Transfer directions under section 48 of the Mental Health Act 1983

10.16.—(1) Where a transfer direction given by the Secretary of State under section 48 of the Mental Health Act 1983 is in force in respect of a person remanded in custody by the High Court or a county court, the court officer must notify—

    (a) the governor of the prison to which that person was remanded; and

    (b) the hospital where that person is detained,

of any committal hearing which that person is required to attend.

(2) The court officer must also give notice in writing of any further remand to the hospital where that person is detained.

(**a**)   Section 51 was amended by section 1(4) of and paragraph 20(1) and (3) of Schedule 1 to the Mental Health Act 2007 (c.12).

(Rules made under section 144 of the Magistrates' Courts Act 1980 make provision for magistrates' courts.)

Recognizances

10.17.—(1) Where, in accordance with paragraph 2(1)(b)(ii) of Schedule 5 to the 1996 Act, the High Court or a county court fixes the amount of any recognizance with a view to it being taken subsequently, the recognizance may be taken by—

(a) a district judge;

(b) a police officer of the rank of inspector or above or in charge of a police station; or

(c) the governor or keeper of a prison where the arrested person is in custody.

(2) The person having custody of an applicant for bail must release that applicant if satisfied that the required recognizances have been taken.

(A magistrates' court has a similar power to require a recognizance under Part 6 of the Magistrates' Courts Act 1980. Section 119 of that Act(**a**) provides a magistrates' court with a power to postpone the taking of a recognizance and rules made under section 144 of the Magistrates' Courts Act 1980 set out the people who may subsequently take the recognizance.)

PART 11

APPLICATIONS UNDER PART 4A OF THE FAMILY LAW ACT 1996

Scope and interpretation

11.1.—(1) The rules in this Part apply to proceedings in the High Court or a county court under Part 4A of the 1996 Act.

(2) In this Part—

"a forced marriage protection order" means an order under section 63A of the 1996 Act(**b**); and

"the person who is the subject of the proceedings" means the person who will be protected by the forced marriage protection order applied for or being considered by the court of its own initiative, if that order is made, or who is being protected by such an order.

Applications

11.2.—(1) An application for a forced marriage protection order may be made without notice.

(2) Where an application is made without notice, it must be supported by a sworn statement explaining why notice has not been given.

(3) An application for a forced marriage protection order made by an organisation must state—

(a) the name and address of the person submitting the application; and

(b) the position which that person holds in the organisation.

Permission to apply

11.3.—(1) Where the permission of the court is required to apply for a forced marriage protection order, the person seeking permission must file—

(a) a Part 18 application notice setting out—

(**a**)   Section 119 was amended by section 77 of and paragraph 55 of Schedule 14 to the Criminal Justice Act 1982 (c.48).
(**b**)   Section 63A was inserted by section 1 of the Forced Marriage (Civil Protection) Act 2007 (c.20).

      (i) the reasons for the application, for the making of which permission is sought ("the proposed application");

      (ii) the applicant's connection with the person to be protected;

     (iii) the applicant's knowledge of the circumstances of the person to be protected; and

     (iv) the applicant's knowledge of the wishes and feelings of the person to be protected;

    and

    (b) a draft of the proposed application, together with sufficient copies for one to be served on each respondent and (if different) the person to be protected.

(2) As soon as practicable after receiving an application under paragraph (1), the court must—

    (a) grant the application; or

    (b) direct that a date be fixed for the hearing of the application and fix the date.

(3) The court officer must inform the following persons of the court's action under paragraph (2)—

    (a) the applicant;

    (b) the respondent;

    (c) (if different) the person to be protected; and

    (d) any other person directed by the court.

(4) Where permission is granted to apply for a forced marriage protection order, the application must proceed in accordance with rule 11.2.

Service of applications on notice

11.4.—(1) Subject to paragraphs (3) and (4A), where an application is made on notice, the applicant must serve a copy of the application, together with the notice of proceedings, personally on—

    (a) the respondent;

    (b) the person who is the subject of the proceedings (if that person is neither the applicant nor a respondent); and

    (c) any other person directed by the court,

not less than 2 days before the date on which the application will be heard.

(2) The court may abridge the period specified in paragraph (1).

(3) Service of the application must be effected by the court if the applicant so requests (this does not affect the court's power to order substituted service).

(4) Where the application is served on the person who is the subject of the proceedings, it must be accompanied by a notice informing that person—

    (a) how to apply to become a party to the proceedings; and

    (b) of that person's right to make representations in writing or orally at any hearing.

(5) Where the person who is the subject of proceedings is not the applicant and is—

    (a) a child;

    (b) a person, not being a party, who lacks or may lack capacity within the meaning of the 2005 Act; or

    (c) a protected party,

the court will give the directions about the persons who are to be served with the application.

(6) Where an application is served by the applicant, the applicant must file a certificate of service stating the date and time of personal service.

Transfer of proceedings

11.5. Subject to any enactment, where proceedings to which this Part applies are pending, the court may transfer the proceedings to another court of its own initiative or on the application of a party or (if not a party) the person who is the subject of the proceedings.

Parties

11.6.—(1) In proceedings under this Part, a person may file a Part 18 application notice for that person or another person to—

    (a) be joined as a party; or

    (b) cease to be a party.

(2) As soon as practicable after receiving an application under paragraph (1), the court must do one of the following—

    (a) in the case only of an application under paragraph (1)(a), grant the application;

    (b) order that the application be considered at a hearing, and fix a date for the hearing; or

    (c) invite written representations as to whether the application should be granted, to be filed within a specified period, and upon expiry of that period act under sub-paragraph (a) or (b) as it sees fit.

(3) The court officer must inform the following persons of the court's action under paragraph (2)—

    (a) the applicant under paragraph (1);

    (b) (if different) the applicant for the forced marriage protection order and the respondent to that application;

    (c) (if different) the person who is the subject of the proceedings; and

    (d) any other person directed by the court.

(4) The court may at any time direct—

    (a) that a person who would not otherwise be a respondent under these rules be joined as a party to the proceedings; or

    (b) that a party to the proceedings cease to be a party,

and such a direction may be made by the court of its own initiative as well as upon an application under paragraph (1).

(5) Where the court directs the addition or removal of a party, it may give consequential directions about—

    (a) service on a new party of a copy of the application for the forced marriage protection order and other relevant documents; and

    (b) the management of the proceedings.

Hearings and service of orders

11.7.—(1) Any hearing relating to an application for a forced marriage protection order must be in private unless the court otherwise directs.

(2) The court may direct the withholding of any submissions made, or any evidence adduced, for or at any hearing in proceedings to which this Part applies—

    (a) in order to protect the person who is the subject of the proceedings or any other person; or

    (b) for any other good reason.

(3) The applicant must, as soon as reasonably practical, serve personally—

    (a) a copy of the order;

    (b) a copy of the record of the hearing; and

(c) where the order is made without notice, a copy of the application together with any statement supporting it,

on the respondent, the person who is the subject of the proceedings (if neither the applicant nor a respondent), and any other person named in the order.

(4) The court must serve the documents listed in paragraph (3) if—

(a) an applicant, acting in person, so requests; or

(b) the court made the order of its own initiative.

Orders made by the court of its own initiative

11.8.—(1) Where the court makes a forced marriage protection order of its own initiative under section 63C of the 1996 Act(**a**), it must set out in the order—

(a) a summary of its reasons for making the order; and

(b) the names of the persons who are to be served with the order.

(2) The court may order service of the order on—

(a) any of the parties to the current proceedings;

(b) (if different) the person who is the subject of the proceedings; and

(c) any other person whom the court considers should be served.

(3) The court must give directions as to how the order is to be served.

Representations in respect of orders

11.9. Where the court makes an order (whether under rule 11.7 or 11.8), it may direct that a hearing (or further hearing) be held in order to consider any representations made by any of the persons named in, or directed to be served with, the order.

Applications to vary, extend or discharge an order

11.10. Rules 11.7 and 11.9 apply to applications to vary, extend or discharge a forced marriage protection order.

Orders containing provisions to which a power of arrest is attached

11.11. Where the court makes a forced marriage protection order containing one or more provisions to which a power of arrest is attached ("relevant provision")—

(a) each relevant provision must be set out in a separate paragraph in the order; and

(b) a paragraph containing a relevant provision must not include a provision of the order to which the power of arrest is not attached.

Service where order contains a power of arrest

11.12.—(1) This rule applies where the court makes a forced marriage protection order consisting of or including a relevant provision (which has the meaning given in rule 11.11).

(2) The following documents must be delivered to the officer for the time being in charge of any police station for the address of the person being protected by the order or of such other police station as the court may specify—

(a) the power of arrest form; and

(**a**) Section 63C was inserted by section 1 of the Forced Marriage (Civil Protection) Act 2007.

(b) a statement showing that the respondents and any persons directed by the court to be served with the order have been so served or informed of its terms (whether by being present when the order was made or by telephone or otherwise).

(3) The documents referred to in paragraph (2) must be delivered by—

(a) the applicant, if the applicant is responsible for serving the order in accordance with rule 11.7(3); or

(b) the court officer, if the court is responsible for serving the order in accordance with rule 11.7(4) or a direction given under rule 11.8(3).

(4) Where an order is made varying, extending or discharging any of the relevant provisions, the court officer must—

(a) immediately inform the officer who received a copy of the power of arrest form under paragraph (2) and, if the address of the person who is the subject of the proceedings has changed, the officer for the time being in charge of the police station for the new address; and

(b) deliver a copy of the order, together with a copy of the order referred to in paragraph (1), to any officer so informed.

Application for issue of warrant for arrest

11.13.—(1) An application under section 63J(2) of the 1996 Act(**a**) for the issue of a warrant for the arrest of a person must be supported by a sworn statement.

(2) An application for the issue of a warrant for arrest made by a person who is neither the person who is the subject of the proceedings nor (if different) the person who applied for the order, shall be treated, in the first instance, as an application for permission to apply for the warrant to be issued, and the court shall either—

(a) grant the application; or

(b) direct that a date be fixed for the hearing of the application and fix a date.

(3) The court officer must inform the following persons of the court's action under paragraph (2)—

(a) the person applying for the issue of the warrant;

(b) the person being protected by the order; and

(c) any other person directed by the court.

Proceedings following arrest

11.14.—(1) This rule applies where a person is arrested pursuant to—

(a) a power of arrest attached to a provision of a forced marriage protection order; or

(b) a warrant of arrest issued on an application under section 63J(2) of the 1996 Act.

(2) The court before whom a person is brought following his arrest may—

(a) determine whether the facts and the circumstances which led to the arrest amounted to disobedience of the order; or

(b) adjourn the proceedings.

(3) Where the proceedings are adjourned, the arrested person may be released and—

(a) unless the court directs otherwise, be dealt with within 14 days of the day on which the person was arrested; and

(b) be given not less than 2 days' notice of the adjourned hearing.

(**a**) Section 63J(2) was inserted by section 1 of the Forced Marriage (Civil Protection) Act 2007.

(4) An application notice seeking the committal for contempt of court of the arrested person may be issued if the arrested person is not dealt with within the period mentioned in paragraph (3)(a).

(The powers of a county court and the High Court to remand in custody or on bail are contained in section 47 of and Schedule 5 to the 1996 Act(**a**).)

Enforcement of orders

11.15.—(1) The following provisions apply, with the necessary modifications, to the enforcement of orders made under this Part—

   (a) RSC Order 52, rule 7 (power to suspend execution of committal order);

   (b) in a case where an application for an order of committal is made to the High Court, RSC Order 52, rule 2 (application to Divisional Court);

   (c) CCR Order 29, rule 1 (enforcement of judgment to do or abstain from doing any act);

   (d) CCR Order 29, rule 1A (undertaking given by party);

   (e) CCR Order 29, rule 3 (discharge of person in custody).

(2) Rule 1 of Order 29 of the CCR (enforcement of judgment to do or abstain from doing any act) has effect as if, for paragraph (3), there were substituted the following—

> "(3) At the time when the order is drawn up, the court officer will, where the order made is (or includes) a forced marriage protection order, issue a copy of the order, indorsed with or incorporating a notice as to the consequences of disobedience, for service in accordance with paragraph (2)."

(For enforcement of an order generally in a county court or the High Court see Part 33.)

Power to adjourn the hearing for consideration of the penalty

11.16. The court may adjourn the hearing for consideration of the penalty to be imposed for any contempt of court found proved and such hearing may be restored if the contemnor does not comply with any conditions specified by the court.

Hospital orders or guardianship orders under the Mental Health Act 1983

11.17.—(1) Where the court makes a hospital order under the Mental Health Act 1983, the court officer must—

   (a) send to the hospital any information which will be of assistance in dealing with the patient; and

   (b) inform the persons directed by the court to be informed about when the patient is being transferred to hospital.

(2) Where the court makes a guardianship order under the Mental Health Act 1983, the court officer must send any information which will be of assistance in dealing with the patient to—

   (a) the patient's guardian; and

   (b) where the guardian is a person other than the local services authority, the local services authority.

Transfer directions under section 48 of the Mental Health Act 1983

11.18.—(1) Where a transfer direction given by the Secretary of State under section 48 of the Mental Health Act 1983 is in force in respect of a person remanded in custody by the court, the court officer must notify—

   (a) the governor of the prison to which that person was remanded; and

---

(**a**)   Section 47 was inserted by section 1 of the Forced Marriage (Civil Protection) Act 2007.

(b) the hospital where that person is detained,

of any committal hearing which that person is required to attend.

(2) The court officer must also give notice in writing of any further remand to the hospital where that person is detained.

Recognizances

11.19.—(1) Where, in accordance with paragraph 2(1)(b)(ii) of Schedule 5 to the 1996 Act, the court fixes the amount of any recognizance with a view to it being taken subsequently, the recognizance may be taken by—

(a) a district judge;

(b) a police officer of the rank of inspector or above or in charge of a police station; or

(c) the governor or keeper of a prison where the arrested person is in the custody of that governor or keeper.

(2) The person having custody of an applicant for bail must release him if satisfied that the required recognizances have been taken.

PART 12

PROCEEDINGS RELATING TO CHILDREN EXCEPT PARENTAL ORDER PROCEEDINGS AND PROCEEDINGS FOR APPLICATIONS IN ADOPTION, PLACEMENT AND RELATED PROCEEDINGS

CHAPTER 1

INTERPRETATION AND APPLICATION OF THIS PART

Application of this Part

12.1.—(1) The rules in this Part apply to—

(a) emergency proceedings;

(b) private law proceedings;

(c) public law proceedings;

(d) proceedings relating to the exercise of the court's inherent jurisdiction (other than applications for the court's permission to start such proceedings);

(e) proceedings relating to child abduction and the recognition and enforcement of decisions relating to custody under the European Convention;

(f) proceedings relating to the Council Regulation or the 1996 Hague Convention in respect of children; and

(g) any other proceedings which may be referred to in a practice direction.

(Part 18 sets out the procedure for making an application for permission to bring proceedings.)

(Part 31 sets out the procedure for making applications for recognition and enforcement of judgments under the Council Regulation or the 1996 Hague Convention.)

(2) The rules in Chapter 7 of this Part also apply to family proceedings which are not within paragraph (1) but which otherwise relate wholly or mainly to the maintenance or upbringing of a minor.

Interpretation

12.2. In this Part—

"the 2006 Act" means the Childcare Act 2006(**a**);

"advocate" means a person exercising a right of audience as a representative of, or on behalf of, a party;

"care proceedings" means proceedings for a care order under section 31(1)(a) of the 1989 Act;

"Case Management Order" means an order in the form referred to in Practice Direction 12A which may contain such of the provisions listed in that practice direction as may be appropriate to the proceedings;

"child assessment order" has the meaning assigned to it by section 43(2) of the 1989 Act;

"contact activity condition" has the meaning assigned to it by section 11C(2) of the 1989 Act;

"contact activity direction" has the meaning assigned to it by section 11A(3) of the 1989 Act;

"contribution order" has the meaning assigned to it by paragraph 23(2) of Schedule 2 to the 1989 Act;

"education supervision order" has the meaning assigned to it by section 36(2) of the 1989 Act;

"emergency proceedings" means proceedings for—

(a) the disclosure of information as to the whereabouts of a child under section 33 of the 1986 Act(**b**);

(b) an order authorising the taking charge of and delivery of a child under section 34 of the 1986 Act(**c**);

(c) an emergency protection order;

(d) an order under section 44(9)(b) of the 1989 Act varying a direction in an emergency protection order given under section 44(6) of that Act;

(e) an order under section 45(5) of the 1989 Act extending the period during which an emergency protection order is to have effect;

(f) an order under section 45(8) of the 1989 Act discharging an emergency protection order;

(g) an order under section 45(8A) of the 1989(**d**) Act varying or discharging an emergency protection order in so far as it imposes an exclusion requirement on a person who is not entitled to apply for the order to be discharged;

(h) an order under section 45(8B) of the 1989 Act(**e**) varying or discharging an emergency protection order in so far as it confers a power of arrest attached to an exclusion requirement;

(i) warrants under sections 48(9) and 102(1) of the 1989 Act and under section 79 of the 2006 Act(**f**); or

(j) a recovery order under section 50 of the 1989 Act(**g**);

"emergency protection order" means an order under section 44 of the 1989 Act;

"enforcement order" has the meaning assigned to it by section 11J(2) of the 1989 Act;

"financial compensation order" means an order made under section 11O(2) of the 1989 Act;

(**a**) 2006 c.21.

(**b**) Section 33 was amended by section 108(5) of and paragraph 62 of Schedule 13 to the Children Act 1989 and section 261(1) of and paragraph 124 of Schedule 27 to the Civil Partnership Act 2004.

(**c**) Section 34 was amended by section 108(5) of and paragraphs 62 and 70 of Schedule 13 to the Children Act 1989 and article 12(3) of Children (Northern Ireland Consequential Amendments) Order 1995 (S.I. 1995/756).

(**d**) Section 45(8A) was inserted by section 52 of and paragraph 4 of Schedule 6 to the Family Law Act 1996.

(**e**) Section 45(8B) was inserted by section 52 of and paragraph 4 of Schedule 6 to the Family Law Act 1996.

(**f**) Section 79 was amended by section 157 of and paragraphs 108 and 114(1) and (2) and (3)(b) of Schedule 14 to the Education and Inspections Act 2006 (c.40).

(**g**) Section 50 was amended by section 261(1) of and paragraph 131 of Schedule 27 to the Civil Partnership Act 2004.

"interim order" means an interim care order or an interim supervision order referred to in section 38(1) of the 1989 Act;

"private law proceedings" means proceedings for—

(a) a section 8 order except a residence order under section 8 of the 1989 Act relating to a child who is the subject of a care order;

(b) a parental responsibility order under sections 4(1)(c)(**a**), 4ZA(1)(c)(**b**) or 4A(1)(b) of the 1989 Act(**c**) or an order terminating parental responsibility under sections 4(2A), 4ZA(5) or 4A(3) of that Act;

(c) an order appointing a child's guardian under section 5(1) of the 1989 Act or an order terminating the appointment under section 6(7) of that Act;

(d) an order giving permission to change a child's surname or remove a child from the United Kingdom under sections 13(1) or 14C(3) of the 1989 Act;

(e) a special guardianship order except where that order relates to a child who is subject of a care order;

(f) an order varying or discharging such an order under section 14D of the 1989 Act(**d**);

(g) an enforcement order;

(h) a financial compensation order;

(i) an order under paragraph 9 of Schedule A1 to the 1989 Act following a breach of an enforcement order;

(j) an order under Part 2 of Schedule A1 to the 1989 Act revoking or amending an enforcement order; or

(k) an order that a warning notice be attached to a contact order;

"public law proceedings" means proceedings for—

(a) a residence order under section 8 of the 1989 Act relating to a child who is the subject of a care order;

(b) a special guardianship order relating to a child who is the subject of a care order;

(c) a secure accommodation order under section 25 of the 1989 Act(**e**);

(d) a care order, or the discharge of such an order under section 39(1) of the 1989 Act;

(e) an order giving permission to change a child's surname or remove a child from the United Kingdom under section 33(7) of the 1989 Act;

(f) a supervision order under section 31(1)(b) of the 1989 Act(**f**), the discharge or variation of such an order under section 39(2) of that Act, or the extension or further extension of such an order under paragraph 6(3) of Schedule 3 to that Act;

(g) an order making provision regarding contact under section 34(2) to (4) of the 1989 Act or an order varying or discharging such an order under section 34(9) of that Act;

(h) an education supervision order, the extension of an education supervision order under paragraph 15(2) of Schedule 3 to the 1989 Act, or the discharge of such an order under paragraph 17(1) of Schedule 3 to that Act(**g**);

(**a**) Section 4(1)(c) was amended by section 111(1) and (2) of the Adoption and Children Act 2002 and section 56 of and paragraphs 21(1) and (2) of Schedule 6 to the Welfare Reform Act 2009 (c.29).

(**b**) Section 4ZA was inserted by section 56 of and paragraph 2 of Schedule 6 to the Human Fertilisation and Embryology Act 2008.

(**c**) Section 4A(1)(b) was amended by section 75(1) and (2) of the Civil Partnership Act 2004.

(**d**) Section 14D was inserted by section 115(1) of the Adoption and Children Act 2002.

(**e**) Section 25 was amended by section 39 of and paragraphs 1 and 15 of Schedule 3 to the Children and Young Persons Act 2008 and section 24 of and paragraph 45 of Schedule 4 to the Access to Justice Act 1999.

(**f**) Section 31(1)(b) was amended by sections 74 and 75 of and paragraphs 87 and 90 of Schedule 7 to the Criminal Justice and Court Services Act 2000 (c.43).

(**g**) Paragraph 17(1) was amended by article 5(1) of and paragraphs 37(1) and (14)(a) of Schedule 2 to the Local Education Authorities and Children's Services Authorities (Intergration of Functions) Order 2010 (S.I. 2010/1158).

(i) an order varying directions made with an interim care order or interim supervision order under section 38(8)(b) of the 1989 Act;

(j) an order under section 39(3) of the 1989 Act varying a supervision order in so far as it affects a person with whom the child is living but who is not entitled to apply for the order to be discharged;

(k) an order under section 39(3A) of the 1989(**a**) Act varying or discharging an interim care order in so far as it imposes an exclusion requirement on a person who is not entitled to apply for the order to be discharged;

(l) an order under section 39(3B)(**b**) of the 1989 Act varying or discharging an interim care order in so far as it confers a power of arrest attached to an exclusion requirement;

(m) the substitution of a supervision order for a care order under section 39(4) of the 1989 Act;

(n) a child assessment order, or the variation or discharge of such an order under section 43(12) of the 1989 Act;

(o) an order permitting the local authority to arrange for any child in its care to live outside England and Wales under paragraph 19(1) of Schedule 2 to the 1989 Act;

(p) a contribution order, or revocation of such an order under paragraph 23(8) of Schedule 2 to the 1989 Act;

(q) an appeal under paragraph 8(1) of Schedule 8 to the 1989 Act;

"special guardianship order" has the meaning assigned to it by section 14A(1) of the 1989 Act(**c**);

"supervision order" has the meaning assigned to it by section 31(11) of the 1989 Act;

"supervision proceedings" means proceedings for a supervision order under section 31(1)(b) of the 1989 Act;

"warning notice" means a notice attached to an order pursuant to section 8(2) of the Children and Adoption Act 2006.

(The 1980 Hague Convention, the 1996 Hague Convention, the Council Regulation, and the European Convention are defined in rule 2.3.)

CHAPTER 2

GENERAL RULES

Who the parties are

12.3.—(1) In relation to the proceedings set out in column 1 of the following table, column 2 sets out who may make the application and column 3 sets out who the respondents to those proceedings will be.

(**a**) Section 39(3A) was inserted by section 52 of and paragraph 2 of Schedule 6 to the Family Law Act 1996.
(**b**) Section 39(3B) was inserted by section 56 of and paragraph 2 of Schedule to the Family Law Act 1996.
(**c**) Section 14A(1) was inserted by section 115(1) of the Adoption and Children Act 2002.

Proceedings for	Applicants	Respondents
A parental responsibility order (section 4(1)(c), 4ZA(1)(c), or section 4A(1)(b) of the 1989 Act).	The child's father; the step parent; or the child's parent (being a woman who is a parent by virtue of section 43 of the Human Fertilisation and Embryology Act 2008 and who is not a person to whom section 1(3) of the Family Law Reform Act 1987(**a**) applies) (sections 4(1)(c), 4ZA(1)(c) and 4A(1)(b) of the 1989 Act).	Every person whom the applicant believes to have parental responsibility for the child; where the child is the subject of a care order, every person whom the applicant believes to have had parental responsibility immediately prior to the making of the care order; in the case of an application to extend, vary or discharge an order, the parties to the proceedings leading to the order which it is sought to have extended, varied or discharged; in the case of specified proceedings, the child.
An order terminating a parental responsibility order or agreement (section 4(2A), 4ZA(5) or section 4A(3) of the 1989 Act(**b**).	Any person who has parental responsibility for the child; or with the court's permission , the child (section 4(3), 4ZA(6) and section 4A(3) of the 1989 Act).	As above.
An order appointing a guardian (section 5(1) of the 1989 Act(**c**)).	An individual who wishes to be appointed as guardian (section 5(1) of the 1989 Act).	As above.
An order terminating the appointment of a guardian (section 6(7) of the 1989 Act).	Any person who has parental responsibility for the child; or with the court's permission, the child (section 6(7) of the 1989 Act).	As above.
A section 8 order.	Any person who is entitled to apply for a section 8 order with respect to the child (section 10(4) to (7) of the 1989 Act(**d**)); or with the court's permission, any person (section10(2)(b) of the 1989 Act).	As above.
An enforcement order (section	A person who is, for the purposes of the contact order, a person with	The person the applicant alleges has failed to comply with the contact order.

(**a**) Section 1(3) was inserted by section 56 of and paragraphs 24(1) and (2) of Schedule 6 to the Human Fertilisation and Embryology Act 2008.

(**b**) Section 4A(3) was inserted by section 112 of the Adoption and Children Act 2002.

(**c**) Section 5(1) was amended by section 115(2), and (4)(a)(i) and (ii) of the Adoption and Children Act 2002.

(**d**) Section 10(4) was amended by section 139(1) of and paragraphs 54, 56(a) and (b) of Schedule 3 to the Adoption and Children Act 2002. Section 10(5) was inserted by section 77 of the Civil Partnership Act 2004. Section 10(5A) was inserted by section 139(1) and paragraphs 54 and 56(c) of Schedule 3 to the Adoption and Children Act 2002. Section 10(5B) was inserted by section 36 of the Children and Young Persons Act 2008. Section 10(7A) was inserted by section 139(1) of and paragraphs 54 and 56(d) of Schedule 3 to the Adoption and Children Act 2002.

Proceedings for	Applicants	Respondents
11J of the 1989 Act(**a**)).	whom the child concerned lives or is to live; any person whose contact with the child concerned is provided for in the contact order; any individual subject to a condition under section 11(7)(b) of the 1989 Act or a contact activity condition imposed by a contact order; or with the court's permission, the child (section 11J(5) of the 1989 Act).	
A financial compensation order (section 11O of the 1989 Act).	Any person who is, for the purposes of the contact order, a person with whom the child concerned lives or is to live; any person whose contact with the child concerned is provided for in the contact order; any individual subject to a condition under section 11(7)(b) of the 1989 Act or a contact activity condition imposed by a contact order; or with the court's permission, the child (section 11O(6) of the 1989 Act).	The person the applicant alleges has failed to comply with the contact order.
An order permitting the child's name to be changed or the removal of the child from the United Kingdom (section 13(1), 14C(3) or 33(7) of the 1989 Act).	Any person (section 13(1), 14C(3), 33(7) of the 1989 Act).	As for a parental responsibility order.

(**a**)   Section 11J was inserted by section 4(1) of the Children and Adoption Act 2006 (c.20).

Proceedings for	Applicants	Respondents
A special guardianship order (section 14A of the 1989 Act).	Any guardian of the child; any individual in whose favour a residence order is in force with respect to the child; any individual listed in subsection (5)(b) or (c) of section 10 (as read with subsection (10) of that section) of the 1989 Act; a local authority foster parent with whom the child has lived for a period of at least one year immediately preceding the application; or any person with the court's permission (section 14A(3) of the 1989 Act) (more than one such individual can apply jointly (section 14A(3) and (5) of that Act)).	As above, and if a care order is in force with respect to the child, the child.
Variation or discharge of a special guardianship order (section 14D of the 1989 Act(**a**)).	The special guardian (or any of them, if there is more than one); any individual in whose favour a residence order is in force with respect to the child; the local authority designated in a care order with respect to the child; any individual within section 14D(1)(d) of the 1989 Act who has parental responsibility for the child; the child, any parent or guardian of the child and any step-parent of the child who has acquired, and has not lost, parental responsibility by virtue of section 4A of that Act with the court's permission; or any individual within section 14D(1)(d) of that Act who immediately before the making of the special guardianship order had, but no longer has, parental responsibility for the child with the court's permission.	As above.

(**a**)   Section 14D was inserted by section 115(1) of the Adoption and Children Act 2002.

Proceedings for	Applicants	Respondents
A secure accommodation order (section 25 section of the 1989 Act).	The local authority which is looking after the child; or the Health Authority, Primary Care Trust, National Health Service Trust established under section 25 of the National Health Service Act 2006(**a**) or section 18(1) of the National Health Service (Wales) Act 2006(**b**), National Health Service Foundation Trust or any local authority providing accommodation for the child (unless the child is looked after by a local authority).	As above.
A care or supervision order (section 31 of the 1989 Act).	Any local authority; the National Society for the Prevention of Cruelty to Children and any of its officers (section 31(1) of the 1989 Act);or any authorised person.	As above.
An order varying directions made with an interim care or interim supervision order (section 38(8)(b) of the 1989 Act).	The parties to proceedings in which directions are given under section 38(6) of the 1989 Act; or any person named in such a direction.	As above.
An order discharging a care order (section 39(1) of the 1989 Act).	Any person who has parental responsibility for the child; the child; or the local authority designated by the order (section 39(1) of the 1989 Act).	As above.
An order varying or discharging an interim care order in so far as it imposes an exclusion requirement (section 39(3A) of the 1989 Act).	A person to whom the exclusion requirement in the interim care order applies who is not entitled to apply for the order to be discharged (section 39(3A) of the 1989 Act).	As above.

(**a**)   2006 c.4.
(**b**)   2006 c.42.

Proceedings for	Applicants	Respondents
An order varying or discharging an interim care order in so far as it confers a power of arrest attached to an exclusion requirement (section 39(3B) of the 1989 Act).	Any person entitled to apply for the discharge of the interim care order in so far as it imposes the exclusion requirement (section 39(3B) of the 1989 Act).	As above.
An order substituting a supervision order for a care order (section 39(4) of the 1989 Act).	Any person entitled to apply for a care order to be discharged under section 39(1) (section 39(4) of the 1989 Act).	As above.
A child assessment order (section 43(1) of the 1989 Act).	Any local authority; the National Society for the Prevention of Cruelty to Children and any of its officers; or any person authorised by order of the Secretary of State to bring the proceedings and any officer of a body who is so authorised (section 43(1) and (13) of the 1989 Act).	As above.
An order varying or discharging a child assessment order (section 43(12) of the 1989 Act).	The applicant for an order that has been made under section 43(1) of the 1989 Act; or the persons referred to in section 43(11) of the 1989 Act (section 43(12) of that Act).	As above.
An emergency protection order (section 44(1) of the 1989 Act).	Any person (section 44(1) of the 1989 Act).	As for a parental responsibility order.
An order extending the period during which an emergency protection order is to have effect (section 45(4) of the 1989 Act).	Any person who— has parental responsibility for a child as the result of an emergency protection order; and is entitled to apply for a care order with respect to the child (section 45(4) of the 1989 Act).	As above.
An order discharging an emergency protection order (section 45(8) of the 1989 Act).	The child; a parent of the child; any person who is not a parent of the child but who has parental responsibility for the child; or any person with whom the child was living before the making of the emergency protection order (section 45(8) of the 1989 Act).	As above.
An order varying	A person to whom the exclusion	As above.

Proceedings for	Applicants	Respondents
or discharging an emergency protection order in so far as it imposes the exclusion requirement (section 45(8A) of the 1989 Act).	requirement in the emergency protection order applies who is not entitled to apply for the emergency protection order to be discharged (section 45(8A) of the 1989 Act).	
An order varying or discharging an emergency protection order in so far as it confers a power of arrest attached to an exclusion requirement (section 45(8B) of the 1989 Act).	Any person entitled to apply for the discharge of the emergency protection order in so far as it imposes the exclusion requirement (section 45(8B) of the 1989 Act).	As above.
An emergency protection order by the police (section 46(7) of the 1989 Act).	The officer designated for the purposes of section 46(3)(e) of the 1989 Act (section 46(7) of the 1989 Act).	As above.
A warrant authorising a constable to assist in exercise of certain powers to search for children and inspect premises (section 48 of the 1989 Act).	Any person attempting to exercise powers under an emergency protection order who has been or is likely to be prevented from doing so by being refused entry to the premises concerned or refused access to the child concerned (section 48(9) of the 1989 Act).	As above.
A warrant authorising a constable to assist in exercise of certain powers to search for children and inspect premises (section 102 of the 1989 Act).	Any person attempting to exercise powers under the enactments mentioned in section 102(6) of the 1989 Act who has been or is likely to be prevented from doing so by being refused entry to the premises concerned or refused access to the child concerned (section 102(1) of that Act).	As above.
An order revoking an enforcement order (paragraph 4 of Schedule A1 to the 1989 Act).	The person subject to the enforcement order.	The person who was the applicant for the enforcement order; and, where the child was a party to the proceedings in which the enforcement order was made, the child.
An order amending an enforcement order (paragraphs	The person subject to the enforcement order.	The person who was the applicant for the enforcement order. (Rule 12.33 makes provision about applications under paragraph 5 of

Proceedings for	Applicants	Respondents
5 to 7 of Schedule A1 to the 1989 Act).		Schedule A1 to the 1989 Act.)
An order following breach of an enforcement order (paragraph 9 of Schedule A1 to the 1989 Act).	Any person who is, for the purposes of the contact order, the person with whom the child lives or is to live; any person whose contact with the child concerned is provided for in the contact order; any individual subject to a condition under section 11(7)(b) of the 1989 Act or a contact activity condition imposed by a contact order; or with the court's permission, the child (paragraph 9 of Schedule A1 to the 1989 Act).	The person the applicant alleges has failed to comply with the unpaid work requirement imposed by an enforcement order; and where the child was a party to the proceedings in which the enforcement order was made, the child.
An order permitting the local authority to arrange for any child in its care to live outside England and Wales (Schedule 2, paragraph 19(1), to the 1989 Act).	The local authority (Schedule 2, paragraph 19(1), to the 1989 Act).	As for a parental responsibility order.
A contribution order (Schedule 2, paragraph 23(1), to the 1989 Act).	The local authority (Schedule 2, paragraph 23(1), to the 1989 Act).	As above and the contributor.
An order revoking a contribution order (Schedule 2, paragraph 23(8), to the 1989 Act).	The contributor; or the local authority.	As above.
An order relating to contact with the child in care and any named person (section 34(2) of the 1989 Act) or permitting the local authority to refuse contact (section 34(4) of that Act).	The local authority; or the child (section 34(2) or 34(4) of the 1989 Act).	As above; and the person whose contact with the child is the subject of the application.

Proceedings for	Applicants	Respondents
An order relating to contact with the child in care (section 34(3) of the 1989 Act).	The child's parents; any guardian or special guardian of the child; any person who by virtue of section 4A of the 1989 Act has parental responsibility for the child; a person in whose favour there was a residence order in force with respect to the child immediately before the care order was made; a person who by virtue of an order made in the exercise of the High Court's inherent jurisdiction with respect to children had care of the child immediately before the care order was made (section 34(3)(a) of the 1989 Act); or with the court's permission, any person (section 34(3) (b) of that Act).	As above; and the person whose contact with the child is the subject of the application.
An order varying or discharging an order for contact with a child in care under section 34 (section 34((9) of the 1989 Act).	The local authority; the child; or any person named in the order (section 34(9) of the 1989 Act).	As above; and the person whose contact with the child is the subject of the application.
An education supervision order (section 36 of the 1989 Act).	Any local authority (section 36(1) of the 1989 Act).	As above; and the child.
An order varying or discharging a supervision order (section 39(2) of the 1989 Act).	Any person who has parental responsibility for the child; the child; or the supervisor (section 39(2) of the 1989 Act).	As above; and the supervisor.
An order varying a supervision order in so far as it affects the person with whom the child is living (section 39(3) of the 1989 Act).	The person with whom the child is living who is not entitled to apply for the order to be discharged (section 39(3) of the 1989 Act).	As above; and the supervisor.
An order varying a direction under section 44(6) of the 1989 Act in an emergency protection order (section 44(9)(b) of that Act).	The parties to the application for the emergency protection order in respect of which it is sought to vary the directions; the children's guardian; the local authority in whose area the child is ordinarily resident; or any person who is named in the directions.	As above, and the parties to the application for the order in respect of which it is sought to vary the directions; any person who was caring for the child prior to the making of the order; and any person whose contact with the child is affected by the direction which

Proceedings for	Applicants	Respondents
		it is sought to have varied.
A recovery order (section 50 of the 1989 Act).	Any person who has parental responsibility for the child by virtue of a care order or an emergency protection order; or where the child is in police protection the officer designated for the purposes of section 46(3)(e) of the 1989 Act (section 50(4) of the 1989 Act).	As above; and the person whom the applicant alleges to have effected or to have been or to be responsible for the taking or keeping of the child.
An order discharging an education supervision order (Schedule 3, paragraph 17(1), to the 1989 Act).	The child concerned; a parent of the child; or the local authority concerned (Schedule 3, paragraph 17(1), to the 1989 Act).	As above; and the local authority concerned; and the child.
An order extending an education supervision order (Schedule 3, paragraph, 15(2), to the 1989 Act).	The local authority in whose favour the education supervision order was made (Schedule 3, paragraph 15(2), to the 1989 Act).	As above; and the child.
An appeal under paragraph (8) of Schedule 8 to the 1989 Act.	A person aggrieved by the matters listed in paragraph 8(1) of Schedule 8 to the 1989 Act.	The appropriate local authority.
An order for the disclosure of information as to the whereabouts of a child under section 33 of the 1986 Act.	Any person with a legitimate interest in proceedings for an order under Part 1 of the 1986 Act; or a person who has registered an order made elsewhere in the United Kingdom or a specified dependent territory.	Any person alleged to have information as to the whereabouts of the child.
An order authorising the taking charge of and delivery of a child under section 34 of the 1986 Act.	The person to whom the child is to be given up under section 34(1) of the 1986 Act.	As above; and the person who is required to give up the child in accordance with section 34(1) of the 1986 Act.
An order relating to the exercise of the court's inherent jurisdiction (including wardship proceedings).	A local authority (with the court's permission); any person with a genuine interest in or relation to the child; or the child (wardship proceedings only).	The parent or guardian of the child; any other person who has an interest in or relationship to the child; and the child (wardship proceedings only and with the court's permission as described at rule 12.37).
A warrant under section 79 of the 2006 Act	Her Majesty's Chief Inspector for Education, Children's Services and Skills.	Any person preventing or likely to prevent Her Majesty's Chief Inspector for Education, Children's Services and

Proceedings for	Applicants	Respondents
authorising any constable to assist Her Majesty's Chief Inspector for Education, Children's Services and Skills in the exercise of powers conferred on him by section 77 of the 2006 Act.		Skills from exercising powers conferred on him by section 77 of the 2006 Act.
An order in respect of a child under the 1980 Hague Convention.	Any person, institution or body who claims that a child has been removed or retained in breach of rights of custody or claims that there has been a breach of rights of access in relation to the child.	The person alleged to have brought the child into the United Kingdom; the person with whom the child is alleged to be; any parent or guardian of the child who is within the United Kingdom and is not otherwise a party; any person in whose favour a decision relating to custody has been made if that person is not otherwise a party; and any other person who appears to the court to have sufficient interest in the welfare of the child.
An order concerning the recognition and enforcement of decisions relating to custody under the European Convention.	Any person who has a court order giving that person rights of custody in relation to the child.	As above.
An application for the High Court to request transfer of jurisdiction under Article 15 of the Council Regulation or Article 9 of the 1996 Hague Convention (rule 12.65).	Any person with sufficient interest in the welfare of the child and who would be entitled to make a proposed application in relation to that child, or who intends to seek the permission of the court to make such application if the transfer is agreed.	As directed by the court in accordance with rule 12.65.
An application under rule 12.71 for a declaration as to the existence, or extent, of parental	Any interested person including a person who holds, or claims to hold, parental responsibility for the child under the law of another State which subsists in accordance with Article 16 of the 1996 Hague Convention following the child	Every person whom the applicant believes to have parental responsibility for the child; any person whom the applicant believes to hold parental responsibility for the child under the law of another State which subsists in accordance with

Proceedings for	Applicants	Respondents
responsibility under Article 16 of the 1996 Convention.	becoming habitually resident in a territorial unit of the United Kingdom.	Article 16 of the 1996 Hague Convention following the child becoming habitually resident in a territorial unit of the United Kingdom; and where the child is the subject of a care order, every person whom the applicant believes to have had parental responsibility immediately prior to the making of the care order.
A warning notice.	The person who is, for the purposes of the contact order, the person with whom the child concerned lives or is to live; the person whose contact with the child concerned is provided for in the contact order; any individual subject to a condition under section 11(7)(b) of the 1989 Act or a contact activity condition imposed by the contact order; or with the court's permission, the child.	Any person who was a party to the proceedings in which the contact order was made. (Rule 12.33 makes provision about applications for warning notices).

(2) The court will direct that a person with parental responsibility be made a party to proceedings where that person requests to be one.

(3) Subject to rule 16.2, the court may at any time direct that—

    (a) any person or body be made a party to proceedings; or

    (b) a party be removed.

(4) If the court makes a direction for the addition or removal of a party under this rule, it may give consequential directions about—

    (a) the service of a copy of the application form or other relevant documents on the new party;

    (b) the management of the proceedings.

(5) In this rule—

"a local authority foster parent" has the meaning assigned to it by section 23(3) of the 1989 Act; and

"care home", "independent hospital", "local authority" and "Primary Care Trust" have the meanings assigned to them by section 105 of the 1989 Act.

(Part 16 contains the rules relating to the representation of children.)

Notice of proceedings to person with foreign parental responsibility

12.4.—(1) This rule applies where a child is subject to proceedings to which this Part applies and —

    (a) a person holds or is believed to hold parental responsibility for the child under the law of another State which subsists in accordance with Article 16 of the 1996 Hague Convention following the child becoming habitually resident in a territorial unit of the United Kingdom; and

    (b) that person is not otherwise required to be joined as a respondent under rule 12.3.

(2) The applicant shall give notice of the proceedings to any person to whom the applicant believes paragraph (1) applies in any case in which a person whom the applicant believed to have parental responsibility under the 1989 Act would be a respondent to those proceedings in accordance with rule 12.3.

(3) The applicant and every respondent to the proceedings shall provide such details as they possess as to the identity and whereabouts of any person they believe to hold parental responsibility for the child in accordance with paragraph (1) to the court officer, upon making, or responding to the application as appropriate.

(4) Where the existence of a person who is believed to have parental responsibility for the child in accordance with paragraph (1) only becomes apparent to a party at a later date during the proceedings, that party must notify the court officer of those details at the earliest opportunity.

(5) Where a person to whom paragraph (1) applies receives notice of proceedings, that person may apply to the court to be joined as a party using the Part 18 procedure.

What the court will do when the application has been issued

12.5. When the proceedings have been issued the court will consider—

(a) setting a date for—

    (i) a directions appointment;

    (ii) in private law proceedings, a First Hearing Dispute Resolution Appointment;

    (iii) in care and supervision proceedings and in so far as practicable other public law proceedings, the First Appointment; or

    (iv) the hearing of the application or an application for an interim order,

    and if the court sets a date it will do so in accordance with rule 12.13 and Practice Directions 12A and 12B;

(b) giving any of the directions listed in rule 12.12 or, where Chapter 6, section 1 applies, rule 12.48; and

(c) doing anything else which is set out in Practice Directions 12A or 12B or any other practice direction.

(Practice Directions 12A and 12B supplementing this Part set out details relating to the First Hearing Dispute Resolution Appointment and the First Appointment.)

Children's guardian, solicitor and reports under section 7 of the 1989 Act

12.6. As soon as practicable after the issue of proceedings or the transfer of the proceedings to the court, the court will—

(a) in specified proceedings, appoint a children's guardian under rule 16.3(1) unless—

    (i) such an appointment has already been made by the court which made the transfer and is subsisting; or

    (ii) the court considers that such an appointment is not necessary to safeguard the interests of the child;

(b) where section 41(3) of the 1989 Act applies, consider whether a solicitor should be appointed to represent the child, and if so, appoint a solicitor accordingly;

(c) consider whether to ask an officer of the service or a Welsh family proceedings officer for advice relating to the welfare of the child;

(d) consider whether a report relating to the welfare of the child is required, and if so, request such a report in accordance with section 7 of the 1989 Act.

(Part 16 sets out the rules relating to representation of children.)

What a court officer will do

12.7.—(1) As soon as practicable after the issue of proceedings the court officer will return to the applicant the copies of the application together with the forms referred to in Practice Direction 5A.

(2) As soon as practicable after the issue of proceedings or the transfer of proceedings to the court or at any other stage in the proceedings the court officer will—

    (a) give notice of any hearing set by the court to the applicant; and

    (b) do anything else set out in Practice Directions 12A or 12B or any other practice direction.

Service of the application

12.8. The applicant will serve—

    (a) the application together with the documents referred to in Practice Direction 12C on the persons referred to and within the time specified in that Practice Direction; and

    (b) notice of any hearing set by the court on the persons referred to in Practice Direction 12C at the same time as serving the application.

Request for transfer from magistrates' court to county court or to another magistrates' court

12.9.—(1) In accordance with the Allocation Order, a magistrates' court may order proceedings before the court (or any part of them) to be transferred to another magistrates' court or to a county court.

(2) Where any request to transfer proceedings to another magistrates' court or to a county court is refused, the court officer will send a copy of the written record of the reasons for refusing the transfer to the parties.

Procedure following refusal of magistrates' court to order transfer

12.10.—(1) Where a request under rule 12.9 to transfer proceedings to a county court in accordance with the provisions of the Allocation Order is refused, a party to the proceedings may apply to a county court for an order transferring proceedings from the magistrates' court.

(2) Such an application must be made in accordance with Part 18 and the Allocation Order.

Transfer of proceedings from one court to another court

12.11. Where proceedings are transferred from one court to another court in accordance with the provisions of the Allocation Order, the court officer from the transferring court will notify the parties of any order transferring the proceedings.

Directions

12.12.—(1) This rule does not apply to proceedings under Chapter 6 of this Part.

(2) At any stage in the proceedings, the court may give directions about the conduct of the proceedings including—

    (a) the management of the case;

    (b) the timetable for steps to be taken between the giving of directions and the final hearing;

    (c) the joining of a child or other person as a party to the proceedings in accordance with rules 12.3(2) and (3);

    (d) the attendance of the child;

(e) the appointment of a children's guardian or of a solicitor under section 41(3) of the 1989 Act;

(f) the appointment of a litigation friend;

(g) the service of documents;

(h) the filing of evidence including experts' reports; and

(i) the exercise by an officer of the Service, Welsh family proceedings officer or local authority officer of any duty referred to in rule 16.38(1)

(3) Paragraph (4) applies where—

(a) an officer of the Service or a Welsh family proceedings officer has filed a report or a risk assessment as a result of exercising a duty referred to in rule 16.38(1)(a); or

(b) a local authority officer has filed a report as a result of exercising a duty referred to in rule 16.38(1)(b).

(4) The court may—

(a) give directions setting a date for a hearing at which that report or risk assessment will be considered; and

(b) direct that the officer who prepared the report or risk assessment attend any such hearing.

(5) The court may exercise the powers in paragraphs (2) and (4) on an application or of its own initiative.

(6) Where the court proposes to exercise its powers of its own initiative the procedure set out in rule 4.3(2) to (6) applies.

(7) Directions of a court which are still in force immediately prior to the transfer of proceedings to another court will continue to apply following the transfer subject to—

(a) any changes of terminology which are required to apply those directions to the court to which the proceedings are transferred; and

(b) any variation or revocation of the direction.

(8) The court or court officer will—

(a) take a note of the giving, variation or revocation of a direction under this rule; and

(b) as soon as practicable serve a copy of the note on every party.

(Rule 12.48 provides for directions in proceedings under the 1980 Hague Convention and the European Convention.)

Setting dates for hearings and setting or confirming the timetable and date for the final hearing

12.13.—(1) At the—

(a) transfer to a court of proceedings;

(b) postponement or adjournment of any hearing; or

(c) conclusion of any hearing at which the proceedings are not finally determined,

the court will set a date for the proceedings to come before the court again for the purposes of giving directions or for such other purposes as the court directs.

(2) At any hearing the court may—

(a) confirm a date for the final hearing or the week within which the final hearing is to begin (where a date or period for the final hearing has already been set);

(b) set a timetable for the final hearing unless a timetable has already been fixed, or the court considers that it would be inappropriate to do so; or

(c) set a date for the final hearing or a period within which the final hearing of the application is to take place.

(3) The court officer will notify the parties of—

    (a) the date of a hearing fixed in accordance with paragraph (1);

    (b) the timetable for the final hearing; and

    (c) the date of the final hearing or the period in which it will take place.

(4) Where the date referred to in paragraph (1) is set at the transfer of proceedings, the date will be as soon as possible after the transfer.

(5) The requirement in paragraph (1) to set a date for the proceedings to come before the court again is satisfied by the court setting or confirming a date for the final hearing.

Attendance at hearings

12.14.—(1) This rule does not apply to proceedings under Chapter 6 of this Part except for proceedings for a declaration under rule 12.71.

(2) Unless the court directs otherwise and subject to paragraph (3), the persons who must attend a hearing are—

    (a) any party to the proceedings;

    (b) any litigation friend for any party or legal representative instructed to act on that party's behalf; and

    (c) any other person directed by the court or required by Practice Directions 12A or 12B or any other practice direction to attend.

(3) Proceedings or any part of them will take place in the absence of a child who is a party to the proceedings if—

    (a) the court considers it in the interests of the child, having regard to the matters to be discussed or the evidence likely to be given; and

    (b) the child is represented by a children's guardian or solicitor.

(4) When considering the interests of the child under paragraph (3) the court will give—

    (a) the children's guardian;

    (b) the solicitor for the child; and

    (c) the child, if of sufficient understanding,

an opportunity to make representations.

(5) Subject to paragraph (6), where at the time and place appointed for a hearing, the applicant appears but one or more of the respondents do not, the court may proceed with the hearing.

(6) The court will not begin to hear an application in the absence of a respondent unless the court is satisfied that—

    (a) the respondent received reasonable notice of the date of the hearing; or

    (b) the circumstances of the case justify proceeding with the hearing.

(7) Where, at the time and place appointed for a hearing one or more of the respondents appear but the applicant does not, the court may—

    (a) refuse the application; or

    (b) if sufficient evidence has previously been received, proceed in the absence of the applicant.

(8) Where at the time and place appointed for a hearing neither the applicant nor any respondent appears, the court may refuse the application.

(9) Paragraphs (5) to (8) do not apply to a hearing where the court—

    (a) is considering—

        (i) whether to make a contact activity direction or to attach a contact activity condition to a contact order; or

(ii) an application for a financial compensation order, an enforcement order or an order under paragraph 9 of Schedule A1 to the 1989 Act following a breach of an enforcement order; and

(b) has yet to obtain sufficient evidence from, or in relation to, the person who may be the subject of the direction, condition or order to enable it to determine the matter.

(10) Nothing in this rule affects the provisions of Article 18 of the Council Regulation in cases to which that provision applies.

(The Council Regulation makes provision in Article 18 for the court to stay proceedings where the respondent is habitually resident in another Member State of the European Union and has not been adequately served with the proceedings as required by that provision.)

Steps taken by the parties

12.15. If—

(a) the parties or any children's guardian agree proposals for the management of the proceedings (including a proposed date for the final hearing or a period within which the final hearing is to take place); and

(b) the court considers that the proposals are suitable,

it may approve them without a hearing and give directions in the terms proposed.

Applications without notice

12.16.—(1) This rule applies to—

(a) proceedings for a section 8 order;

(b) emergency proceedings; and

(c) proceedings relating to the exercise of the court's inherent jurisdiction (other than an application for the court's permission to start such proceedings and proceedings for collection, location and passport orders where Chapter 6 applies).

(2) An application in proceedings referred to in paragraph (1) may, in the High Court or a county court, be made without notice in which case the applicant must file the application—

(a) where the application is made by telephone, the next business day after the making of the application; or

(b) in any other case, at the time when the application is made.

(3) An application in proceedings referred to in paragraph (1)(a) or (b) may, in a magistrates' court, be made with the permission of the court, without notice, in which case the applicant must file the application at the time when the application is made or as directed by the court.

(4) Where—

(a) a section 8 order;

(b) an emergency protection order;

(c) an order for the disclosure of information as to the whereabouts of a child under section 33 of the 1986 Act; or

(d) an order authorising the taking charge of and delivery of a child under section 34 of the 1986 Act,

is made without notice, the applicant must serve a copy of the application on each respondent within 48 hours after the order is made.

(5) Within 48 hours after the making of an order without notice, the applicant must serve a copy of the order on—

(a) the parties, unless the court directs otherwise;

(b) any person who has actual care of the child or who had such care immediately prior to the making of the order; and

(c) in the case of an emergency protection order and a recovery order, the local authority in whose area the child lives or is found.

(6) Where the court refuses to make an order on an application without notice it may direct that the application is made on notice in which case the application will proceed in accordance with rules 12.3 to 12.15.

(7) Where the hearing takes place outside the hours during which the court office is normally open, the court or court officer will take a note of the proceedings.

(Practice Direction 12E (Urgent Business) provides further details of the procedure for out of hours applications. See also Practice Direction 12D (Inherent Jurisdiction (including Wardship Proceedings).)

(Rule 12.47 provides for without-notice applications in proceedings under Chapter 6, section 1 of this Part, (proceedings under the 1980 Hague Convention and the European Convention).)

Investigation under section 37 of the 1989 Act

12.17.—(1) This rule applies where a direction is given to an appropriate authority by the court under section 37(1) of the 1989 Act.

(2) On giving the direction the court may adjourn the proceedings.

(3) As soon as practicable after the direction is given the court will record the direction.

(4) As soon as practicable after the direction is given the court officer will—

    (a) serve the direction on—

        (i) the parties to the proceedings in which the direction is given; and

        (ii) the appropriate authority where it is not a party;

    (b) serve any documentary evidence directed by the court on the appropriate authority.

(5) Where a local authority informs the court of any of the matters set out in section 37(3)(a) to (c) of the 1989 Act it will do so in writing.

(6) Unless the court directs otherwise, the court officer will serve a copy of any report to the court under section 37 of the 1989 Act on the parties.

(Section 37 of the 1989 Act refers to the appropriate authority and section 37(5) of that Act sets out which authority should be named in a particular case.)

Disclosure of a report under section 14A(8) or (9) of the 1989 Act

12.18.—(1) In proceedings for a special guardianship order, the local authority must file the report under section 14A(8) or (9) of the 1989 Act(**a**) within the timetable fixed by the court.

(2) The court will consider whether to give a direction that the report under section 14A(8) or (9) of the 1989 Act be disclosed to each party to the proceedings.

(3) Before giving a direction for the report to be disclosed, the court must consider whether any information should be deleted from the report.

(4) The court may direct that the report must not be disclosed to a party.

(5) The court officer must serve a copy of the report in accordance with any direction under paragraph (2).

(6) In paragraph (3), information includes information which a party has declined to reveal under rule 29.1(1).

(**a**) Sections 14A(8) and (9) were inserted by section 115(1) of the Adoption and Children Act 2002.

Additional evidence

12.19.—(1) This rule applies to proceedings for a section 8 order or a special guardianship order.

(2) Unless the court directs otherwise, a party must not—

(a) file or serve any document other than in accordance with these rules or any practice direction;

(b) in completing a form prescribed by these rules or any practice direction, give information or make a statement which is not required or authorised by that form; or

(c) file or serve at a hearing—

(i) any witness statement of the substance of the oral evidence which the party intends to adduce; or

(ii) any copy of any document (including any experts' report) which the party intends to rely on.

(3) Where a party fails to comply with the requirements of this rule in relation to any witness statement or other document, the party cannot seek to rely on that statement or other document unless the court directs otherwise.

Expert evidence-examination of child

12.20.—(1) No person may cause the child to be medically or psychiatrically examined, or otherwise assessed, for the purpose of preparation of expert evidence for use in the proceedings without the court's permission.

(2) Where the court's permission has not been given under paragraph (1), no evidence arising out of an examination or assessment referred to in that paragraph may be adduced without the court's permission.

Hearings

12.21.—(1) The court may give directions about the order of speeches and the evidence at a hearing.

(2) Subject to any directions given under paragraph (1), the parties and the children's guardian must adduce their evidence at a hearing in the following order—

(a) the applicant;

(b) any party with parental responsibility for the child;

(c) other respondents;

(d) the children's guardian;

(e) the child, if the child is a party to proceedings and there is no children's guardian.

CHAPTER 3

SPECIAL PROVISIONS ABOUT PUBLIC LAW PROCEEDINGS

Application of rules 12.23 to 12.26

12.22. Rules 12.23 to 12.26 apply to care and supervision proceedings and in so far as practicable other public law proceedings.

Timetable for the Child

12.23.—(1) The court will set the timetable for the proceedings in accordance with the Timetable for the Child.

(2) The "Timetable for the Child" means the timetable set by the court in accordance with its duties under section 1 and 32 of the 1989 Act(**a**) and will—

(a) take into account dates of the significant steps in the life of the child who is the subject of the proceedings; and

(b) be appropriate for that child.

Directions

12.24. The court will direct the parties to—

(a) monitor compliance with the court's directions; and

(b) tell the court or court officer about—

(i) any failure to comply with a direction of the court; and

(ii) any other delay in the proceedings.

First Appointment, Case Management Conference and Issues Resolution Hearing

12.25.—(1) The court may set the date for the First Appointment, Case Management Conference and Issues Resolution Hearing at the times and in the circumstances referred to in Practice Direction 12A.

(2) The matters which the court will consider at the hearings referred to in paragraph (1) are set out in Practice Direction 12A.

Discussion between advocates

12.26.—(1) When setting a date for a Case Management Conference or an Issues Resolution Hearing the court will direct a discussion between the parties' advocates to—

(a) discuss the provisions of a draft of the Case Management Order; and

(b) consider any other matter set out in Practice Direction 12A.

(2) Where there is a litigant in person the court will give directions about how that person may take part in the discussions between the parties' advocates.

(3) The court will direct that following a discussion between advocates they must prepare or amend a draft of the Case Management Order for the court to consider.

(4) Where it is not possible for the advocates to agree the terms of a draft of the Case Management Order, the advocates should specify on a draft of the Case Management Order or on a separate document if more practicable—

(a) those provisions on which they agree; and

(b) those provisions on which they disagree.

(5) Unless the court directs otherwise—

(a) any discussion between advocates must take place no later than 2 days; and

(b) a draft of the Case Management Order must be filed with the court no later than 1 day,

before the Case Management Conference or the Issues Resolution Hearing whichever may be appropriate.

(6) For the purposes of this rule "advocate" includes a litigant in person.

(**a**) Section 1 was amended by section 115(2) and (3) of the Adoption and Children Act 2002.

(3) On receipt of a statement filed in accordance with paragraph (2) above, a court officer will notify the relegant authority in or before which the application is pending and will subsequently notify the relevant authority of the result of the proceedings.

(4) On receipt by the relevant authority of a notification under paragraph (3) from the High Court or equivalent notification from the Court of Session, the High Court in Northern Ireland or the High Court of Justice of the Isle of Man—

(a) all further proceedings in the action will be stayed^(GL) unless and until the proceedings under the 1980 Hague Convention in the High Court, Court of Session, the High Court in Northern Ireland or the High Court of Justice of the Isle of Man are dismissed; and

(b) the parties to the action will be notified by the court officer of the stay^(GL) and dismissal.

Stay of proceedings where application made under s.16 of the 1985 Act (registration of decisions under the European Convention)

12.53.—(1) A person who—

(a) is a party to—

(i) proceedings under section 16 of the 1985 Act; or

(ii) proceedings as a result of which a decision relating to custody has been registered under section 16 of the 1985 Act; and

(b) knows that an application is pending under—

(i) section 20(2) of the 1985 Act;

(ii) Article 21(2) of the Child Abduction and Custody (Jersey) Law 2005; or

(iii) section 42(2) of the Child Custody Act 1987 (an Act of Tynwald),

must file within the proceedings under section 16 of the 1985 Act a concise statement of the nature of the pending application.

(2) On receipt of a statement filed in accordance with paragraph (1) above, a court officer will notify the relevant authority in or before which the application is pending and will subsequently notify the relevant authority of the result of the proceedings.

(3) On receipt by the relevant authority of a notification under paragraph (2) from the High Court or equivalent notification from the Court of Session, the High Court in Northern Ireland or the High Court of Justice of the Isle of Man, the court officer will notify the parties to the action.

Transfer of proceedings

12.54.—(1) At any stage in proceedings under the 1985 Act the court may-

(a) of its own initiative; or

(b) on the application of a party with a minimum of two days' notice;

order that the proceedings be transferred to a court listed in paragraph (4).

(2) Where the court makes an order for transfer under paragraph (1)—

(a) the court will state its reasons on the face of the order;

(b) a court officer will send a copy of the order, the application and the accompanying documents (if any) and any evidence to the court to which the proceedings are transferred; and

(c) the costs of the proceedings both before and after the transfer will be at the discretion of the court to which the proceedings are transferred.

(3) Where proceedings are transferred to the High Court from a court listed in paragraph (4), a court officer will notify the parties of the transfer and the proceedings will continue as if they had been commenced in the High Court.

(4) The listed courts are the Court of Session, the High Court in Northern Ireland, the Royal Court of Jersey or the High Court of Justice of the Isle of Man.

Revocation and variation of registered decisions

12.55.—(1) This rule applies to decisions which—

    (a) have been registered under section 16 of the 1985 Act; and

    (b) are subsequently varied or revoked by an authority in the Contracting State in which they were made.

(2) The court will, on cancelling the registration of a decision which has been revoked, notify—

    (a) the person appearing to the court to have care of the child;

    (b) the person on whose behalf the application for registration of the decision was made; and

    (c) any other party to the application.

(3) The court will, on being informed of the variation of a decision, notify—

    (a) the party appearing to the court to have care of the child; and

    (b) any party to the application for registration of the decision;

and any such person may apply to make representations to the court before the registration is varied.

(4) Any person appearing to the court to have an interest in the proceedings may apply for the registration of a decision for the cancellation or variation of the decision referred to in paragraph (1).

The central index of decisions registered under the 1985 Act

12.56. A central index of decisions registered under section 16 of the 1985 Act, together with any variation of those decisions made under section 17 of that Act, will be kept by the principal registry.

Disclosure of information in proceedings under the European Convention

12.57. At any stage in proceedings under the European Convention the court may, if it has reason to believe that any person may have relevant information about the child who is the subject of those proceedings, order that person to disclose such information and may for that purpose order that the person attend before it or file affidavit[(GL)] evidence.

SECTION 2

Applications relating to the Council Regulation and the 1996 Hague Convention

Interpretation

12.58.—(1) In this section —

    "Central Authority" means, in relation to England and Wales, the Lord Chancellor;

    "Contracting State" means a State party to the 1996 Hague Convention;

    "judgment" has the meaning given in Article 2(4) of the Council Regulation;

    "Member State" means a Member State bound by the Council Regulation or a country which has subsequently adopted the Council Regulation;

    "parental responsibility" has the meaning given in —

    (a) Article 2(7) of the Council Regulation in relation to proceedings under that Regulation; and

    (b) Article 1(2) of the 1996 Hague Convention in relation to proceedings under that Convention; and

    "seised" has the meaning given in Article 16 of the Council Regulation.

(2) In rules 12.59 to 12.70, references to the court of another member State or Contracting State include authorities within the meaning of "court" in Article 2(1) of the Council Regulation, and

CHAPTER 4

SPECIAL PROVISIONS ABOUT PRIVATE LAW PROCEEDINGS

The First Hearing Dispute Resolution Appointment

12.31.—(1) The court may set a date for the First Hearing Dispute Resolution Appointment after the proceedings have been issued.

(2) The court officer will give notice of any of the dates so fixed to the parties.

(Provisions relating to the timing of and issues to be considered at the First Hearing Dispute Resolution Appointment are contained in Practice Direction 12B.)

Answer

12.32. A respondent must file and serve on the parties an answer to the application for an order in private law proceedings within 14 days beginning with the date on which the application is served.

Applications for warning notices or applications to amend enforcement orders by reason of change of residence

12.33.—(1) This rule applies in relation to an application to the High Court or a county court for—

    (a) a warning notice to be attached to a contact order; or

    (b) an order under paragraph 5 of Schedule A1 to the 1989 Act to amend an enforcement order by reason of change of residence.

(2) The application must be made without notice.

(3) The court may deal with the application without a hearing.

(4) If the court decides to deal with the application at a hearing, rules 12.5, 12.7 and 12.8 will apply.

Service of a risk assessment

12.34.—(1) Where an officer of the Service or a Welsh family proceedings officer has filed a risk assessment with the court, subject to paragraph (2), the court officer will as soon as practicable serve copies of the risk assessment on each party.

(2) Before serving the risk assessment, the court must consider whether, in order to prevent a risk of harm to the child, it is necessary for—

    (a) information to be deleted from a copy of the risk assessment before that copy is served on a party; or

    (b) service of a copy of the risk assessment (whether with information deleted from it or not) on a party to be delayed for a specified period,

and may make directions accordingly.

Service of enforcement orders or orders amending or revoking enforcement orders

12.35.—(1) Paragraphs (2) and (3) apply where the High Court or a county court makes—

    (a) an enforcement order; or

    (b) an order under paragraph 9(2) of Schedule A1 to the 1989 Act (enforcement order made following a breach of an enforcement order).

(2) As soon as practicable after an order has been made, a copy of it must be served by the court officer on—

    (a) the parties, except the person against whom the order is made;

(b) the officer of the Service or the Welsh family proceedings officer who is to comply with a request under section 11M of the 1989 Act(**a**) to monitor compliance with the order; and

(c) the responsible officer.

(3) Unless the court directs otherwise, the applicant must serve a copy of the order personally on the person against whom the order is made.

(4) The court officer must send a copy of an order made under paragraph 4, 5, 6 or 7 of Schedule A1 to the 1989 Act (revocation or amendment of an enforcement order) to—

(a) the parties;

(b) the officer of the Service or the Welsh family proceedings officer who is to comply with a request under section 11M of the 1989 Act to monitor compliance with the order;

(c) the responsible officer; and

(d) in the case of an order under paragraph 5 of Schedule A1 to the 1989 Act (amendment of enforcement order by reason of change of residence), the responsible officer in the former local justice area.

(5) In this rule, "responsible officer" has the meaning given in paragraph 8(8) of Schedule A1 to the 1989 Act.

CHAPTER 5

SPECIAL PROVISIONS ABOUT INHERENT JURISDICTION PROCEEDINGS

Where to start proceedings

12.36.—(1) An application for proceedings under the Inherent Jurisdiction of the court must be started in the High Court.

(2) Wardship proceedings, except applications for an order that a child be made or cease to be a ward of court, may be transferred to the county court unless the issues of fact or law make them more suitable for hearing in the High Court.

(The question of suitability for hearing in the High Court is explained in Practice Direction 12D (Inherent Jurisdiction (including Wardship Proceedings)).)

Child as respondent to wardship proceedings

12.37.—(1) A child who is the subject of wardship proceedings must not be made a respondent to those proceedings unless the court gives permission following an application under paragraph (2).

(2) Where nobody other than the child would be a suitable respondent to wardship proceedings, the applicant may apply without notice for permission to make the wardship application—

(a) without notice; or

(b) with the child as the respondent.

Registration requirements

12.38. The court officer will send a copy of every application for a child to be made a ward of court to the principal registry for recording in the register of wards.

Notice of child's whereabouts

12.39.—(1) Every respondent, other than a child, must file with the acknowledgment of service a notice stating—

(**a**) Section 11M was inserted by section 4(1) of the Children and Adoption Act 2006.

Application by a court of another Member State or another Contracting State for transfer of the proceedings

12.63.—(1) This rule applies where a court of another Member State or another Contracting State makes an application under Article 15(2)(c) of the Council Regulation or under Article 9 of the 1996 Hague Convention that the court having jurisdiction in relation to the proceedings transfer the proceedings or a specific part of the proceedings to the applicant court.

(2) When the court receives the application, the court officer will—

(a) as soon as practicable, notify the Central Authority for England and Wales of the application; and

(b) serve the application, and notice of the hearing on all other parties in England and Wales not less than 5 days before the hearing of the application.

Exercise by the court of its own initiative of powers to seek to transfer the proceedings

12.64.—(1) The court having jurisdiction in relation to the proceedings may exercise its powers of its own initiative under Article 15 of the Council Regulation or Article 8 of the 1996 Hague Convention in relation to the proceedings or a specified part of the proceedings.

(2) Where the court proposes to exercise its powers, the court officer will give the parties not less than 5 days' notice of the hearing.

Application to High Court to make request under Article 15 of the Council Regulation or Article 9 of the 1996 Hague Convention to request transfer of jurisdiction

12.65.—(1) An application for the court to request transfer of jurisdiction in a matter concerning a child from another Member State or another Contracting State under Article 15 of the Council Regulation, or Article 9 of the 1996 Hague Convention (as the case may be) must be made to the principal registry and heard in the High Court.

(2) An application must be made without notice to any other person and the court may give directions about joining any other party to the application.

(3) Where there is agreement between the court and the court or competent authority to which the request under paragraph (1) is made to transfer the matter to the courts of England and Wales, the court will consider with that other court or competent authority the specific timing and conditions for the transfer.

(4) Upon receipt of agreement to transfer jurisdiction from the court or other competent authority in the Member State, or Contracting State to which the request has been made, the court officer will serve on the applicant a notice that jurisdiction has been accepted by the courts of England and Wales.

(5) The applicant must attach the notice referred to in paragraph (3) to any subsequent application in relation to the child.

(6) Nothing in this rule requires an application with respect to a child commenced following a transfer of jurisdiction to be made to or heard in the High Court.

(7) Upon allocation, the court to which the proceedings are allocated must immediately fix a directions hearing to consider the future conduct of the case.

Procedure where the court receives a request from the authorities of another Member State or Contracting State to assume jurisdiction in a matter concerning a child

12.66.—(1) Where any court other than the High Court receives a request to assume jurisdiction in a matter concerning a child from a court or other authority which has jurisdiction in another Member State or Contracting State, that court must immediately refer the request to a Judge of the High Court for a decision regarding acceptance of jurisdiction to be made.

(2) Upon the High Court agreeing to the request under paragraph (1), the court officer will notify the parties to the proceedings before the other Member State or Contracting State of that decision, and the case must be allocated as if the application had been made in England and Wales.

(3) Upon allocation, the court to which the proceedings are allocated must immediately fix a directions hearing to consider the future conduct of the case.

(4) The court officer will serve notice of the directions hearing on all parties to the proceedings in the other Member State or Contracting State no later than 5 days before the date of that hearing.

Service of the court's order or request relating to transfer of jurisdiction under the Council Regulation or the 1996 Hague Convention

12.67. The court officer will serve an order or request relating to transfer of jurisdiction on all parties, the Central Authority of the other Member State or Contracting State, and the Central Authority for England and Wales.

Questions as to the court's jurisdiction or whether the proceedings should be stayed

12.68.—(1) If at any time after issue of the application it appears to the court that under any of Articles 16 to 18 of the Council Regulation it does not or may not have jurisdiction to hear an application, or that under Article 19 of the Council Regulation or Article 13 of the 1996 Hague Convention it is or may be required to stay(GL) the proceedings or to decline jurisdiction, the court must—

    (a) stay(GL) the proceedings; and

    (b) fix a date for a hearing to determine jurisdiction or whether there should be a stay(GL) or other order.

(2) The court officer will serve notice of the hearing referred to at paragraph (1)(b) on the parties to the proceedings.

(3) The court must, in writing—

    (a) give reasons for its decision under paragraph (1); and

    (b) where it makes a finding of fact, state such finding.

(4) The court may with the consent of all the parties deal with any question as to the jurisdiction of the court, or as to whether the proceedings should be stayed(GL), without a hearing.

Request for consultation as to contemplated placement of child in England and Wales

12.69.—(1) This rule applies to a request made —

    (a) under Article 56 of the Council Regulation, by a court in another Member State; or

    (b) under Article 33 of the 1996 Hague Convention by a court in another Contracting State

for consultation on or consent to the contemplated placement of a child in England and Wales.

(2) Where the court receives a request directly from a court in another Member State or Contracting State, the court shall, as soon as practicable after receipt of the request, notify the Central Authority for England and Wales of the request and take the appropriate action under paragraph (4).

(3) Where it appears to the court officer that no proceedings relating to the child are pending before a court in England and Wales, the court officer must inform the Central Authority for England and Wales of that fact and forward to the Central Authority all documents relating to the request sent by the court in the other Member State or Contracting State.

(4) Where the court receives a request forwarded by the Central Authority for England and Wales, the court must, as soon as practicable after receipt of the request, either—

    (a) where proceedings relating to the child are pending before the court, fix a directions hearing; or

(b) in any other case, at the time when the application is made.

(3) Where an order is made without notice, the applicant must serve a copy of the order on the other parties as soon as practicable after the making of the order, unless the court otherwise directs.

(4) Where the court refuses to make an order on an application without notice, it may direct that the application is made on notice.

(5) Where any hearing takes place outside the hours during which the court office is usually open—

    (a) if the hearing takes place by telephone, the applicant's solicitors will, if practicable, arrange for the hearing to be recorded; and

    (b) in all other cases, the court or court officer will take a note of the proceedings.

(Practice Direction 12E (Urgent Business) provides further details of the procedure for out of hours applications. See also Practice Direction 12D (Inherent Jurisdiction (including Wardship Proceedings)).)

Directions

12.48.—(1) As soon as practicable after an application to which this section applies has been made, the court may give directions as to the following matters, among others—

    (a) whether service of the application may be dispensed with;

    (b) whether the proceedings should be transferred to another court under rule 12.54;

    (c) expedition of the proceedings or any part of the proceedings (and any direction for expedition may specify a date by which the court must issue its final judgment in the proceedings or a specified part of the proceedings);

    (d) the steps to be taken in the proceedings and the time by which each step is to be taken;

    (e) whether the child or any other person should be made a party to the proceedings;

    (f) if the child is not made a party to the proceedings, the manner in which the child's wishes and feelings are to be ascertained, having regard to the child's age and maturity and in particular whether an officer of the Service or a Welsh family proceedings officer should report to the court for that purpose;

    (g) where the child is made a party to the proceedings, the appointment of a children's guardian for that child unless a children's guardian has already been appointed;

    (h) the attendance of the child or any other person before the court;

    (i) the appointment of a litigation friend for a child or for any protected party, unless a litigation friend has already been appointed;

    (j) the service of documents;

    (k) the filing of evidence including expert evidence; and

    (l) whether the parties and their representatives should meet at any stage of the proceedings and the purpose of such a meeting.

(Rule 16.2 provides for when the court may make the child a party to the proceedings and rule 16.4 for the appointment of a children's guardian for the child who is made a party. Rule 16.5 (without prejudice to rule 16.6) requires a child who is a party to the proceedings but not the subject of those proceedings to have a litigation friend.)

(2) Directions of a court which are in force immediately prior to the transfer of proceedings to another court under rule 12.54 will continue to apply following the transfer subject to—

    (a) any changes of terminology which are required to apply those directions to the court to which the proceedings are transferred; and

    (b) any variation or revocation of the directions.

(3) The court or court officer will—

    (a) take a note of the giving, variation or revocation of directions under this rule; and

(b) as soon as practicable serve a copy of the directions order on every party.

Answer

12.49.—(1) Subject to paragraph (2) and to any directions given under rule 12.48, a respondent must file and serve on the parties an answer to the application within 7 days beginning with the date on which the application is served.

(2) The court may direct a longer period for service where the respondent has been made a party solely on one of the following grounds—

(a) a decision relating to custody has been made in the respondent's favour; or

(b) the respondent appears to the court to have sufficient interest in the welfare of the child.

Filing and serving written evidence

12.50.—(1) The respondent to an application to which this section applies may file and serve with the answer a statement verified by a statement of truth, together with any further evidence on which the respondent intends to rely.

(2) The applicant may, within 7 days beginning with the date on which the respondent's evidence was served under paragraph (1), file and serve a statement in reply verified by a statement of truth, together with any further evidence on which the applicant intends to rely.

Adjournment

12.51. The court will not adjourn the hearing of an application to which this section applies for more than 21 days at at any one time.

Stay of proceedings upon notification of wrongful removal etc.

12.52.—(1) In this rule and in rule 12.53—

(a) "relevant authority" means —

(i) the High Court;

(ii) a county court;

(iii) a magistrates' court;

(iv) the Court of Session;

(v) a sheriff court;

(vi) a children's hearing within the meaning of section 93 of the Children (Scotland) Act 1995;

(vii) the High Court in Northern Ireland;

(viii) a county court in Northern Ireland;

(ix) a court of summary jurisdiction in Northern Ireland;

(x) the Royal Court of Jersey;

(xi) a court of summary jurisdiction in Jersey;

(xii) the High Court of Justice of the Isle of Man;

(xiii) a court of summary jurisdiction in the Isle of Man; or

(xiv) the Secretary of State; and

(b) "rights of custody" has the same meaning as in the 1980 Hague Convention.

(2) Where a party to proceedings under the 1980 Hague Convention knows that an application relating to the merits of rights of custody is pending in or before a relevant authority, that party must file within the proceedings under the 1980 Hague Convention a concise statement of the nature of that application, including the relevant authority in or before which it is pending.

Matters prescribed for the purposes of the Act

12.27.—(1) Proceedings for an order under any of the following provisions of the 1989 Act—

    (a) a secure accommodation order under section 25;

    (b) an order giving permission to change a child's surname or remove a child from the United Kingdom under section 33(7);

    (c) an order permitting the local authority to arrange for any child in its care to live outside England and Wales under paragraph 19(1) of Schedule 2;

    (d) the extension or further extension of a supervision order under paragraph 6(3) of Schedule 3;

    (e) appeals against the determination of proceedings of a kind set out in sub-paragraphs (a) to (d);

are specified for the purposes of section 41 of that Act in accordance with section 41(6)(i) of that Act.

(2) The persons listed as applicants in the table set out in rule 12.3 to proceedings for the variation of directions made with interim care or interim supervision orders under section 38(8) of the 1989 Act are the prescribed class of persons for the purposes of that section.

(3) The persons listed as applicants in the table set out in rule 12.3 to proceedings for the variation of a direction made under section 44(6) of the 1989 Act in an emergency protection order are the prescribed class of persons for the purposes of section 44(9) of that Act.

Exclusion requirements: interim care orders and emergency protection orders

12.28.—(1) This rule applies where the court includes an exclusion requirement in an interim care order or an emergency protection order.

(2) The applicant for an interim care order or emergency protection order must—

    (a) prepare a separate statement of the evidence in support of the application for an exclusion requirement;

    (b) serve the statement personally on the relevant person with a copy of the order containing the exclusion requirement (and of any power of arrest which is attached to it);

    (c) inform the relevant person of that person's right to apply to vary or discharge the exclusion requirement.

(3) Where a power of arrest is attached to an exclusion requirement in an interim care order or an emergency protection order, the applicant will deliver—

    (a) a copy of the order; and

    (b) a statement showing that the relevant person has been served with the order or informed of its terms (whether by being present when the order was made or by telephone or otherwise),

to the officer for the time being in charge of the police station for the area in which the dwelling-house in which the child lives is situated (or such other police station as the court may specify).

(4) Rules 10.6(2) and 10.10 to 10.17 will apply, with the necessary modifications, for the service, variation, discharge and enforcement of any exclusion requirement to which a power of arrest is attached as they apply to an order made on an application under Part 4 of the 1996 Act.

(5) The relevant person must serve the parties to the proceedings with any application which that person makes for the variation or discharge of the exclusion requirement.

(6) Where an exclusion requirement ceases to have effect whether—

(a) as a result of the removal of a child under section 38A(10) or 44A(10) of the 1989 Act(**a**);

(b) because of the discharge of the interim care order or emergency protection order; or

(c) otherwise,

the applicant must inform—

(i) the relevant person;

(ii) the parties to the proceedings;

(iii) any officer to whom a copy of the order was delivered under paragraph (3); and

(iv) (where necessary) the court.

(7) Where the court includes an exclusion requirement in an interim care order or an emergency protection order of its own motion, paragraph (2) will apply with the omission of any reference to the statement of the evidence.

(8) In this rule, "the relevant person" has the meaning assigned to it by sections 38A(2) and 44A(2) of the 1989 Act.

Notification of consent

12.29.—(1) Consent for the purposes of the following provisions of the 1989 Act—

(a) section 16(3)(**b**);

(b) section 38A(2)(b)(ii) or 44A(2)(b)(ii); or

(c) paragraph 19(3)(c) or (d) of Schedule 2,

must be given either—

(i) orally to the court; or

(ii) in writing to the court signed by the person giving consent.

(2) Any written consent for the purposes of section 38A(2) or 44A(2) of the 1989 Act must include a statement that the person giving consent—

(a) is able and willing to give to the child the care which it would be reasonable to expect a parent to give; and

(b) understands that the giving of consent could lead to the exclusion of the relevant person from the dwelling-house in which the child lives.

Proceedings for secure accommodation orders: copies of reports

12.30. In proceedings under section 25 of the 1989 Act, the court will, if practicable, arrange for copies of all written reports filed in the case to be made available before the hearing to—

(a) the applicant;

(b) the parent or guardian of the child to whom the application relates;

(c) any legal representative of the child;

(d) the children's guardian; and

(e) the child, unless the court directs otherwise,

and copies of the reports may, if the court considers it desirable, be shown to any person who is entitled to notice of any hearing in accordance with Practice Direction 12C.

(**a**) Sections 38A(10) and 44A(10) were inserted by section 52 of and paragraphs 1 and 3 of Schedule 6 to the Family Law Act 1996.

(**b**) Paragraph (a) was repealed by sections 6(1), (2), 15(2) of and Schedule 3 to the Children and Adoption Act 2006.

authorities of Contracting States which have jurisdiction to take measures directed to the protection of the person or property of the child within the meaning of the 1996 Hague Convention.

Procedure under Article 11(6) of the Council Regulation where the court makes a non-return order under Article 13 of the 1980 Hague Convention

12.59.—(1) Where the court makes an order for the non-return of a child under Article 13 of the 1980 Hague Convention, it must immediately transmit the documents referred to in Article 11(6) of the Council Regulation —

    (a) directly to the court with jurisdiction or the central authority in the Member State where the child was habitually resident immediately before the wrongful removal to, or wrongful retention in, England and Wales; or

    (b) to the Central Authority for England and Wales for onward transmission to the court with jurisdiction or the central authority in the other Member State mentioned in sub-paragraph (a).

(2) The documents required by paragraph (1) must be transmitted by a method which, in the case of direct transmission to the court with jurisdiction in the other Member State, ensures and, in any other case, will not prevent, their receipt by that court within one month of the date of the non-return order.

Procedure under Article 11(7) of the Council Regulation where the court receives a non-return order made under Article 13 of the 1980 Hague Convention by a court in another Member State

12.60.—(1) This rule applies where the court receives an order made by a court in another Member State for the non-return of a child.

(2) In this rule, the order for non-return of the child and the papers transmitted with that order from the court in the other Member State are referred to as "the non-return order".

(3) Where, at the time of receipt of the non-return order, the court is already seised of a question of parental responsibility in relation to the child, —

    (a) the court officer shall immediately —

        (i) serve copies of the non-return order on each party to the proceedings in which a question of parental responsibility in relation to the child is at issue; and

        (ii) where the non-return order was received directly from the court or the central authority in the other Member State, transmit to the Central Authority for England and Wales a copy of the non-return order.

    (b) the court shall immediately invite the parties to the 1980 Hague Convention proceedings to file written submissions in respect of the question of custody by a specified date, or to attend a hearing to consider the future conduct of the proceedings in the light of the non-return order.

(4) Where, at the time of receipt of the non-return order, the court is not already seised of the question of parental responsibility in relation to the child, it shall immediately—

    (a) open a court file in respect of the child and assign a court reference to the file;

    (b) serve a copy of the non-return order on each party to the proceedings before the court in the Member State which made that order;

    (c) invite each party to file, within 3 months of notification to that party of receipt of the non-return order, submissions in the form of—

        (i) an application for an order under—

            (aa) the 1989 Act; or

            (bb) (in the High Court only) an application under the inherent jurisdiction in respect of the child; or

(ii) where permission is required to make an application for the order in question, an application for that permission;

(d) where the non-return order was received directly from the court or central authority in the other Member State, transmit to the Central Authority for England and Wales a copy of the non-return order.

(5) In a case to which paragraph (4) applies where no application is filed within the 3 month period provided for by paragraph (4)(c) the court must close its file in respect of the child.

(Enforcement of a subsequent judgment requiring the return of the child, made under Article 11(8) by a court examining custody of the child under Article 11(7), is dealt with in Part 31 below.)

Transfer of proceedings under Article 15 of the Council Regulation or under Article 8 of the 1996 Hague Convention

12.61.—(1) Where the court is considering the transfer of proceedings to the court of another Member State or Contracting State under rules 12.62 to 12.64 it will—

(a) fix a date for a hearing for the court to consider the question of transfer; and

(b) give directions as to the manner in which the parties may make representations.

(2) The court may, with the consent of all parties, deal with the question of transfer without a hearing.

(3) Directions which are in force immediately prior to the transfer of proceedings to a court in another Member State or Contracting State under rules 12.62 to 12.64 will continue to apply until the court in that other State accepts jurisdiction in accordance with the provisions of the Council Regulation or the 1996 Hague Convention (as appropriate), subject to any variation or revocation of the directions.

(4) The court or court officer will—

(a) take a note of the giving, variation or revocation of directions under this rule; and

(b) as soon as practicable serve a copy of the directions order on every party.

(5) A register of all applications and requests for transfer of jurisdiction to or from another Member State or Contracting State will be kept by the principal registry.

Application by a party for transfer of the proceedings

12.62.—(1) A party may apply to the court under Article 15(1) of the Council Regulation or under Article 8(1) of the 1996 Hague Convention —

(a) to stay$^{(GL)}$ the proceedings or a specified part of the proceedings and to invite the parties to introduce a request before a court of another Member State or Contracting State; or

(b) to make a request to a court of another Member State or another Contracting State to assume jurisdiction for the proceedings, or a specified part of the proceedings.

(2) An application under paragraph (1) must be made—

(a) to the court in which the relevant parental responsibility proceedings are pending; and

(b) using the Part 18 procedure.

(3) The applicant must file the application notice and serve it on the respondents—

(a) where the application is also made under Article 11 of the Council Regulation, not less than 5 days, and

(b) in any other case, not less than 42 days,

before the hearing of the application.

(a) the respondent's address; and

(b) either—

    (i) the whereabouts of the child; or

    (ii) that the respondent is unaware of the child's whereabouts if that is the case.

(2) Unless the court directs otherwise, the respondent must serve a copy of that notice on the applicant.

(3) Every respondent other than a child must immediately notify the court in writing of—

(a) any subsequent changes of address; or

(b) any change in the child's whereabouts,

and, unless the court directs otherwise, serve a copy of that notice on the applicant.

(4) In this rule a reference to the whereabouts of a child is a reference to—

(a) the address at which the child is living;

(b) the person with whom the child is living; and

(c) any other information relevant to where the child may be found.

Enforcement of orders in wardship proceedings

12.40. The High Court may secure compliance with any direction relating to a ward of court by an order addressed to the tipstaff.

(The role of the tipstaff is explained in Practice Direction 12D (Inherent Jurisdiction (including Wardship Proceedings)).)

Child ceasing to be ward of court

12.41.—(1) A child who, by virtue of section 41(2) of the Senior Courts Act 1981, automatically becomes a ward of court on the making of a wardship application will cease to be a ward on the determination of the application unless the court orders that the child be made a ward of court.

(2) Nothing in paragraph (1) affects the power of the court under section 41(3) of the Senior Courts Act 1981 to order that any child cease to be a ward of court.

Adoption of a child who is a ward of court

12.42. An application for permission—

(a) to start proceedings to adopt a child who is a ward of court;

(b) to place such a child for adoption with parental consent; or

(c) to start proceedings for a placement order in relation to such a child,

may be made without notice in accordance with Part 18.

CHAPTER 6

PROCEEDINGS UNDER THE 1980 HAGUE CONVENTION, THE EUROPEAN CONVENTION, THE COUNCIL REGULATION, AND THE 1996 HAGUE CONVENTION

Scope

12.43. This Chapter applies to —

(a) proceedings relating to children under the 1980 Hague Convention or the European Convention; and

(b) applications relating to the Council Regulation or the 1996 Hague Convention in respect of children.

SECTION 1

Proceedings under the 1980 Hague Convention or the European Convention

Interpretation

12.44. In this section—

"the 1985 Act" means the Child Abduction and Custody Act 1985;

"Central Authority" means, in relation to England and Wales, the Lord Chancellor;

"Contracting State" has the meaning given in—

(a) section 2 of the 1985 Act in relation to the 1980 Hague Convention; and

(b) section 13 of the 1985 Act in relation to the European Convention; and

"decision relating to custody" has the same meaning as in the European Convention.

("the 1980 Hague Convention" and the "the European Convention" are defined in rule 2.3)

Where to start proceedings

12.45. Every application under the 1980 Hague Convention or the European Convention must be—

(a) made in the High Court and issued in the principal registry; and

(b) heard by a Judge of the High Court unless the application is;

(i) to join a respondent; or

(ii) to dispense with service or extend the time for acknowledging service.

Evidence in support of application

12.46. Where the party making an application under this section does not produce the documents referred to in Practice Direction 12F, the court may—

(a) fix a time within which the documents are to be produced;

(b) accept equivalent documents; or

(c) dispense with production of the documents if the court considers it has sufficient information.

Without-notice applications

12.47.—(1) This rule applies to applications—

(a) commencing or in proceedings under this section;

(b) for interim directions under section 5 or 19 of the 1985 Act(**a**);

(c) for the disclosure of information about the child and for safeguarding the child's welfare, under rule 12.57;

(d) for the disclosure of relevant information as to where the child is, under section 24A of the 1985 Act(**b**); or

(e) for a collection order, location order or passport order.

(2) Applications under this rule may be made without notice, in which case the applicant must file the application—

(a) where the application is made by telephone, the next business day after the making of the application; or

---

(**a**) Section 5 was amended by section 115(2), (4)(a) (i), (4)(b) and 4(c) of the Adoption and Children Act 2002.

(**b**) Section 24A was inserted by section 67(4) of the Family Law Act 1986.

(b) where proceedings relating to the child are pending before another court in England and Wales, send a copy of the request to that court.

Request made by court in England and Wales for consultation as to contemplated placement of child in another Member State or Contracting State

12.70.—(1) This rule applies where the court is contemplating the placement of a child in another Member State under Article 56 of the Council Regulation or another Contracting State under Article 33 of the 1996 Hague Convention, and proposes to send a request for consultation with or for the consent of the central authority or other authority having jurisdiction in the other State in relation to the contemplated placement.

(2) In this rule, a reference to "the request" includes a reference to a report prepared for purposes of Article 33 of the 1996 Hague Convention where the request is made under that Convention.

(3) Where the court sends the request directly to the central authority or other authority having jurisdiction in the other State, it shall at the same time send a copy of the request to the Central Authority for England and Wales.

(4) The court may send the request to the Central Authority for England and Wales for onward transmission to the central authority or other authority having jurisdiction in the other Member State.

(5) The court should give consideration to the documents which should accompany the request.

(See Chapters 1 to 3 of this Part generally, for the procedure governing applications for an order under paragraph 19(1) of Schedule 2 to the 1989 Act permitting a local authority to arrange for any child in its care to live outside England and Wales.)

(Part 14 sets out the procedure governing applications for an order under section 84 (giving parental responsibility prior to adoption abroad) of the Adoption and Children Act 2002.)

Application for a declaration as to the extent, or existence, of parental responsibility in relation to a child under Article 16 of the 1996 Hague Convention

12.71.—(1) Any interested person may apply for a declaration —

(a) that a person has, or does not have, parental responsibility for a child; or

(b) as to the extent of a person's parental responsibility for a child,

where the question arises by virtue of the application of Article 16 of the 1996 Hague Convention.

(2) An application for a declaration as to the extent, or existence of a person's parental responsibility for a child by virtue of Article 16 of the 1996 Hague Convention must be made in the principal registry and heard in the High Court.

(3) An application for a declaration referred to in paragraph (1) may not be made where the question raised is otherwise capable of resolution in any other family proceedings in respect of the child.

CHAPTER 7

COMMUNICATION OF INFORMATION: PROCEEDINGS RELATING TO CHILDREN

Interpretation

12.72.—(1) In this Chapter "independent reviewing officer" means a person appointed in respect of a child in accordance with regulation 2A of the Review of Children's Cases Regulations 1991(**a**), or regulation 3 of the Review of Children's Cases (Wales) Regulations 2007(**b**).

(**a**) S.I. 1991/895.
(**b**) S.I. 2007/307.

Communication of information: general

12.73.—(1) For the purposes of the law relating to contempt of court, information relating to proceedings held in private (whether or not contained in a document filed with the court) may be communicated—

    (a) where the communication is to—

        (i) a party;

       (ii) the legal representative of a party;

      (iii) a professional legal adviser;

      (iv) an officer of the service or a Welsh family proceedings officer;

       (v) the welfare officer;

      (vi) the Legal Services Commission;

     (vii) an expert whose instruction by a party has been authorised by the court for the purposes of the proceedings;

    (viii) a professional acting in furtherance of the protection of children;

      (ix) an independent reviewing officer appointed in respect of a child who is, or has been, subject to proceedings to which this rule applies;

    (b) where the court gives permission; or

    (c) subject to any direction of the court, in accordance with rule 12.75 and Practice Direction 12G.

(2) Nothing in this Chapter permits the communication to the public at large, or any section of the public, of any information relating to the proceedings.

(3) Nothing in rule 12.75 and Practice Direction 12G permits the disclosure of an unapproved draft judgment handed down by any court.

Instruction of experts

12.74.—(1) No party may instruct an expert for any purpose relating to proceedings, including to give evidence in those proceedings, without the permission of the court.

(2) Where the permission of the court has not been given under paragraph (1), no evidence arising out of an unauthorised instruction may be introduced without permission of the court.

Communication of information for purposes connected with the proceedings

12.75.—(1) A party or the legal representative of a party, on behalf of and upon the instructions of that party, may communicate information relating to the proceedings to any person where necessary to enable that party—

    (a) by confidential discussion, to obtain support, advice or assistance in the conduct of the proceedings;

    (b) to engage in mediation or other forms of alternative dispute resolution;

    (c) to make and pursue a complaint against a person or body concerned in the proceedings; or

    (d) to make and pursue a complaint regarding the law, policy or procedure relating to a category of proceedings to which this Part applies.

(2) Where information is communicated to any person in accordance with paragraph (1)(a) of this rule, no further communication by that person is permitted.

(3) When information relating to the proceedings is communicated to any person in accordance with paragraphs (1)(b),(c) or (d) of this rule—

    (a) the recipient may communicate that information to a further recipient, provided that—

(i) the party who initially communicated the information consents to that further communication; and

(ii) the further communication is made only for the purpose or purposes for which the party made the initial communication; and

(b) the information may be successively communicated to and by further recipients on as many occasions as may be necessary to fulfil the purpose for which the information was initially communicated, provided that on each such occasion the conditions in sub-paragraph (a) are met.

PART 13

PROCEEDINGS UNDER SECTION 54 OF THE HUMAN FERTILISATION AND EMBRYOLOGY ACT 2008

Interpretation and application

13.1.—(1) A reference in this Part to the 2002 Act is a reference to that Act as applied with modifications by the Human Fertilisation and Embryology (Parental Order) Regulations 2010.

(2) In this Part—

"the other parent" means any person who is a parent of the child but is not one of the applicants or the woman who carried the child (including any man who is the father by virtue of section 35 or 36 of the 2008 Act or any woman who is a parent by virtue of section 42 or 43 of that Act);

"parental order" means an order under section 54 of the 2008 Act;

"parental order proceedings" means proceedings for the making of a parental order under the 2008 Act or an order under any provision of the 2002 Act;

"parental order reporter" means an officer of the service or a Welsh family proceedings officer appointed to act on behalf of a child who is the subject of parental order proceedings;

"provision for contact" means a contact order under section 8 or 34 of the 1989 Act(**a**).

(3) Except where the contrary intention appears, the rules in this Part apply to parental order proceedings.

Application of Part 12

13.2. Rules 12.9 to 12.11, 12.19 and 12.21 apply as appropriate, with any necessary modifications, to parental order proceedings.

Who the parties are

13.3.—(1) An application for a parental order may be made by such of the following who satisfy the conditions set out in section 54(1) of the 2008 Act—

(a) a husband and wife;

(b) civil partners of each other; or

(c) two persons who are living as partners in an enduring family relationship and are not within the prohibited degrees of relationship in relation to each other.

(2) The respondents to an application for a parental order are—

(a) the woman who carried the child;

(**a**) Section 34 was amended by section 139(1) of and paragraphs 54, 64(a) and (b) of Schedule 3 to the Adoption and Children Act 2002.

(b) the other parent (if any);

(c) any person in whose favour there is provision for contact; and

(d) any other person or body with parental responsibility for the child at the date of the application.

(3) The court will direct that a person with parental responsibility for the child be made a party to proceedings where that person requests to be one.

(4) The court may at any time direct that—

(a) any other person or body be made a respondent to the proceedings; or

(b) a respondent be removed from the proceedings.

(5) If the court makes a direction for the addition or removal of a party, it may give consequential directions about—

(a) serving a copy of the application form on any new respondent;

(b) serving relevant documents on the new party; and

(c) the management of the proceedings.

Notice of proceedings to person with foreign parental responsibility

13.4.—(1) This rule applies where a child is subject to proceedings to which this Part applies and at the date of the application –

(a) a person holds or is believed to hold parental responsibility for the child under the law of another State which subsists in accordance with Article 16 of the 1996 Hague Convention following the child becoming habitually resident in a territorial unit of the United Kingdom; and

(b) that person is not otherwise required to be joined as a respondent under rule 13.3.

(2) The applicant shall give notice of the proceedings to any person to whom the applicant believes paragraph (1) applies.

(3) The applicant and every respondent to the proceedings shall provide such details as they possess as to the identity and whereabouts of any person they believe to hold parental responsibility for the child in accordance with paragraph (1) to the court officer, upon making, or responding to the application as appropriate.

(4) Where the existence of such a person only becomes apparent to a party at a later date during the proceedings, that party must notify the court officer of those details at the earliest opportunity.

(5) Where a person to whom paragraph (1) applies receives notice of proceedings, that person may apply to the court to be joined as a party using the Part 18 procedure.

What the court or a court officer will do when the application has been issued

13.5.—(1) As soon as practicable after the issue of proceedings—

(a) the court will—

(i) if section 48(1) of the 2002 Act applies (restrictions on making parental orders), consider whether it is proper to hear the application;

(ii) subject to paragraph (2), set a date for the first directions hearing;

(iii) appoint a parental order reporter; and

(iv) set a date for the hearing of the application; and

(b) a court officer will—

(i) return to the applicants the copies of the application together with any other documents the applicant is required to serve; and

(ii) send a certified copy of the entry in the register of live births to the parental order reporter.

(2) Where it considers it appropriate the court may, instead of setting a date for a first directions appointment, give the directions provided for in rule 13.9.

Service of the application and other documents

13.6.—(1) The applicants must, within 14 days before the hearing or first directions hearing, serve on the respondents —

    (a) the application;

    (b) a form for acknowledging service; and

    (c) a notice of proceedings.

(2) The applicants must serve a notice of proceedings on any local authority or voluntary organisation that has at any time provided accommodation for the child.

Acknowledgement

13.7. Within 7 days of the service of an application for a parental order, each respondent must file an acknowledgment of service and serve it on all the other parties.

Date for first directions hearing

13.8. Unless the court directs otherwise, the first directions hearing must be within 4 weeks beginning with the date on which the application is issued.

The first directions hearing

13.9.—(1) At the first directions hearing in the proceedings the court will—

    (a) fix a timetable for the filing of—

        (i) any report from a parental order reporter;

        (ii) if a statement of facts has been filed, any amended statement of facts; and

        (iii) any other evidence;

    (b) give directions relating to the report of the parental order reporter and other evidence;

    (c) consider whether any other person should be a party to the proceedings and, if so, give directions in accordance with rule 13.3(3) or (4) joining that person as a party;

    (d) give directions relating to the appointment of a litigation friend for any protected party unless a litigation friend has already been appointed;

    (e) consider whether the case needs to be transferred to another court and, if so, give directions to transfer the proceedings to another court in accordance with the Allocation Order;

    (f) give directions about—

        (i) tracing the other parent or the woman who carried the child;

        (ii) service of documents;

        (iii) subject to paragraph (2), disclosure as soon as possible of information and evidence to the parties; and

        (iv) the final hearing.

(2) Rule 13.12 (reports of the parental order reporter and disclosure to parties) applies to any direction given under paragraph (1)(f)(iii) as it applies to a direction given under rule 13.12(1).

(3) The parties or their legal representatives must attend the first directions hearing unless the court directs otherwise.

(4) Directions may also be given at any stage in the proceedings—

    (a) of the court's own initiative; or

(b) on the application of a party or the parental order reporter.

(5) Where the court proposes to exercise its powers in paragraph (1) of its own initiative the procedure set out in rule 4.3(2) to (7) applies.

(6) For the purposes of giving directions or for such purposes as the court directs—

(a) the court may set a date for a further directions hearing or other hearing; and

(b) the court officer will give notice of any date so fixed to the parties and to the parental order reporter.

(7) Directions of a court which are still in force immediately prior to the transfer of proceedings to another court shall continue to apply following the transfer subject to—

(a) any changes of terminology which are required to apply those directions to the court to which the proceedings are transferred; and

(b) any variation or revocation of the direction.

(8) The court or court officer will—

(a) take a note of the giving, variation or revocation of a direction under this rule; and

(b) as soon as practicable serve a copy of the note on every party.

(9) After the first directions hearing the court will monitor compliance by the parties with the court's timetable and directions.

Where the agreement of the other parent or the woman who carried the child is not required

13.10.—(1) This rule applies where the agreement of the other parent or the woman who carried the child to the making of the parental order is not required as the person in question cannot be found or is incapable of giving agreement.

(2) The applicants must—

(a) state that the agreement is not required in the application form, or at any later stage by filing a written note with the court;

(b) file a statement of facts setting out a summary of the history of the case and any other facts to satisfy the court that the other parent or the woman who carried the child cannot be found or is incapable of giving agreement.

(3) On receipt of the application form or written note—

(a) a court officer will—

(i) unless the other parent or the woman who carried the child cannot be found, inform the other parent or the woman who carried the child that their agreement is not required;

(ii) send a copy of the statement of facts filed in accordance with paragraph (2)(b) to—

(aa) the other parent unless the other parent cannot be found;

(bb) the woman who carried the child unless the woman cannot be found; and

(cc) the parental order reporter; and

(b) if the applicants consider that the other parent or the woman who carried the child is incapable of giving agreement the court will consider whether to—

(i) appoint a litigation friend for the other parent or the woman who carried the child under rule 15.6(1) or

(ii) give directions for an application to be made under rule 15.6(3),

unless a litigation friend is already appointed for the other parent or the woman who carried the child.

Agreement

13.11.—(1) Unless the court directs otherwise, the agreement of the other parent or the woman who carried the child to the making of the parental order may be given in the form referred to in Practice Direction 5A or a form to the like effect.

(2) Any form of agreement executed in Scotland must be witnessed by a Justice of the Peace or a Sheriff.

(3) Any form of agreement executed in Northern Ireland must be witnessed by a Justice of the Peace.

(4) Any form of agreement executed outside the United Kingdom must be witnessed by—

(a) any person for the time being authorised by law in the place where the document is executed to administer an oath for any judicial or other legal purpose;

(b) a British Consular officer;

(c) a notary public; or

(d) if the person executing the document is serving in any of the regular armed forces of the Crown, an officer holding a commission in any of those forces.

Reports of the parental order reporter and disclosure to the parties

13.12.—(1) The court will consider whether to give a direction that a confidential report of the parental order reporter be disclosed to each party to the proceedings.

(2) Before giving such a direction the court will consider whether any information should be deleted including information which discloses the particulars referred to in rule 29.1(1) where a party has given notice under rule 29.1(2) (disclosure of personal details).

(3) The court may direct that the report shall not be disclosed to a party.

Notice of final hearing

13.13. A court officer will give notice to the parties and to the parental order reporter—

(a) of the date and place where the application will be heard; and

(b) of the fact that, unless the person wishes or the court requires, the person need not attend.

The final hearing

13.14.—(1) Any person who has been given notice in accordance with rule 13.13 may attend the final hearing and be heard on the question of whether an order should be made.

(2) The court may direct that any person must attend a final hearing.

Proof of identity of the child

13.15.—(1) Unless the contrary is shown, the child referred to in the application will be deemed to be the child referred to in the form of agreement to the making of the parental order where the conditions in paragraph (2) apply.

(2) The conditions are—

(a) the application identifies the child by reference to a full certified copy of an entry in the registers of live-births;

(b) the form of agreement identifies the child by reference to a full certified copy of an entry in the registers of live-births attached to the form; and

(c) the copy of the entry in the registers of live-births referred to in sub-paragraph (a) is the same or relates to the same entry in the registers of live-births as the copy of the entry in the registers of live-births attached to the form of agreement.

(3) Where the precise date of the child's birth is not proved to the satisfaction of the court, the court will determine the probable date of birth.

(4) The probable date of the child's birth may be specified in the parental order as the date of the child's birth.

(5) Where the child's place of birth cannot be proved to the satisfaction of the court—

    (a) the child may be treated as having been born in the registration district of the court where it is probable that the child may have been born in—

        (i) the United Kingdom;

        (ii) the Channel Islands; or

        (iii) the Isle of Man; or

    (b) in any other case, the particulars of the country of birth may be omitted from the parental order.

Disclosing information to an adult who was subject to a parental order

13.16.—(1) Subject to paragraph (2), the person who is subject to the parental order has the right to receive from the court which made the parental order a copy of the following—

    (a) the application form for a parental order (but not the documents attached to that form);

    (b) the parental order and any other orders relating to the parental order proceedings;

    (c) a transcript of the court's decision; and

    (d) a report made to the court by the parental order reporter.

(2) The court will not provide a copy of a document or order referred to in paragraph (1) unless the person making the request has completed the certificate relating to counselling in the form for that purpose referred to in Practice Direction 5A.

(3) This rule does not apply to a person under the age of 18 years.

Application for recovery orders

13.17.—(1) An application for any of the orders referred to in section 41(2) of the 2002 Act (recovery orders) may—

    (a) in the High Court or a county court, be made without notice in which case the applicant must file the application—

        (i) where the application is made by telephone, the next business day after the making of the application; or

        (ii) in any other case, at the time when the application is made; and

    (b) in a magistrates' court, be made, with the permission of the court, without notice in which case the applicant must file the application at the time when the application is made or as directed by the court.

(2) Where the court refuses to make an order on an application without notice it may direct that the application is made on notice in which case the application shall proceed in accordance with rules 13.1 to 13.14.

(3) The respondents to an application under this rule are—

    (a) in a case where parental order proceedings are pending, all parties to those proceedings;

    (b) any person having parental responsibility for the child;

    (c) any person in whose favour there is provision for contact;

    (d) any person who was caring for the child immediately prior to the making of the application; and

    (e) any person whom the applicant alleges to have effected, or to have been or to be responsible for, the taking or keeping of the child.

Keeping of registers, custody, inspection and disclosure of documents and information

13.18.—(1) Such part of the register kept in a family proceedings court in pursuance of rules made under the Magistrates' Courts Act 1980 as relates to parental order proceedings, must be kept in a separate book and the book must not contain particulars of any other proceedings.

(2) All documents relating to parental order proceedings and related proceedings under the 2002 Act including, in a family proceedings court, the book kept in accordance with paragraph (1), must, while they are in the custody of the court, be kept in a place of special security.

(3) Any person who obtains any information in the course of, or relating to, parental order proceedings must treat that information as confidential and must only disclose it if—

    (a) the disclosure is necessary for the proper exercise of that person's duties; or

    (b) the information is requested by—

        (i) a court or public authority (whether in Great Britain or not) having power to determine parental order proceedings and related matters, for the purpose of that court or authority discharging its duties relating to those proceedings and matters; or

        (ii) a person who is authorised in writing by the Secretary of State to obtain the information for the purposes of research.

Documents held by the court not to be inspected or copied without the court's permission

13.19. Subject to the provisions of these rules, any practice direction or any direction given by the court—

    (a) no document or order held by the court in parental order proceedings and related proceedings under the 2002 Act will be open to inspection by any person; and

    (b) no copy of any such document or order, or of an extract from any such document or order, shall be taken by or given to any person.

Orders

13.20.—(1) A parental order takes effect from the date when it is made, or such later date as the court may specify.

(2) In proceedings in Wales a party may request that an order be drawn up in Welsh as well as English.

Copies of orders

13.21.—(1) Within 7 days beginning with the date on which the final order was made in proceedings, or such shorter time as the court may direct, a court officer will send—

    (a) a copy of the order to the applicant;

    (b) a copy, which is sealed^(GL), authenticated with the stamp of the court or certified as a true copy of a parental order, to the Registrar General;

    (c) a notice of the making or refusal of—

        (i) the final order; or

        (ii) an order quashing or revoking a parental order or allowing an appeal against an order in proceedings,

    to every respondent and, with the permission of the court, any other person.

(2) The court officer will also send notice of the making of a parental order to—

    (a) any court in Great Britain which appears to the court officer to have made any such order as is referred to in section 46(2) of the 2002 Act (order relating to parental responsibility for, and maintenance of, the child); and

    (b) the principal registry, if it appears to the court officer that a parental responsibility agreement has been recorded at the principal registry.

(3) A copy of any final order may be sent to any other person with the permission of the court.

(4) The court officer will send a copy of any order made during the course of the proceedings to all the parties to those proceedings unless the court directs otherwise.

(5) If an order has been drawn up in Welsh as well as in English in accordance with rule 13.20(2), any reference in this rule to sending an order is to be taken as a reference to sending both the Welsh and English orders.

Amendment and revocation of orders

13.22.—(1) This rule applies to an application under paragraph 4 of Schedule 1 to the 2002 Act (amendment of a parental order and revocation of direction).

(2) If the application is made in a family proceedings court it must be made to a family proceedings court for the same local justice area as the family proceedings court which made the parental order, by delivering it or sending it by post to the designated officer of the court.

(3) Subject to paragraph (4), an application may be made without serving a copy of the application notice.

(4) The court may direct that an application notice be served on such persons as it thinks fit.

(5) Where the court makes an order granting the application, a proper officer shall send the Registrar General a notice—

(a) specifying the amendments; or

(b) informing the Registrar General of the revocation,

giving sufficient particulars of the order to enable the Registrar General to identify the case.

PART 14

PROCEDURE FOR APPLICATIONS IN ADOPTION, PLACEMENT AND RELATED PROCEEDINGS

Application of this Part and interpretation

14.1.—(1) The rules in this Part apply to the following proceedings—

(a) adoption proceedings;

(b) placement proceedings; and

(c) proceedings for—

(i) the making of a contact order under section 26 of the 2002 Act(**a**);

(ii) the variation or revocation of a contact order under section 27 of the 2002 Act;

(iii) an order giving permission to change a child's surname or remove a child from the United Kingdom under section 28(2) and (3) of the 2002 Act;

(iv) a section 84 order;

(v) a section 88 direction;

(vi) a section 89 order; or

(vii) any other order that may be referred to in a practice direction.

(2) In this Part—

"Central Authority" means—

(a) in relation to England, the Secretary of State; and

(**a**) Section 26 was amended by section 15(1) of and paragraphs 13 and 14(1) to (3) of Schedule 2 to the Children and Adoption Act 2006.

(b) in relation to Wales, the Welsh Ministers;

"Convention adoption order" means an adoption order under the 2002 Act which, by virtue of regulations under section 1 of the Adoption (Intercountry Aspects) Act 1999(**a**) (regulations giving effect to the Convention on Protection of Children and Co-operation in Respect of Intercountry Adoption, concluded at the Hague on 29th May 1993), is made as a Convention adoption order;

"guardian" means—

(a) a guardian (other than the guardian of the estate of a child) appointed in accordance with section 5 of the 1989 Act(**b**); and

(b) a special guardian within the meaning of section 14A of the 1989 Act(**c**);

"provision for contact" means a contact order under section 8 or 34 of the 1989 Act or a contact order under section 26 of the 2002 Act;

"section 88 direction" means a direction given by the High Court under section 88 of the 2002 Act that section 67(3) of that Act (status conferred by adoption) does not apply or does not apply to any extent specified in the direction.

Application for a serial number

14.2.—(1) This rule applies to any application in proceedings by a person who intends to adopt the child.

(2) If, before the proceedings have started, the applicant requests a court officer to assign a serial number to identify the applicant in connection with the proceedings in order for the applicant's identity to be kept confidential in those proceedings, a serial number will be so assigned.

(3) The court may at any time direct that a serial number identifying the applicant in the proceedings referred to in paragraph (2) must be removed.

(4) If a serial number has been assigned to a person under paragraph (2)—

(a) the court officer will ensure that any application form or application notice sent in accordance with these rules does not contain information which discloses, or is likely to disclose, the identity of that person to any other party to that application who is not already aware of that person's identity; and

(b) the proceedings on the application will be conducted with a view to securing that the applicant is not seen by or made known to any party who is not already aware of the applicant's identity except with the applicant's consent.

Who the parties are

14.3.—(1) In relation to the proceedings set out in column 1 of the following table, column 2 sets out who the application may be made by and column 3 sets out who the respondents to those proceedings will be.

Proceedings for	Applicants	Respondents
An adoption order (section 46 of the 2002 Act).	The prospective adopters (sections 50 and 51 of the 2002 Act)(**d**).	Each parent who has parental responsibility for the child unless that parent has given notice under section 20(4)(a) of the 2002 Act (statement of wish not to be informed of any application for an adoption order) which has effect;

(**a**) 1999 c. 18 Section 1 was inserted by section 120(1) of and paragraph 10 of Schedule 2 to the Adoption and Children (Scotland) Act 2007 (2007 asp 4).

(**b**) Section 5 was amended by section 115(2), (4)(a)(i),(ii),(4)(b) and (4)(c) of the Adoption and Children Act 2002.

(**c**) Section 14A was inserted by section 115 of the Adoption and Children Act 2002.

(**d**) Section 51 was amended by section 79(1), (4) and (5) of the Civil Partnership Act 2004 and by section 56 of and paragraphs 39(1), (2) and (3) of Schedule 6 to the Human Fertilisation and Embryology Act 2008.

		any guardian of the child unless that guardian has given notice under section 20(4)(a) of the 2002 Act (statement of wish not to be informed of any application for an adoption order) which has effect;
		any person in whose favour there is provision for contact;
		any adoption agency having parental responsibility for the child under section 25 of the 2002 Act;
		any adoption agency which has taken part at any stage in the arrangements for adoption of the child;
		any local authority to whom notice under section 44 of the 2002 Act (notice of intention to adopt or apply for a section 84 order) has been given;
		any local authority or voluntary organisation which has parental responsibility for, is looking after or is caring for, the child; and
		the child where—

the child where—

— permission has been granted to a parent or guardian to oppose the making of the adoption order (section 47(3) or 47(5) of the 2002 Act);

— the child opposes the making of an adoption order;

— a children and family reporter recommends that it is in the best interests of the child to be a party to the proceedings and that recommendation is accepted by the court;

— the child is already an adopted child;

— any party to the proceedings or the child is opposed to the arrangements for allowing any person contact with the child, or a person not being allowed contact with the child after the making of the adoption order;

— the application is for a Convention adoption order or a section 84 order;

— the child has been brought into the United Kingdom in the circumstances where section 83(1) of the 2002 Act applies (restriction on bringing children in);

		— the application is for an adoption order other than a Convention adoption order and the prospective adopters intend the child to live in a country or territory outside the British Islands after the making of the adoption order; or — the prospective adopters are relatives of the child.
A section 84 order.	The prospective adopters asking for parental responsibility prior to adoption abroad.	As for an adoption order.
A placement order (section 21 of the 2002 Act).	A local authority (section 22 of the 2002 Act).	Each parent who has parental responsibility for the child: any guardian of the child; any person in whose favour an order under the 1989 Act is in force in relation to the child; any adoption agency or voluntary organisation which has parental responsibility for, is looking after, or is caring for, the child; the child; and the parties or any persons who are or have been parties to proceedings for a care order in respect of the child where those proceedings have led to the application for the placement order.
An order varying a placement order (section 23 of the 2002 Act).	The joint application of the local authority authorised by the placement order to place the child for adoption and the local authority which is to be substituted for that authority (section 23 of the 2002 Act).	The parties to the proceedings leading to the placement order which it is sought to have varied except the child who was the subject of those proceedings; and any person in whose favour there is provision for contact.
An order revoking a placement order (section 24 of the 2002 Act).	The child; the local authority authorised to place the child for adoption; or where the child is not placed for adoption by the authority, any other person who has the permission of the court to apply (section 24 of the 2002 Act).	The parties to the proceedings leading to the placement order which it is sought to have revoked; and any person in whose favour there is provision for contact.
A contact order (section 26 of the 2002 Act(**a**)).	The child; the adoption agency; any parent, guardian or relative; any person in whose favour there was provision for contact under the 1989 Act which ceased to have	The adoption agency authorised to place the child for adoption or which has placed the child for adoption; the person with whom the child lives or is to live; each parent with parental responsibility

---

(**a**)   Section 26 was amended by section 15(1) of and paragraphs 13, 14(1), (2) and (3) of Schedule 2 to the Children and Adoption Act 2006.

	effect on an adoption agency being authorised to place a child for adoption, or placing a child for adoption who is less than six weeks old (section 26(1) of the 2002 Act); a person in whose favour there was a residence order in force immediately before the adoption agency was authorised to place the child for adoption or placed the child for adoption at a time when the child was less than six weeks old; a person who by virtue of an order made in the exercise of the High Court's inherent jurisdiction with respect to children had care of the child immediately before that time; or any person who has the permission of the court to make the application (section 26 of the 2002 Act).	for the child; any guardian of the child; and the child where— — the adoption agency authorised to place the child for adoption or which has placed the child for adoption or a parent with parental responsibility for the child opposes the making of the contact order under section 26 of the 2002 Act; — the child opposes the making of the contact order under section 26 of the 2002 Act; — existing provision for contact is to be revoked; — relatives of the child do not agree to the arrangements for allowing any person contact with the child, or a person not being allowed contact with the child; or — the child is suffering or is at risk of suffering harm within the meaning of the 1989 Act.
An order varying or revoking a contact order (section 27 of the 2002 Act).	The child; the adoption agency; or any person named in the contact order (section 27(1) of the 2002 Act).	The parties to the proceedings leading to the contact order which it is sought to have varied or revoked; and any person named in the contact order.
An order permitting the child's name to be changed or the removal of the child from the United Kingdom (section 28(2) and (3) of the 2002 Act).	Any person including the adoption agency or the local authority authorised to place, or which has placed, the child for adoption (section 28(2) of the 2002 Act).	The parties to proceedings leading to any placement order; the adoption agency authorised to place the child for adoption or which has placed the child for adoption; any prospective adopters with whom the child is living; each parent with parental responsibility for the child; and any guardian of the child.
A section 88 direction.	The adopted child; the adopters; any parent; or any other person.	The adopters; the parents; the adoption agency; the local authority to whom notice under section 44 of the 2002 Act (notice of intention to apply for a section 84 order) has been given; and the Attorney-General.
A section 89 order.	The adopters; the adopted person; any parent; the relevant Central Authority;	The adopters; the parents; the adoption agency; and the local authority to whom notice

	the adoption agency; the local authority to whom notice under section 44 of the 2002 Act (notice of intention to adopt or apply for a section 84 order) has been given; the Secretary of State for the Home Department; or any other person.	under section 44 of the 2002 Act (notice of intention to adopt or apply for a section 84 order) has been given.

(2) The court may at any time direct that a child, who is not already a respondent to proceedings, be made a respondent to proceedings where—

    (a) the child—

        (i) wishes to make an application; or

        (ii) has evidence to give to the court or a legal submission to make which has not been given or made by any other party; or

    (b) there are other special circumstances.

(3) The court may at any time direct that—

    (a) any other person or body be made a respondent to proceedings; or

    (b) a party be removed.

(4) If the court makes a direction for the addition or removal of a party, it may give consequential directions about—

    (a) serving a copy of the application form on any new respondent;

    (b) serving relevant documents on the new party; and

    (c) the management of the proceedings.

Notice of proceedings to person with foreign parental responsibility

14.4.—(1) This rule applies where a child is subject to proceedings to which this Part applies and –

    (a) a parent of the child holds or is believed to hold parental responsibility for the child under the law of another State which subsists in accordance with Article 16 of the 1996 Hague Convention following the child becoming habitually resident in a territorial unit of the United Kingdom; and

    (b) that parent is not otherwise required to be joined as a respondent under rule 14.3.

(2) The applicant shall give notice of the proceedings to any parent to whom the applicant believes paragraph (1) applies in any case in which a person who was a parent with parental responsibility under the 1989 Act would be a respondent to the proceedings in accordance with rule 14.3.

(3) The applicant and every respondent to the proceedings shall provide such details as they possess as to the identity and whereabouts of any parent they believe to hold parental responsibility for the child in accordance with paragraph (1) to the court officer, upon making, or responding to the application as appropriate.

(4) Where the existence of such a parent only becomes apparent to a party at a later date during the proceedings, that party must notify the court officer of those details at the earliest opportunity.

(5) Where a parent to whom paragraph (1) applies receives notice of proceedings, that parent may apply to the court to be joined as a party using the Part 18 procedure.

Who is to serve

14.5.—(1) The general rules about service in Part 6 are subject to this rule.

(2) In proceedings to which this Part applies, a document which has been issued or prepared by a court officer will be served by the court officer except where—

(a) a practice direction provides otherwise; or

(b) the court directs otherwise.

(3) Where a court officer is to serve a document, it is for the court to decide which of the methods of service specified in rule 6.23 is to be used.

What the court or a court officer will do when the application has been issued

14.6.—(1) As soon as practicable after the application has been issued in proceedings—

(a) the court will—

(i) if section 48(1) of the 2002 Act (restrictions on making adoption orders) applies, consider whether it is proper to hear the application;

(ii) subject to paragraph (4), set a date for the first directions hearing;

(iii) appoint a children's guardian in accordance with rule 16.3(1);

(iv) appoint a reporting officer in accordance with rule 16.30;

(v) consider whether a report relating to the welfare of the child is required, and if so, request such a report in accordance with rule 16.33;

(vi) set a date for the hearing of the application; and

(vii) do anything else that may be set out in a practice direction; and

(b) a court officer will—

(i) subject to receiving confirmation in accordance with paragraph (2)(b)(ii), give notice of any directions hearing set by the court to the parties and to any children's guardian, reporting officer or children and family reporter;

(ii) serve a copy of the application form (but, subject to sub-paragraphs (iii) and (iv), not the documents attached to it) on the persons referred to in Practice Direction 14A;

(iii) send a copy of the certified copy of the entry in the register of live-births or Adopted Children Register and any health report attached to an application for an adoption order to—

(aa) any children's guardian, reporting officer or children and family reporter; and

(bb) the local authority to whom notice under section 44 of the 2002 Act (notice of intention to adopt or apply for a section 84 order) has been given;

(iv) if notice under rule 14.9(2) has been given (request to dispense with consent of parent or guardian), in accordance with that rule inform the parent or guardian of the request and send a copy of the statement of facts to—

(aa) the parent or guardian;

(bb) any children's guardian, reporting officer or children and family reporter;

(cc) any local authority to whom notice under section 44 of the 2002 Act (notice of intention to adopt or apply for a section 84 order) has been given; and

(dd) any adoption agency which has placed the child for adoption; and

(v) do anything else that may be set out in a practice direction.

(2) In addition to the matters referred to in paragraph (1), as soon as practicable after an application for an adoption order or a section 84 order has been issued the court or the court officer will—

(a) where the child is not placed for adoption by an adoption agency—

(i) ask either the Service or the Assembly to file any relevant form of consent to an adoption order or a section 84 order; and

(ii) ask the local authority to prepare a report on the suitability of the prospective adopters if one has not already been prepared; and

(b) where the child is placed for adoption by an adoption agency, ask the adoption agency to—

    (i) file any relevant form of consent to—

        (aa) the child being placed for adoption;

        (bb) an adoption order;

        (cc) a future adoption order under section 20 of the 2002 Act; or

        (dd) a section 84 order;

    (ii) confirm whether a statement has been made under section 20(4)(a) of the 2002 Act (statement of wish not to be informed of any application for an adoption order) and if so, to file that statement;

    (iii) file any statement made under section 20(4)(b) of the 2002 Act (withdrawal of wish not to be informed of any application for an adoption order) as soon as it is received by the adoption agency; and

    (iv) prepare a report on the suitability of the prospective adopters if one has not already been prepared.

(3) In addition to the matters referred to in paragraph (1), as soon as practicable after an application for a placement order has been issued—

    (a) the court will consider whether a report giving the local authority's reasons for placing the child for adoption is required, and if so, will direct the local authority to prepare such a report; and

    (b) the court or the court officer will ask either the Service or the Assembly to file any form of consent to the child being placed for adoption.

(4) Where it considers it appropriate the court may, instead of setting a date for a first directions hearing, give the directions provided for by rule 14.8.

Date for first directions hearing

14.7. Unless the court directs otherwise, the first directions hearing must be within 4 weeks beginning with the date on which the application is issued.

The first directions hearing

14.8.—(1) At the first directions hearing in the proceedings the court will—

    (a) fix a timetable for the filing of—

        (i) any report relating to the suitability of the applicants to adopt a child;

        (ii) any report from the local authority;

        (iii) any report from a children's guardian, reporting officer or children and family reporter;

        (iv) if a statement of facts has been filed, any amended statement of facts;

        (v) any other evidence, and

        (vi) give directions relating to the reports and other evidence;

    (b) consider whether the child or any other person should be a party to the proceedings and, if so, give directions in accordance with rule 14.3(2) or (3) joining that child or person as a party;

    (c) give directions relating to the appointment of a litigation friend for any protected party or child who is a party to, but not the subject of, proceedings unless a litigation friend has already been appointed;

    (d) consider whether the case needs to be transferred to another court and, if so, give directions to transfer the proceedings to another court in accordance with any order made by the Lord Chancellor under Part 1 of Schedule 11 to the 1989 Act;

(e) give directions about—

    (i) tracing parents or any other person the court considers to be relevant to the proceedings;

    (ii) service of documents;

    (iii) subject to paragraph (2), disclosure as soon as possible of information and evidence to the parties; and

    (iv) the final hearing.

(By rule 3.3 the court may also direct that the case be adjourned if it considers that alternative dispute resolution is appropriate.)

(2) Rule 14.13(2) applies to any direction given under paragraph (1)(e)(iii) as it applies to a direction given under rule 14.13(1).

(3) In addition to the matters referred to in paragraph (1), the court will give any of the directions listed in Practice Direction 14B in proceedings for—

    (a) a Convention adoption order;

    (b) a section 84 order;

    (c) a section 88 direction;

    (d) a section 89 order; or

    (e) an adoption order where section 83(1) of the 2002 Act applies (restriction on bringing children in).

(4) The parties or their legal representatives must attend the first directions hearing unless the court directs otherwise.

(5) Directions may also be given at any stage in the proceedings—

    (a) of the court's own initiative; or

    (b) on the application of a party or any children's guardian or, where the direction concerns a report by a reporting officer or children and family reporter, the reporting officer or children and family reporter.

(6) For the purposes of giving directions or for such purposes as the court directs—

    (a) the court may set a date for a further directions hearing or other hearing; and

    (b) the court officer will give notice of any date so fixed to the parties and to any children's guardian, reporting officer or children and family reporter.

(7) After the first directions hearing the court will monitor compliance by the parties with the court's timetable and directions.

Requesting the court to dispense with the consent of any parent or guardian

14.9.—(1) This rule applies where the applicant wants to ask the court to dispense with the consent of any parent or guardian of a child to—

    (a) the child being placed for adoption;

    (b) the making of an adoption order except a Convention adoption order; or

    (c) the making of a section 84 order.

(2) The applicant requesting the court to dispense with the consent must—

    (a) give notice of the request in the application form or at any later stage by filing a written request setting out the reasons for the request; and

    (b) file a statement of facts setting out a summary of the history of the case and any other facts to satisfy the court that—

        (i) the parent or guardian cannot be found or is incapable of giving consent; or

        (ii) the welfare of the child requires the consent to be dispensed with.

(3) If a serial number has been assigned to the applicant under rule 14.2, the statement of facts supplied under paragraph (2)(b) must be framed so that it does not disclose the identity of the applicant.

(4) On receipt of the notice of the request—

    (a) a court officer will—

        (i) inform the parent or guardian of the request unless the parent or guardian cannot be found; and

        (ii) send a copy of the statement of facts filed in accordance with paragraph (2)(b) to—

            (aa) the parent or guardian unless the parent or guardian cannot be found;

            (bb) any children's guardian, reporting officer or children and family reporter;

            (cc) any local authority to whom notice under section 44 of the 2002 Act (notice of intention to adopt or apply for a section 84 order) has been given; and

            (dd) any adoption agency which has placed the child for adoption; and

    (b) if the applicant considers that the parent or guardian is incapable of giving consent, the court will consider whether to—

        (i) appoint a litigation friend for the parent or guardian under rule 15.6(1); or

        (ii) give directions for an application to be made under rule 15.6(3),

        (iii) unless a litigation friend is already appointed for that parent or guardian.

Consent

14.10.—(1) Consent of any parent or guardian of a child—

    (a) under section 19 of the 2002 Act, to the child being placed for adoption; and

    (b) under section 20 of the 2002 Act, to the making of a future adoption order,

must be given in the form referred to in Practice Direction 5A or a form to the like effect.

(2) Subject to paragraph (3), consent—

    (a) to the making of an adoption order; or

    (b) to the making of a section 84 order,

may be given in the form referred to in Practice Direction 5A or a form to the like effect or otherwise as the court directs.

(3) Any consent to a Convention adoption order must be in a form which complies with the internal law relating to adoption of the Convention country of which the child is habitually resident.

(4) Any form of consent executed in Scotland must be witnessed by a Justice of the Peace or a Sheriff.

(5) Any form of consent executed in Northern Ireland must be witnessed by a Justice of the Peace.

(6) Any form of consent executed outside the United Kingdom must be witnessed by—

    (a) any person for the time being authorised by law in the place where the document is executed to administer an oath for any judicial or other legal purpose;

    (b) a British Consular officer;

    (c) a notary public; or

    (d) if the person executing the document is serving in any of the regular armed forces of the Crown, an officer holding a commission in any of those forces.

Reports by the adoption agency or local authority

14.11.—(1) The adoption agency or local authority must file the report on the suitability of the applicant to adopt a child within the timetable fixed by the court.

(2) A local authority that is directed to prepare a report on the placement of the child for adoption must file that report within the timetable fixed by the court.

(3) The reports must cover the matters specified in Practice Direction 14C.

(4) The court may at any stage request a further report or ask the adoption agency or local authority to assist the court in any other manner.

(5) A court officer will send a copy of any report referred to in this rule to any children's guardian, reporting officer or children and family reporter.

(6) A report to the court under this rule is confidential.

Health reports

14.12.—(1) Reports by a registered medical practitioner ("health reports") made not more than 3 months earlier on the health of the child and of each applicant must be attached to an application for an adoption order or a section 84 order except where—

    (a) the child was placed for adoption with the applicant by an adoption agency;

    (b) the applicant or one of the applicants is a parent of the child; or

    (c) the applicant is the partner of a parent of the child.

(2) Health reports must contain the matters set out in Practice Direction 14D.

(3) A health report is confidential.

Confidential reports to the court and disclosure to the parties

14.13.—(1) The court will consider whether to give a direction that a confidential report be disclosed to each party to the proceedings.

(2) Before giving such a direction the court will consider whether any information should be deleted including information which—

    (a) discloses, or is likely to disclose, the identity of a person who has been assigned a serial number under rule 14.2(2); or

    (b) discloses the particulars referred to in rule 29.1(1) where a party has given notice under rule 29.1(2) (disclosure of personal details).

(3) The court may direct that the report will not be disclosed to a party.

Communication of information relating to proceedings

14.14. For the purposes of the law relating to contempt of court, information (whether or not it is recorded in any form) relating to proceedings held in private may be communicated—

    (a) where the court gives permission;

    (b) unless the court directs otherwise, in accordance with Practice Direction 14E; or

    (c) where the communication is to—

        (i) a party;

        (ii) the legal representative of a party;

        (iii) a professional legal adviser;

        (iv) an officer of the service or a Welsh family proceedings officer;

        (v) a welfare officer;

        (vi) the Legal Services Commission;

        (vii) an expert whose instruction by a party has been authorised by the court for the purposes of the proceedings; or

        (viii) a professional acting in furtherance of the protection of children.

Notice of final hearing

14.15. A court officer will give notice to the parties, any children's guardian, reporting officer or children and family reporter and to any other person to whom a practice direction may require such notice to be given—

(a) of the date and place where the application will be heard; and

(b) of the fact that, unless the person wishes or the court requires, the person need not attend.

The final hearing

14.16.—(1) Any person who has been given notice in accordance with rule 14.15 may attend the final hearing and, subject to paragraph (2), be heard on the question of whether an order should be made.

(2) A person whose application for the permission of the court to oppose the making of an adoption order under section 47(3) or (5) of the 2002 Act has been refused is not entitled to be heard on the question of whether an order should be made.

(3) Any member or employee of a party which is a local authority, adoption agency or other body may address the court at the final hearing if authorised to do so.

(4) The court may direct that any person must attend a final hearing.

(5) Paragraphs (6) and (7) apply to—

(a) an adoption order;

(b) a section 84 order; or

(c) a section 89 order.

(6) Subject to paragraphs (7) and (8), the court cannot make an order unless the applicant and the child personally attend the final hearing.

(7) The court may direct that the applicant or the child need not attend the final hearing.

(8) In a case of adoption by a couple under section 50 of the 2002 Act, the court may make an adoption order after personal attendance of one only of the applicants if there are special circumstances.

(9) The court cannot make a placement order unless a legal representative of the applicant attends the final hearing.

Proof of identity of the child

14.17.—(1) Unless the contrary is shown, the child referred to in the application will be deemed to be the child referred to in the form of consent—

(a) to the child being placed for adoption;

(b) to the making of an adoption order; or

(c) to the making of a section 84 order,

where the conditions in paragraph (2) apply.

(2) The conditions are—

(a) the application identifies the child by reference to a full certified copy of an entry in the registers of live-births;

(b) the form of consent identifies the child by reference to a full certified copy of an entry in the registers of live-births attached to the form; and

(c) the copy of the entry in the registers of live-births referred to in sub-paragraph (a) is the same or relates to the same entry in the registers of live-births as the copy of the entry in the registers of live-births attached to the form of consent.

(3) Where the child is already an adopted child paragraph (2) will have effect as if for the references to the registers of live-births there were substituted references to the Adopted Children Register.

(4) Subject to paragraph (7), where the precise date of the child's birth is not proved to the satisfaction of the court, the court will determine the probable date of birth.

(5) The probable date of the child's birth may be specified in the placement order, adoption order or section 84 order as the date of the child's birth.

(6) Subject to paragraph (7), where the child's place of birth cannot be proved to the satisfaction of the court—

(a) the child may be treated as having been born in the registration district of the court where it is probable that the child may have been born in—

(i) the United Kingdom;

(ii) the Channel Islands; or

(iii) the Isle of Man; or

(b) in any other case, the particulars of the country of birth may be omitted from the placement order, adoption order or section 84 order.

(7) A placement order identifying the probable date and place of birth of the child will be sufficient proof of the date and place of birth of the child in adoption proceedings and proceedings for a section 84 order.

Disclosing information to an adopted adult

14.18.—(1) The adopted person has the right, on request, to receive from the court which made the adoption order a copy of the following—

(a) the application form for an adoption order (but not the documents attached to that form);

(b) the adoption order and any other orders relating to the adoption proceedings;

(c) orders allowing any person contact with the child after the adoption order was made; and

(d) any other document or order referred to in Practice Direction 14F.

(2) The court will remove any protected information from any copy of a document or order referred to in paragraph (1) before the copies are given to the adopted person.

(3) This rule does not apply to an adopted person under the age of 18 years.

(4) In this rule "protected information" means information which would be protected information under section 57(3) of the 2002 Act if the adoption agency gave the information and not the court.

Translation of documents

14.19.—(1) Where a translation of any document is required for the purposes of proceedings for a Convention adoption order the translation must—

(a) unless the court directs otherwise, be provided by the applicant; and

(b) be signed by the translator to certify that the translation is accurate.

(2) This rule does not apply where the document is to be served in accordance with the Service Regulation.

Application for recovery orders

14.20.—(1) An application for any of the orders referred to in section 41(2) of the 2002 Act (recovery orders) may—

(a) in the High Court or a county court, be made without notice in which case the applicant must file the application—

(i) where the application is made by telephone, the next business day after the making of the application; or

(ii) in any other case, at the time when the application is made; and

(b) in a magistrates' court, be made, with the permission of the court, without notice in which case the applicant must file the application at the time when the application is made or as directed by the court.

(2) Where the court refuses to make an order on an application without notice it may direct that the application is made on notice in which case the application will proceed in accordance with rules 14.1 to 14.17.

(3) The respondents to an application under this rule are—

(a) in a case where—

(i) placement proceedings;

(ii) adoption proceedings; or

(iii) proceedings for a section 84 order,

are pending, all parties to those proceedings;

(b) any adoption agency authorised to place the child for adoption or which has placed the child for adoption;

(c) any local authority to whom notice under section 44 of the 2002 Act (notice of intention to adopt or apply for a section 84 order) has been given;

(d) any person having parental responsibility for the child;

(e) any person in whose favour there is provision for contact;

(f) any person who was caring for the child immediately prior to the making of the application; and

(g) any person whom the applicant alleges to have effected, or to have been or to be responsible for, the taking or keeping of the child.

Inherent jurisdiction and fathers without parental responsibility

14.21. Where no proceedings have started an adoption agency or local authority may ask the High Court for directions on the need to give a father without parental responsibility notice of the intention to place a child for adoption.

Timing of applications for section 89 order

14.22. An application for a section 89 order must be made within 2 years beginning with the date on which—

(a) the Convention adoption or Convention adoption order; or

(b) the overseas adoption or determination under section 91 of the 2002 Act,

to which it relates was made.

Custody of documents

14.23. All documents relating to proceedings under the 2002 Act must, while they are in the custody of the court, be kept in a place of special security.

Documents held by the court not to be inspected or copied without the court's permission

14.24. Subject to the provisions of these rules, any practice direction or any direction given by the court—

(a) no document or order held by the court in proceedings under the 2002 Act will be open to inspection by any person; and

(b) no copy of any such document or order, or of an extract from any such document or order, will be taken by or given to any person.

Orders

14.25.—(1) An order takes effect from the date when it is made, or such later date as the court may specify.

(2) In proceedings in Wales a party may request that an order be drawn up in Welsh as well as English.

Copies of orders

14.26.—(1) Within 7 days beginning with the date on which the final order was made in proceedings, or such shorter time as the court may direct, a court officer will send—

    (a) a copy of the order to the applicant;

    (b) a copy, which is sealed[(GL)], authenticated with the stamp of the court or certified as a true copy, of—

        (i) an adoption order;

        (ii) a section 89 order; or

        (iii) an order quashing or revoking an adoption order or allowing an appeal against an adoption order,

    to the Registrar General;

    (c) a copy of a Convention adoption order to the relevant Central Authority;

    (d) a copy of a section 89 order relating to a Convention adoption order or a Convention adoption to the—

        (i) relevant Central Authority;

        (ii) adopters;

        (iii) adoption agency; and

        (iv) local authority;

    (e) unless the court directs otherwise, a copy of a contact order under section 26 of the 2002 Act or a variation or revocation of a contact order under section 27 of the 2002 Act to the—

        (i) person with whom the child is living;

        (ii) adoption agency; and

        (iii) local authority; and

    (f) a notice of the making or refusal of—

        (i) the final order; or

        (ii) an order quashing or revoking an adoption order or allowing an appeal against an order in proceedings,

    to every respondent and, with the permission of the court, any other person.

(2) The court officer will also send notice of the making of an adoption order or a section 84 order to—

    (a) any court in Great Britain which appears to the court officer to have made any such order as is referred to in section 46(2) of the 2002 Act (order relating to parental responsibility for, and maintenance of, the child); and

    (b) the principal registry, if it appears to the court officer that a parental responsibility agreement has been recorded at the principal registry.

(3) A copy of any final order may be sent to any other person with the permission of the court.

(4) The court officer will send a copy of any order made during the course of the proceedings to the following persons or bodies, unless the court directs otherwise—

(a) all the parties to those proceedings;

(b) any children and family reporter appointed in those proceedings;

(c) any adoption agency or local authority which has prepared a report on the suitability of an applicant to adopt a child;

(d) any local authority which has prepared a report on placement for adoption.

(5) If an order has been drawn up in Welsh as well as English in accordance with rule 14.25(2) any reference in this rule to sending an order is to be taken as a reference to sending both the Welsh and English orders.

Amendment and revocation of orders

14.27.—(1) Subject to paragraph (2), an application under—

(a) section 55 of the 2002 Act(**a**) (revocation of adoptions on legitimation); or

(b) paragraph 4 of Schedule 1 to the 2002 Act (amendment of adoption order and revocation of direction),

may be made without serving a copy of the application notice.

(2) The court may direct that an application notice be served on such persons as it thinks fit.

(3) Where the court makes an order granting the application, a court officer will send the Registrar General a notice—

(a) specifying the amendments; or

(b) informing the Registrar General of the revocation,

giving sufficient particulars of the order to enable the Registrar General to identify the case.

Keeping registers in the family proceedings court

14.28.—(1) A magistrates' court officer will keep a register in which there will be entered a minute or memorandum of every adjudication of the court in proceedings to which this Part applies.

(2) The register may be stored in electronic form on the court computer system and entries in the register will include, where relevant, the following particulars—

(a) the name and address of the applicant;

(b) the name of the child including, in adoption proceedings, the name of the child prior to, and after, adoption;

(c) the age and sex of the child;

(d) the nature of the application; and

(e) the minute of adjudication.

(3) The part of the register relating to adoption proceedings will be kept separately to any other part of the register and will—

(a) not contain particulars of any other proceedings; and

(b) be kept by the court in a place of special security.

(**a**) Section 55 was amended by section 109(1) of and paragraph 412 of Schedule 8 to the Courts Act 2003.

PART 15

REPRESENTATION OF PROTECTED PARTIES

Application of this Part

15.1. This Part contains special provisions which apply in proceedings involving protected parties.

Requirement for litigation friend in proceedings

15.2. A protected party must have a litigation friend to conduct proceedings on that party's behalf.

Stage of proceedings at which a litigation friend becomes necessary

15.3.—(1) A person may not without the permission of the court take any step in proceedings except—

(a) filing an application form; or

(b) applying for the appointment of a litigation friend under rule 15.6,

until the protected party has a litigation friend.

(2) If during proceedings a party lacks capacity (within the meaning of the 2005 Act) to continue to conduct proceedings, no party may take any step in proceedings without the permission of the court until the protected party has a litigation friend.

(3) Any step taken before a protected party has a litigation friend has no effect unless the court orders otherwise.

Who may be a litigation friend for a protected party without a court order

15.4.—(1) This rule does not apply if the court has appointed a person to be a litigation friend.

(2) A person with authority as a deputy to conduct the proceedings in the name of a protected party or on that party's behalf is entitled to be the litigation friend of the protected party in any proceedings to which that person's authority extends.

(3) If there is no person with authority as a deputy to conduct the proceedings in the name of a protected party or on that party's behalf, a person may act as a litigation friend if that person—

(a) can fairly and competently conduct proceedings on behalf of the protected party;

(b) has no interest adverse to that of the protected party; and

(c) subject to paragraph (4), undertakes to pay any costs which the protected party may be ordered to pay in relation to the proceedings, subject to any right that person may have to be repaid from the assets of the protected party.

(4) Paragraph (3)(c) does not apply to the Official Solicitor.

("deputy" is defined in rule 2.3.)

How a person becomes a litigation friend without a court order

15.5.—(1) If the court has not appointed a litigation friend, a person who wishes to act as a litigation friend must follow the procedure set out in this rule.

(2) A person with authority as a deputy to conduct the proceedings in the name of a protected party or on that party's behalf must file an official copy$^{(GL)}$ of the order, declaration or other document which confers that person's authority to act.

(3) Any other person must file a certificate of suitability stating that that person satisfies the conditions specified in rule 15.4(3).

(4) A person who is to act as a litigation friend must file—

    (a) the document conferring that person's authority to act; or

    (b) the certificate of suitability,

at the time when that person first takes a step in the proceedings on behalf of the protected party.

(5) A court officer will send the certificate of suitability to every person on whom, in accordance with rule 6.28, the application form should be served.

(6) This rule does not apply to the Official Solicitor.

How a person becomes a litigation friend by court order

15.6.—(1) The court may, if the person to be appointed so consents, make an order appointing—

    (a) a person other than the Official Solicitor; or

    (b) the Official Solicitor,

as a litigation friend.

(2) An order appointing a litigation friend may be made by the court of its own initiative or on the application of—

    (a) a person who wishes to be a litigation friend; or

    (b) a party to the proceedings.

(3) The court may at any time direct that a party make an application for an order under paragraph (2).

(4) An application for an order appointing a litigation friend must be supported by evidence.

(5) Unless the court directs otherwise, a person appointed under this rule to be a litigation friend for a protected party will be treated as a party for the purpose of any provision in these rules requiring a document to be served on, or sent to, or notice to be given to, a party to the proceedings.

(6) Subject to rule 15.4(4), the court may not appoint a litigation friend under this rule unless it is satisfied that the person to be appointed complies with the conditions specified in rule 15.4(3).

Court's power to change litigation friend and to prevent person acting as litigation friend

15.7.—(1) The court may—

    (a) direct that a person may not act as a litigation friend;

    (b) terminate a litigation friend's appointment; or

    (c) appoint a new litigation friend in substitution for an existing one.

(2) An application for an order or direction under paragraph (1) must be supported by evidence.

(3) Subject to rule 15.4(4), the court may not appoint a litigation friend under this rule unless it is satisfied that the person to be appointed complies with the conditions specified in rule 15.4(3).

Appointment of litigation friend by court order – supplementary

15.8.—(1) A copy of the application for an order under rule 15.6 or 15.7 must be sent by a court officer to—

    (a) every person on whom, in accordance with rule 6.28, the application form should be served; and

    (b) unless the court directs otherwise, the protected party.

(2) A copy of an application for an order under rule 15.7 must also be sent to—

    (a) the person who is the litigation friend, or who is purporting to act as the litigation friend when the application is made; and

    (b) the person, if not the applicant, who it is proposed should be the litigation friend.

Procedure where appointment of litigation friend comes to an end

15.9.—(1) When a party ceases to be a protected party, the litigation friend's appointment continues until it is brought to an end by a court order.

(2) An application for an order under paragraph (1) may be made by—

(a) the former protected party;

(b) the litigation friend; or

(c) a party.

(3) On the making of an order under paragraph (1), the court officer will send a notice to the other parties stating that the appointment of the protected party's litigation friend to act has ended.

PART 16

REPRESENTATION OF CHILDREN AND REPORTS IN PROCEEDINGS INVOLVING CHILDREN

CHAPTER 1

APPLICATION OF THIS PART

Application of this Part

16.1. This Part—

(a) sets out when the court will make a child a party in family proceedings; and

(b) contains special provisions which apply in proceedings involving children.

CHAPTER 2

CHILD AS PARTY IN FAMILY PROCEEDINGS

When the court may make a child a party to proceedings

16.2.—(1) The court may make a child a party to proceedings if it considers it is in the best interests of the child to do so.

(2) This rule does not apply to a child who is the subject of proceedings—

(a) which are specified proceedings; or

(b) to which Part 14 applies.

(The Practice Direction 16A sets out the matters which the court will take into consideration before making a child a party under this rule.)

CHAPTER 3

WHEN A CHILDREN'S GUARDIAN OR LITIGATION FRIEND WILL BE APPOINTED

Appointment of a children's guardian in specified proceedings or proceedings to which Part 14 applies

16.3.—(1) Unless it is satisfied that it is not necessary to do so to safeguard the interests of the child, the court must appoint a children's guardian for a child who is—

(a) the subject of; and

(b) a party to,

proceedings—

(i) which are specified proceedings; or

(ii) to which Part 14 applies.

(Rules 12.6 and 14.6 set out the point in the proceedings when the court will appoint a children's guardian in specified proceedings and proceedings to which Part 14 applies respectively.)

(2) At any stage in the proceedings—

    (a) a party may apply, without notice to the other parties unless the court directs otherwise, for the appointment of a children's guardian; or

    (b) the court may of its own initiative appoint a children's guardian.

(3) Where the court refuses an application under paragraph (2)(a) it will give reasons for the refusal and the court or a court officer will—

    (a) record the refusal and the reasons for it; and

    (b) as soon as practicable, notify the parties and either the Service or the Assembly of a decision not to appoint a children's guardian.

(4) When appointing a children's guardian the court will consider the appointment of anyone who has previously acted as a children's guardian of the same child.

(5) Where the court appoints a children's guardian in accordance with this rule, the provisions of Chapter 6 of this Part apply.

Appointment of a children's guardian in proceedings not being specified proceedings or proceedings to which Part 14 applies

16.4.—(1) Without prejudice to rule 8.42 or 16.6, the court must appoint a children's guardian for a child who is the subject of proceedings, which are not proceedings of a type referred to in rule 16.3(1), if—

    (a) the child is an applicant in the proceedings;

    (b) a provision in these rules provides for the child to be a party to the proceedings; or

    (c) the court has made the child a party in accordance with rule 16.2.

(2) The provisions of Chapter 7 of this Part apply where the appointment of a children's guardian is required in accordance with paragraph (1).

("children's guardian" is defined in rule 2.3.)

Requirement for a litigation friend

16.5.—(1) Without prejudice to rule 16.6, where a child is—

    (a) a party to proceedings; but

    (b) not the subject of those proceedings,

the child must have a litigation friend to conduct proceedings on the child's behalf.

(2) The provisions of Chapter 5 of this Part apply where a litigation friend is required in accordance with paragraph (1).

CHAPTER 4

WHERE A CHILDREN'S GUARDIAN OR LITIGATION FRIEND IS NOT REQUIRED

Circumstances in which a child does not need a children's guardian or litigation friend

16.6.—(1) Subject to paragraph (2), a child may conduct proceedings without a children's guardian or litigation friend where the proceedings are proceedings—

    (a) under the 1989 Act;

    (b) to which Part 11 (applications under Part 4A of the Family Law Act 1996) or Part 14 (applications in adoption, placement and related proceedings) of these rules apply; or

    (c) relating to the exercise of the court's inherent jurisdiction with respect to children,

and one of the conditions set out in paragraph (3) is satisfied.

(2) Paragraph (1) does not apply where the child is the subject of and a party to proceedings—

    (a)   which are specified proceedings; or

    (b)   to which Part 14 applies.

(3) The conditions referred to in paragraph (1) are that either—

    (a)   the child has obtained the court's permission; or

    (b)   a solicitor—

        (i)   considers that the child is able, having regard to the child's understanding, to give instructions in relation to the proceedings; and

        (ii)   has accepted instructions from that child to act for that child in the proceedings and, if the proceedings have begun, the solicitor is already acting.

(4) An application for permission under paragraph (3)(a) may be made by the child without notice.

(5) Where a child—

    (a)   has a litigation friend or children's guardian in proceedings to which this rule applies; and

    (b)   wishes to conduct the remaining stages of the proceedings without the litigation friend or children's guardian,

the child may apply to the court, on notice to the litigation friend or children's guardian, for permission for that purpose and for the removal of the litigation friend or children's guardian.

(6) The court will grant an application under paragraph (3)(a) or (5) if it considers that the child has sufficient understanding to conduct the proceedings concerned or proposed without a litigation friend or children's guardian.

(7) In exercising its powers under paragraph (6) the court may require the litigation friend or children's guardian to take such part in the proceedings as the court directs.

(8) The court may revoke any permission granted under paragraph (3)(a) where it considers that the child does not have sufficient understanding to participate as a party in the proceedings concerned without a litigation friend or children's guardian.

(9) Where a solicitor is acting for a child in proceedings without a litigation friend or children's guardian by virtue of paragraph (3)(b) and either of the conditions specified in paragraph (3)(b)(i) or (ii) cease to be fulfilled, the solicitor must inform the court immediately.

(10) Where—

    (a)   the court revokes any permission under paragraph (8); or

    (b)   either of the conditions specified in paragraph (3)(b)(i) or (ii) is no longer fulfilled,

the court may, if it considers it necessary in order to protect the interests of the child concerned, appoint a person to be that child's litigation friend or children's guardian.

CHAPTER 5

LITIGATION FRIEND

Application of this Chapter

16.7. This Chapter applies where a child must have a litigation friend to conduct proceedings on the child's behalf in accordance with rule 16.5.

Stage of proceedings at which a litigation friend becomes necessary

16.8.—(1) This rule does not apply in relation to a child who is conducting proceedings without a litigation friend in accordance with rule 16.6.

(2) A person may not without the permission of the court take any step in proceedings except—

    (a)   filing an application form; or

(b) applying for the appointment of a litigation friend under rule 16.11,

until the child has a litigation friend.

(3) Any step taken before a child has a litigation friend has no effect unless the court orders otherwise.

Who may be a litigation friend for a child without a court order

16.9.—(1) This rule does not apply if the court has appointed a person to be a litigation friend.

(2) A person may act as a litigation friend if that person—

(a) can fairly and competently conduct proceedings on behalf of the child;

(b) has no interest adverse to that of the child; and

(c) subject to paragraph (3), undertakes to pay any costs which the child may be ordered to pay in relation to the proceedings, subject to any right that person may have to be repaid from the assets of the child.

(3) Paragraph (2)(c) does not apply to the Official Solicitor, an officer of the Service or a Welsh family proceedings officer.

How a person becomes a litigation friend without a court order

16.10.—(1) If the court has not appointed a litigation friend, a person who wishes to act as such must file a certificate of suitability stating that that person satisfies the conditions specified in rule 16.9(2).

(2) The certificate of suitability must be filed at the time when the person who wishes to act as litigation friend first takes a step in the proceedings on behalf of the child.

(3) A court officer will send the certificate of suitability to every person on whom, in accordance with rule 6.28, the application form should be served.

(4) This rule does not apply to the Official Solicitor, an officer of the Service or a Welsh family proceedings officer.

Appointment of litigation friend by the court

16.11.—(1) The court may, if the person to be appointed consents, make an order appointing as a litigation friend—

(a) the Official Solicitor;

(b) an officer of the Service or a Welsh family proceedings officer; or

(c) some other person.

(2) An order appointing a litigation friend may be made by the court of its own initiative or on the application of—

(a) a person who wishes to be a litigation friend; or

(b) a party to the proceedings.

(3) The court may at any time direct that a party make an application for an order under paragraph (2).

(4) An application for an order appointing a litigation friend must be supported by evidence.

(5) Unless the court directs otherwise, a person appointed under this rule to be a litigation friend for a child will be treated as a party for the purpose of any provision in these rules requiring a document to be served on, or sent to, or notice to be given to, a party to the proceedings.

(6) Subject to rule 16.9(3), the court may not appoint a litigation friend under this rule unless it is satisfied that the person to be appointed complies with the conditions specified in rule 16.9(2).

(7) This rule is without prejudice to rule 16.6.

Court's power to change litigation friend and to prevent person acting as litigation friend

16.12.—(1) The court may—

    (a) direct that a person may not act as a litigation friend;

    (b) terminate a litigation friend's appointment; or

    (c) appoint a new litigation friend in substitution for an existing one.

(2) An application for an order or direction under paragraph (1) must be supported by evidence.

(3) Subject to rule 16.9(3), the court may not appoint a litigation friend under this rule unless it is satisfied that the person to be appointed complies with the conditions specified in rule 16.9(2).

Appointment of litigation friend by court order – supplementary

16.13.—(1) A copy of the application for an order under rule 16.11 or 16.12 must be sent by a court officer to every person on whom, in accordance with rule 6.28, the application form should be served.

(2) A copy of an application for an order under rule 16.12 must also be sent to—

    (a) the person who is the litigation friend, or who is purporting to act as the litigation friend when the application is made; and

    (b) the person, if not the applicant, who it is proposed should be the litigation friend.

Powers and duties of litigation friend

16.14.—(1) The litigation friend—

    (a) has the powers and duties set out in Practice Direction 16A; and

    (b) must exercise those powers and duties in accordance with Practice Direction 16A.

(2) Where the litigation friend is an officer of the Service or a Welsh family proceedings officer, rule 16.20 applies as it applies to a children's guardian appointed in accordance with Chapter 6.

Procedure where appointment of litigation friend comes to an end

16.15.—(1) When a child who is not a protected party reaches the age of 18, a litigation friend's appointment comes to an end.

(2) A court officer will send a notice to the other parties stating that the appointment of the child's litigation friend to act has ended.

CHAPTER 6

CHILDREN'S GUARDIAN APPOINTED UNDER RULE 16.3

Application of this Chapter

16.16. This Chapter applies where the court must appoint a children's guardian in accordance with rule 16.3.

Who may be a children's guardian

16.17. Where the court is appointing a children's guardian under rule 16.3 it will appoint an officer of the Service or a Welsh family proceedings officer.

What the court or a court officer will do once the court has made a decision about appointing a children's guardian

16.18.—(1) Where the court appoints a children's guardian under rule 16.3 a court officer will record the appointment and, as soon as practicable, will—

(a) inform the parties and either the Service or the Assembly; and

(b) unless it has already been sent, send the children's guardian a copy of the application and copies of any document filed with the court in the proceedings.

(2) A court officer has a continuing duty to send the children's guardian a copy of any other document filed with the court during the course of the proceedings.

Termination of the appointment of the children's guardian

16.19.—(1) The appointment of a children's guardian under rule 16.3 continues for such time as is specified in the appointment or until terminated by the court.

(2) When terminating an appointment in accordance with paragraph (1), the court will give reasons for doing so, a note of which will be taken by the court or a court officer.

Powers and duties of the children's guardian

16.20.—(1) The children's guardian is to act on behalf of the child upon the hearing of any application in proceedings to which this Chapter applies with the duty of safeguarding the interests of the child.

(2) The children's guardian must also provide the court with such other assistance as it may require.

(3) The children's guardian, when carrying out duties in relation to specified proceedings, other than placement proceedings, must have regard to the principle set out in section 1(2) and the matters set out in section 1(3)(a) to (f) of the 1989 Act as if for the word "court" in that section there were substituted the words "children's guardian".

(4) The children's guardian, when carrying out duties in relation to proceedings to which Part 14 applies, must have regard to the principle set out in section 1(3) and the matters set out in section 1(4)(a) to (f) of the 2002 Act as if for the word "court" in that section there were substituted the words "children's guardian".

(5) The children's guardian's duties must be exercised in accordance with Practice Direction 16A.

(6) A report to the court by the children's guardian is confidential.

Where the child instructs a solicitor or conducts proceedings on the child's own behalf

16.21.—(1) Where it appears to the children's guardian that the child—

(a) is instructing a solicitor direct; or

(b) intends to conduct and is capable of conducting the proceedings on that child's own behalf,

the children's guardian must inform the court of that fact.

(2) Where paragraph (1) applies the children's guardian—

(a) must perform such additional duties as the court may direct;

(b) must take such part in the proceedings as the court may direct; and

(c) may, with the permission of the court, have legal representation in the conduct of those duties.

CHAPTER 7

CHILDREN'S GUARDIAN APPOINTED UNDER RULE 16.4

Application of this Chapter

16.22. This Chapter applies where the court must appoint a children's guardian under rule 16.4.

Stage of proceedings at which a children's guardian becomes necessary

16.23.—(1) This rule does not apply in relation to a child who is conducting proceedings without a children's guardian in accordance with rule 16.6.

(2) A person may not without the permission of the court take any step in proceedings except—

    (a) filing an application form; or

    (b) applying for the appointment of a children's guardian under rule 16.24,

until the child has a children's guardian.

(3) Any step taken before a child has a children's guardian has no effect unless the court orders otherwise.

Appointment of a children's guardian

16.24.—(1) The court may make an order appointing as a children's guardian, an officer of the Service or a Welsh family proceedings officer or, if the person to be appointed consents —

    (a) a person other than the Official Solicitor; or

    (b) the Official Solicitor.

(2) An order appointing a children's guardian may be made by the court of its own initiative or on the application of—

    (a) a person who wishes to be a children's guardian; or

    (b) a party to the proceedings.

(3) The court may at any time direct that a party make an application for an order under paragraph (2).

(4) An application for an order appointing a children's guardian must be supported by evidence.

(5) The court may not appoint a children's guardian under this rule unless it is satisfied that that person—

    (a) can fairly and competently conduct proceedings on behalf of the child;

    (b) has no interest adverse to that of the child; and

    (c) subject to paragraph (6), undertakes to pay any costs which the child may be ordered to pay in relation to the proceedings, subject to any right that person may have to be repaid from the assets of the child.

(6) Paragraph (5)(c) does not apply to the Official Solicitor, an officer of the Service or a Welsh family proceedings officer.

(7) This rule is without prejudice to rule 16.6 and rule 9.11.

(Rule 9.11 provides for a child to be separately represented in certain applications for a financial remedy.)

Court's power to change children's guardian and to prevent person acting as children's guardian

16.25.—(1) The court may—

    (a) direct that a person may not act as a children's guardian;

    (b) terminate the appointment of a children's guardian; or

    (c) appoint a new children's guardian in substitution for an existing one.

(2) An application for an order or direction under paragraph (1) must be supported by evidence.

(3) Subject to rule 16.24(6), the court may not appoint a children's guardian under this rule unless it is satisfied that the person to be appointed complies with the conditions specified in rule 16.24(5).

Appointment of children's guardian by court order – supplementary

16.26.—(1) A copy of the application for an order under rule 16.24 or 16.25 must be sent by a court officer to every person on whom, in accordance with rule 6.28, the application form should be served.

(2) A copy of an application for an order under rule 16.25 must also be sent to—

(a) the person who is the children's guardian, or who is purporting to act as the children's guardian when the application is made; and

(b) the person, if not the applicant, who it is proposed should be the children's guardian.

Powers and duties of children's guardian

16.27.—(1) The children's guardian—

(a) has the powers and duties set out in Practice Direction 16A; and

(b) must exercise those powers and duties in accordance with Practice Direction 16A.

(2) Where the children's guardian is an officer of the Service or a Welsh family proceedings officer, rule 16.20 applies to a children's guardian appointed in accordance with this Chapter as it applies to a children's guardian appointed in accordance with Chapter 6.

Procedure where appointment of children's guardian comes to an end

16.28.—(1) When a child reaches the age of 18, the appointment of a children's guardian comes to an end.

(2) A court officer will send a notice to the other parties stating that the appointment of the child's children's guardian to act has ended.

CHAPTER 8

DUTIES OF SOLICITOR ACTING FOR THE CHILD

Solicitor for child

16.29.—(1) Subject to paragraphs (2) and (4), a solicitor appointed—

(a) under section 41(3) of the 1989 Act; or

(b) by the children's guardian in accordance with the Practice Direction 16A,

must represent the child in accordance with instructions received from the children's guardian.

(2) If a solicitor appointed as mentioned in paragraph (1) considers, having taken into account the matters referred to in paragraph (3), that the child—

(a) wishes to give instructions which conflict with those of the children's guardian; and

(b) is able, having regard to the child's understanding, to give such instructions on the child's own behalf,

the solicitor must conduct the proceedings in accordance with instructions received from the child.

(3) The matters the solicitor must take into account for the purposes of paragraph (2) are—

(a) the views of the children's guardian; and

(b) any direction given by the court to the children's guardian concerning the part to be taken by the children's guardian in the proceedings.

(4) Where—

(a) no children's guardian has been appointed; and

(b) the condition in section 41(4)(b) of the 1989 Act is satisfied,

a solicitor appointed under section 41(3) of the 1989 Act must represent the child in accordance with instructions received from the child.

(5) Where a solicitor appointed as mentioned in paragraph (1) receives no instructions under paragraphs (1), (2) or (4), the solicitor must represent the child in furtherance of the best interests of the child.

(6) A solicitor appointed under section 41(3) of the 1989 Act or by the children's guardian in accordance with Practice Direction 16A must serve documents, and accept service of documents, on behalf of the child in accordance with rule 6.31 and, where the child has not been served separately and has sufficient understanding, advise the child of the contents of any document so served.

(7) Where the child wishes an appointment of a solicitor—

    (a) under section 41(3) of the 1989 Act; or

    (b) by the children's guardian in accordance with the Practice Direction 16A,

to be terminated—

        (i) the child may apply to the court for an order terminating the appointment; and

        (ii) the solicitor and the children's guardian will be given an opportunity to make representations.

(8) Where the children's guardian wishes an appointment of a solicitor under section 41(3) of the 1989 Act to be terminated—

    (a) the children's guardian may apply to the court for an order terminating the appointment; and

    (b) the solicitor and, if of sufficient understanding, the child, will be given an opportunity to make representations.

(9) When terminating an appointment in accordance with paragraph (7) or (8), the court will give its reasons for so doing, a note of which will be taken by the court or a court officer.

(10) The court or a court officer will record the appointment under section 41(3) of the 1989 Act or the refusal to make the appointment.

CHAPTER 9

REPORTING OFFICER

When the court appoints a reporting officer

16.30. In proceedings to which Part 14 applies, the court will appoint a reporting officer where—

    (a) it appears that a parent or guardian of the child is willing to consent to the placing of the child for adoption, to the making of an adoption order or to a section 84 order; and

    (b) that parent or guardian is in England or Wales.

Appointment of the same reporting officer in respect of two or more parents or guardians

16.31. The same person may be appointed as the reporting officer for two or more parents or guardians of the child.

The duties of the reporting officer

16.32.—(1) The reporting officer must witness the signature by a parent or guardian on the document in which consent is given to—

    (a) the placing of the child for adoption;

    (b) the making of an adoption order; or

    (c) the making of a section 84 order.

(2) The reporting officer must carry out such other duties as are set out in Practice Direction 16A.

(3) A report to the court by the reporting officer is confidential.

(4) The reporting officer's duties must be exercised in accordance with Practice Direction 16A.

CHAPTER 10

CHILDREN AND FAMILY REPORTER AND WELFARE OFFICER

Request by court for a welfare report in respect of the child

16.33.—(1) Where the court is considering an application for an order in proceedings, the court may ask—

(a) in proceedings to which Parts 12 and 14 apply, a children and family reporter; or

(b) in proceedings to which Part 12 applies, a welfare officer,

to prepare a report on matters relating to the welfare of the child, and, in this rule, the person preparing the report is called "the officer".

(2) It is the duty of the officer to—

(a) comply with any request for a report under this rule; and

(b) provide the court with such other assistance as it may require.

(3) A report to the court under this rule is confidential.

(4) The officer, when carrying out duties in relation to proceedings under the 1989 Act, must have regard to the principle set out in section 1(2) and the matters set out in section 1(3)(a) to (f) of that Act as if for the word "court" in that section there were substituted the words "children and family reporter" or "welfare officer" as the case may be.

(5) A party may question the officer about oral or written advice tendered by that officer to the court.

(6) The court officer will notify the officer of a direction given at a hearing at which—

(a) the officer is not present; and

(b) the welfare report is considered.

(7) The officer's duties must be exercised in accordance with Practice Direction 16A

("children and family reporter" and "welfare officer" are defined in rule 2.3)

CHAPTER 11

PARENTAL ORDER REPORTER

When the court appoints a parental order reporter

16.34. In proceedings to which Part 13 applies, the court will appoint a parental order reporter in accordance with rule 13.5.

Powers and duties of the parental order reporter

16.35.—(1) The parental order reporter is to act on behalf of the child upon the hearing of any application in proceedings to which Part 13 applies with the duty of safeguarding the interests of the child.

(2) The parental order reporter must—

(a) investigate the matters set out in sections 54(1) to (8) of the 2008 Act;

(b) so far as the parental order reporter considers necessary, investigate any matter contained in the application form or other matter which appears relevant to the making of the parental order; and

(c) advise the court on whether there is any reason under section 1 of the 2002 Act (as applied with modifications by the Human Fertilisation and Embryology (Parental Orders) Regulations 2010) to refuse the parental order.

(3) The parental order reporter must also provide the court with such other assistance as it may require.

(4) The parental order reporter's duties must be exercised in accordance with Practice Direction 16A.

(5) A report to the court by the parental order reporter is confidential.

CHAPTER 12

SUPPLEMENTARY APPOINTMENT PROVISIONS

Persons who may not be appointed as children's guardian, reporting officer or children and family reporter

16.36.—(1) In adoption proceedings or proceedings for a section 84 order or a section 89 order, no person may be appointed as a children's guardian, reporting officer or children and family reporter who—

(a) is a member, officer or servant of a local authority which is a party to the proceedings;

(b) is, or has been, a member, officer or servant of a local authority or voluntary organisation who has been directly concerned in that capacity in arrangements relating to the care, accommodation or welfare of the child during the 5 years prior to the start of the proceedings; or

(c) is a serving probation officer who has, in that capacity, been previously concerned with the child or the child's family.

(2) In placement proceedings, a person described in paragraph (1)(b) or (c) may not be appointed as a children's guardian, reporting officer or children and family reporter.

Appointment of the same person as children's guardian, reporting officer and children and family reporter

16.37. The same person may be appointed to act as one or more of the following—

(a) the children's guardian;

(b) the reporting officer; and

(c) the children and family reporter.

CHAPTER 13

OFFICERS OF THE SERVICE, WELSH FAMILY PROCEEDINGS OFFICERS AND LOCAL AUTHORITY OFFICERS: FURTHER DUTIES

Officers of the Service, Welsh family proceedings officers and local authority officers acting under certain duties

16.38.—(1) This rule applies when—

(a) an officer of the Service or a Welsh family proceedings officer is acting under a duty in accordance with—

(i) section 11E(7) of the 1989 Act(**a**) (providing the court with information as to the making of a contact activity direction or a contact activity condition);

(ii) section 11G(2) of the 1989 Act(**b**) (monitoring compliance with a contact activity direction or a contact activity condition);

(iii) section 11H(2) of the 1989 Act(**c**) (monitoring compliance with a contact order);

(iv) section 11L(5) of the 1989 Act (providing the court with information as to the making of an enforcement order);

(**a**)   Section 11E was inserted by section 1 of the Children and Adoption Act 2006.
(**b**)   Section 11G was inserted by section 1 of the Children and Adoption Act 2006.
(**c**)   Section 11H was inserted by section 1 of the Children and Adoption Act 2006.

> (v) section 11M(1) of the 1989 Act (monitoring compliance with an enforcement order);
>
> (vi) section 16(6) of the 1989 Act(**a**) (providing a report to the court in accordance with a direction in a family assistance order); and
>
> (vii) section 16A of the 1989 Act(**b**) (making a risk assessment); and

(b) a local authority officer is acting under a duty in accordance with section 16(6) of the 1989 Act (providing a report to the court in accordance with a direction in a family assistance order).

(2) In this rule,—

(a) "contact activity direction", "contact activity condition" and "enforcement order" have the meanings given in rule 12.2; and

(b) references to "the officer" are to the officer of the Service, Welsh family proceedings officer or local authority officer referred to in paragraph (1).

(3) In exercising the duties referred to in paragraph (1), the officer must have regard to the principle set out in section 1(2) of the 1989 Act and the matters set out in section 1(3)(a) to (f) of the 1989 Act as if for the word "court" in that section there were substituted the words "officer of the Service, Welsh family proceedings officer or local authority officer".

(4) The officer's duties referred to in paragraph (1) must be exercised in accordance with Practice Direction 16A.

CHAPTER 14

ENFORCEMENT ORDERS AND FINANCIAL COMPENSATION ORDERS: PERSONS NOTIFIED

Application for enforcement orders and financial compensation orders: duties of the person notified

16.39.—(1) This rule applies where a person who was the child's children's guardian, litigation friend or legal representative in the proceedings in which a contact order was made has been notified of an application for an enforcement order or for a financial compensation order as required by Practice Direction 12C.

(2) The person who has been notified of the application must—

(a) consider whether it is in the best interests of the child for the child to be made a party to the proceedings for an enforcement order or a financial compensation order (as applicable); and

(b) before the date fixed for the first hearing in the case notify the court, orally or in writing, of the opinion reached on the question, together with the reasons for this opinion.

(3) In this rule, "enforcement order" and "financial compensation order" have the meanings given in rule 12.2.

PART 17

STATEMENTS OF TRUTH

Interpretation

17.1. In this Part "statement of case" has the meaning given to it in Part 4 except that a statement of case does not include an application for a matrimonial order or a civil partnership order or an answer to such an application.

(**a**) Section 16(6) was amended by section 6(1) and (5) of the Children and Adoption Act 2006.
(**b**) Section 16A was inserted by section 7 of the Children and Adoption Act 2006.

(Rule 4.1 defines "statement of case" for the purposes of Part 4.)

Documents to be verified by a statement of truth

17.2.—(1) Subject to paragraph (9), the following documents must be verified by a statement of truth—

    (a) a statement of case;

    (b) a witness statement;

    (c) an acknowledgement of service in a claim begun by the Part 19 procedure;

    (d) a certificate of service;

    (e) a statement of arrangements for children;

    (f) a statement of information filed under rule 9.26(1)(b); and

    (g) any other document where a rule or practice direction requires it.

(2) Where a statement of case is amended, the amendments must be verified by a statement of truth unless the court orders otherwise.

(3) If an applicant wishes to rely on matters set out in the application form or application notice as evidence, the application form or notice must be verified by a statement of truth.

(4) Subject to paragraph (5), a statement of truth is a statement that—

    (a) the party putting forward the document;

    (b) in the case of a witness statement, the maker of the witness statement; or

    (c) in the case of a certificate of service, the person who signs the certificate,

believes the facts stated in the document are true.

(5) If a party is conducting proceedings with a litigation friend, the statement of truth in—

    (a) a statement of case; or

    (b) an application notice,

is a statement that the litigation friend believes the facts stated in the document being verified are true.

(6) The statement of truth must be signed by—

    (a) in the case of a statement of case—

        (i) the party or litigation friend; or

        (ii) the legal representative on behalf of the party or litigation friend; and

    (b) in the case of a witness statement or statement of arrangements for children, the maker of the statement.

(7) A statement of truth, which is not contained in the document which it verifies, must clearly identify that document.

(8) A statement of truth in a statement of case may be made by—

    (a) a person who is not a party; or

    (b) by two parties jointly,

where this is permitted by a practice direction.

(9) An application that does not contain a statement of facts need not be verified by a statement of truth.

(Practice Direction 17A sets out the form of statement of truth.)

Failure to verify a statement of case

17.3.—(1) If a party fails to verify that party's statement of case by a statement of truth—

    (a) the statement of case shall remain effective unless struck out; but

(b) the party may not rely on the statement of case as evidence of any of the matters set out in it.

(2) The court may strike out$^{(GL)}$ a statement of case which is not verified by a statement of truth.

(3) Any party may apply for an order under paragraph (2).

Failure to verify a witness statement

17.4. If the maker of a witness statement fails to verify the witness statement by a statement of truth, the court may direct that it shall not be admissible as evidence.

Power of the court to require a document to be verified

17.5.—(1) The court may order a person who has failed to verify a document in accordance with rule 17.2 to verify the document.

(2) Any party may apply for an order under paragraph (1).

False statements

17.6.—(1) Proceedings for contempt of court may be brought against a person who makes, or causes to be made, a false statement in a document verified by a statement of truth without an honest belief in its truth.

(2) Proceedings under this rule may be brought only—

(a) by the Attorney General; or

(b) with the permission of the court.

(3) This rule does not apply to proceedings in a magistrates' court.

PART 18

PROCEDURE FOR OTHER APPLICATIONS IN PROCEEDINGS

Types of application for which Part 18 procedure may be followed

18.1.—(1) The Part 18 procedure is the procedure set out in this Part.

(2) An applicant may use the Part 18 procedure if the application is made—

(a) in the course of existing proceedings;

(b) to start proceedings except where some other Part of these rules prescribes the procedure to start proceedings; or

(c) in connection with proceedings which have been concluded.

(3) Paragraph (2) does not apply—

(a) to applications where any other rule in any other Part of these rules sets out the procedure for that type of application;

(b) if a practice direction provides that the Part 18 procedure may not be used in relation to the type of application in question.

Applications for permission to start proceedings

18.2. An application for permission to start proceedings must be made to the court where the proceedings will be started if permission is granted.

Respondents to applications under this Part

18.3.—(1) The following persons are to be respondents to an application under this Part—

(a) where there are existing proceedings or the proceedings have been concluded—

    (i) the parties to those proceedings; and

    (ii) if the proceedings are proceedings under Part 11, the person who is the subject of those proceedings;

(b) where there are no existing proceedings—

    (i) if notice has been given under section 44 of the 2002 Act (notice of intention to adopt or apply for an order under section 84 of that Act), the local authority to whom notice has been given; and

    (ii) if an application is made for permission to apply for an order in proceedings, any person who will be a party to the proceedings brought if permission is granted; and

(c) any other person as the court may direct.

Application notice to be filed

18.4.—(1) Subject to paragraph (2), the applicant must file an application notice.

(2) An applicant may make an application without filing an application notice if—

    (a) this is permitted by a rule or practice direction; or

    (b) the court dispenses with the requirement for an application notice.

Notice of an application

18.5.—(1) Subject to paragraph (2), a copy of the application notice must be served on—

    (a) each respondent;

    (b) in relation to proceedings under Part 11, the person who is, or, in the case of an application to start proceedings, it is intended will be, the subject of the proceedings; and

    (c) in relation to proceedings under Parts 12 and 14, the children's guardian (if any).

(2) An application may be made without serving a copy of the application notice if this is permitted by—

    (a) a rule;

    (b) a practice direction; or

    (c) the court.

(Rule 18.8 deals with service of a copy of the application notice.)

Time when an application is made

18.6. When an application must be made within a specified time, it is so made if the court receives the application notice within that time.

What an application notice must include

18.7.—(1) An application notice must state—

    (a) what order the applicant is seeking; and

    (b) briefly, why the applicant is seeking the order.

(2) A draft of the order sought must be attached to the application notice.

(Part 17 requires an application notice to be verified by a statement of truth if the applicant wishes to rely on matters set out in his application as evidence.)

Service of a copy of an application notice

18.8.—(1) Subject to rule 2.4, a copy of the application notice must be served in accordance with the provisions of Part 6—

(a) as soon as practicable after it is filed; and

(b) in any event—

   (i) where the application is for an interim order under rule 9.7 at least 14 days; and

   (ii) in any other case, at least 7 days;

   before the court is to deal with the application.

(2) The applicant must, when filing the application notice, file a copy of any written evidence in support.

(3) If a copy of an application notice is served by a court officer it must be accompanied by—

(a) a notice of the date and place where the application will be heard;

(b) a copy of any witness statement in support; and

(c) a copy of the draft order which the applicant has attached to the application.

(4) If—

(a) an application notice is served; but

(b) the period of notice is shorter than the period required by these rules or a practice direction,

the court may direct that, in the circumstances of the case, sufficient notice has been given and hear the application.

(5) This rule does not require written evidence—

(a) to be filed if it has already been filed; or

(b) to be served on a party on whom it has already been served.

Applications which may be dealt with without a hearing

18.9.—(1) The court may deal with an application without a hearing if—

(a) the court does not consider that a hearing would be appropriate; or

(b) the parties agree as to the terms of the order sought or the parties agree that the court should dispose of the application without a hearing and the court does not consider that a hearing would be appropriate.

(2) Where—

(a) an application is made for permission to make an application in proceedings under the 1989 Act; and

(b) the court refuses the application without a hearing in accordance with paragraph (1)(a),

the court must, at the request of the applicant, re-list the application and fix a date for a hearing.

(3) Paragraph (2) does not apply to magistrates' courts.

Service of application notice following court order where application made without notice

18.10.—(1) This rule applies where the court has disposed of an application which it permitted to be made without service of a copy of the application notice.

(2) Where the court makes an order, whether granting or dismissing the application, a copy of the application notice and any evidence in support must unless the court orders otherwise, be served with the order on—

(a) all the parties in proceedings; and

(b) in relation to proceedings under Part 11, the person who is, or, in the case of an application to start proceedings, it is intended will be, the subject of the proceedings.

(3) The order must contain a statement of the right to make an application to set aside^(GL) or vary the order under rule 18.11.

Application to set aside or vary order made without notice

18.11.—(1) A person who was not served with a copy of the application notice before an order was made under rule 18.10 may apply to have the order set aside^(GL) or varied.

(2) An application under this rule must be made within 7 days beginning with the date on which the order was served on the person making the application.

Power of the court to proceed in the absence of a party

18.12.—(1) Where the applicant or any respondent fails to attend the hearing of an application, the court may proceed in the absence of that person.

(2) Where—

    (a) the applicant or any respondent fails to attend the hearing of an application; and

    (b) the court makes an order at the hearing,

the court may, on application or of its own initiative, re-list the application.

(3) Paragraph (2) does not apply to magistrates' courts.

Dismissal of totally without merit applications

18.13. If the High Court or a county court dismisses an application (including an application for permission to appeal) and it considers that the application is totally without merit—

    (a) the court's order must record that fact; and

    (b) the court must at the same time consider whether it is appropriate to make a civil restraint order.

PART 19

ALTERNATIVE PROCEDURE FOR APPLICATIONS

Types of application for which Part 19 procedure may be followed

19.1.—(1) The Part 19 procedure is the procedure set out in this Part.

(2) An applicant may use the Part 19 procedure where the Part 18 procedure does not apply and—

    (a) there is no form prescribed by a rule or referred to in Practice Direction 5A in which to make the application;

    (b) the applicant seeks the court's decision on a question which is unlikely to involve a substantial dispute of fact; or

    (c) paragraph (5) applies.

(3) The court may at any stage direct that the application is to continue as if the applicant had not used the Part 19 procedure and, if it does so, the court may give any directions it considers appropriate.

(4) Paragraph (2) does not apply if a practice direction provides that the Part 19 procedure may not be used in relation to the type of application in question.

(5) A rule or practice direction may, in relation to a specified type of proceedings—

    (a) require or permit the use of the Part 19 procedure; and

    (b) disapply or modify any of the rules set out in this Part as they apply to those proceedings.

Applications for which the Part 19 procedure must be followed

19.2.—(1) The Part 19 procedure must be used in an application made in accordance with—

    (a) section 60(3) of the 2002 Act (order to prevent disclosure of information to an adopted person);

    (b) section 79(4) of the 2002 Act (order for Registrar General to give any information referred to in section 79(3) of the 2002 Act); and

    (c) rule 14.21 (directions of High Court regarding fathers without parental responsibility).

(2) The respondent to an application made in accordance with paragraph (1)(b) is the Registrar General.

Contents of the application

19.3. Where the applicant uses the Part 19 procedure, the application must state—

    (a) that this Part applies;

    (b) either—

        (i) the question which the applicant wants the court to decide; or

        (ii) the order which the applicant is seeking and the legal basis of the application for that order;

    (c) if the application is being made under an enactment, what that enactment is;

    (d) if the applicant is applying in a representative capacity, what that capacity is; and

    (e) if the respondent appears or is to appear in a representative capacity, what that capacity is.

(Part 17 requires a statement of case to be verified by a statement of truth.)

Issue of application without naming respondents

19.4.—(1) A practice direction may set out circumstances in which an application may be issued under this Part without naming a respondent.

(2) The practice direction may set out those cases in which an application for permission must be made by application notice before the application is issued.

(3) The application for permission—

    (a) need not be served on any other person; and

    (b) must be accompanied by a copy of the application which the applicant proposes to issue.

(4) Where the court gives permission, it will give directions about the future management of the application.

Acknowledgment of service

19.5.—(1) Subject to paragraph (2), each respondent must—

    (a) file an acknowledgment of service within 14 days beginning with the date on which the application is served; and

    (b) serve the acknowledgment of service on the applicant and any other party.

(2) If the application is to be served out of the jurisdiction, the respondent must file and serve an acknowledgment of service within the period set out in Practice Direction 6B.

(3) The acknowledgment of service must—

    (a) state whether the respondent contests the application;

    (b) state, if the respondent seeks a different order from that set out in the application, what that order is; and

(c) be signed by the respondent or the respondent's legal representative.

Consequence of not filing an acknowledgment of service

19.6.—(1) This rule applies where—

(a) the respondent has failed to file an acknowledgment of service; and

(b) the time period for doing so has expired.

(2) The respondent may attend the hearing of the application but may not take part in the hearing unless the court gives permission.

Filing and serving written evidence

19.7.—(1) The applicant must, when filing the application, file the written evidence on which the applicant intends to rely.

(2) The applicant's evidence must be served on the respondent with the application.

(3) A respondent who wishes to rely on written evidence must file it when filing the acknowledgment of service.

(4) A respondent who files written evidence must also, at the same time, serve a copy of that evidence on the other parties.

(5) Within 14 days beginning with the date on which a respondent's evidence was served on the applicant, the applicant may file further written evidence in reply.

(6) An applicant who files further written evidence must also, within the same time limit, serve a copy of that evidence on the other parties.

Evidence – general

19.8.—(1) No written evidence may be relied on at the hearing of the application unless—

(a) it has been served in accordance with rule 19.7; or

(b) the court gives permission.

(2) The court may require or permit a party to give oral evidence at the hearing.

(3) The court may give directions requiring the attendance for cross-examination[(GL)] of a witness who has given written evidence.

(Rule 22.1 contains a general power for the court to control evidence.)

Procedure where respondent objects to use of the Part 19 procedure

19.9.—(1) A respondent who contends that the Part 19 procedure should not be used because—

(a) there is a substantial dispute of fact; and

(b) the use of the Part 19 procedure is not required or permitted by a rule or practice direction,

must state the reasons for that contention when filing the acknowledgment of service.

(2) When the court receives the acknowledgment of service and any written evidence, it will give directions as to the future management of the case.

(Rule 19.7 requires a respondent who wishes to rely on written evidence to file it when filing the acknowledgment of service.)

(Rule 19.1(3) allows the court to make an order that the application continue as if the applicant had not used the Part 19 procedure.)

PART 20

INTERIM REMEDIES AND SECURITY FOR COSTS

CHAPTER 1

INTERIM REMEDIES

Scope of this Part

20.1. The rules in this Part do not apply to proceedings in a magistrates' court.

Orders for interim remedies

20.2.—(1) The court may grant the following interim remedies—

(a) an interim injunction(GL);

(b) an interim declaration;

(c) an order—

    (i) for the detention, custody or preservation of relevant property;

    (ii) for the inspection of relevant property;

    (iii) for the taking of a sample of relevant property;

    (iv) for the carrying out of an experiment on or with relevant property;

    (v) for the sale of relevant property which is of a perishable nature or which for any other good reason it is desirable to sell quickly; and

    (vi) for the payment of income from relevant property until an application is decided;

(d) an order authorising a person to enter any land or building in the possession of a party to the proceedings for the purposes of carrying out an order under sub-paragraph (c);

(e) an order under section 4 of the Torts (Interference with Goods) Act 1977(**a**) to deliver up goods;

(f) an order (referred to as a 'freezing injunction(GL)')—

    (i) restraining a party from removing from the jurisdiction assets located there; or

    (ii) restraining a party from dealing with any assets whether located within the jurisdiction or not;

(g) an order directing a party to provide information about the location of relevant property or assets or to provide information about relevant property or assets which are or may be the subject of an application for a freezing injunction(GL);

(h) an order (referred to as a "search order") under section 7 of the Civil Procedure Act 1997(**b**) (order requiring a party to admit another party to premises for the purpose of preserving evidence etc.);

(i) an order under section 34 of the Senior Courts Act 1981(**c**) or section 53 of the County Courts Act 1984(**d**) (order in certain proceedings for disclosure of documents or inspection of property against a non-party);

(j) an order for a specified fund to be paid into court or otherwise secured, where there is a dispute over a party's right to the fund;

(**a**) 1977 c. 32.

(**b**) Section 7 of the Civil Procedure Act 1997 (c.12) was amended by section 261(1) of and paragraph 154 of Schedule 27 to the Civil Partnership Act 2004.

(**c**) 1981 c.54. Section 34 was amended by section 148(3) of and Schedule 4 to the County Courts Act 1984 and article 5(b) of the Civil Procedure (Modification of Enactments) Order 1998 (S.I. 1998/2940).

(**d**) Section 53 was amended by article 6(c)(i) of the Civil Procedure (Modification of Enactments) Order 1998 and section 10 of and paragraph 2(2) of Schedule 2 to the Civil Procedure Act 1997 (c.12) and by section 125(3) of and paragraph 44 of Schedule 18 to the Courts and Legal Services Act 1990.

(k) an order permitting a party seeking to recover personal property to pay money into court pending the outcome of the proceedings and directing that, if money is paid into court, the property must be given up to that party;

(l) an order directing a party to prepare and file accounts relating to the dispute;

(m) an order directing any account to be taken or inquiry to be made by the court.

(2) In paragraph (1)(c) and (g), 'relevant property' means property (including land) which is the subject of an application or as to which any question may arise on an application.

(3) The fact that a particular kind of interim remedy is not listed in paragraph (1) does not affect any power that the court may have to grant that remedy.

Time when an order for an interim remedy may be made

20.3.—(1) An order for an interim remedy may be made at any time, including—

(a) before proceedings are started; and

(b) after judgment has been given.

(Rule 5.3 provides that proceedings are started when the court issues an application form.)

(2) However—

(a) paragraph (1) is subject to any rule, practice direction or other enactment which provides otherwise; and

(b) the court may grant an interim remedy before an application has been started only if—

(i) the matter is urgent; or

(ii) it is otherwise desirable to do so in the interests of justice.

(3) Where the court grants an interim remedy before an application has been started, it will give directions requiring an application to be started.

(4) The court need not direct that an application be started where the application is made under section 33 of the Senior Courts Act 1981 or section 52 of the County Courts Act 1984(**a**) (order for disclosure, inspection etc. before starting an application).

How to apply for an interim remedy

20.4.—(1) The court may grant an interim remedy on an application made without notice if it appears to the court that there are good reasons for not giving notice.

(2) An application for an interim remedy must be supported by evidence, unless the court orders otherwise.

(3) If the applicant makes an application without giving notice, the evidence in support of the application must state the reasons why notice has not been given.

(Part 4 lists general case-management powers of the court.)

(Part 18 contains general rules about making an application.)

Interim injunction to cease if application is stayed

20.5. If—

(a) the court has granted an interim injunction^(GL) other than a freezing injunction^(GL); and

(b) the application is stayed^(GL) other than by agreement between the parties,

the interim injunction^(GL) will be set aside^(GL) unless the court orders that it should continue to have effect even though the application is stayed^(GL).

(**a**) Section 52 was amended by section 10 of and paragraph 2(2) of Schedule 2 to the Civil Procedure Act 1997 and by article 6(b) of the Civil Procedure (Modification of Enactments) Order 1998 and by section 125(3) of and paragraph 43 of Schedule 18 to the Courts and Legal Services Act 1990.

CHAPTER 2

SECURITY FOR COSTS

Security for costs

20.6.—(1) A respondent to any application may apply under this Chapter of this Part for security for costs of the proceedings.

(Part 4 provides for the court to order payment of sums into court in other circumstances.)

(2) An application for security for costs must be supported by written evidence.

(3) Where the court makes an order for security for costs, it will—

    (a) determine the amount of security; and

    (b) direct—

        (i) the manner in which; and

        (ii) the time within which,

    the security must be given.

Conditions to be satisfied

20.7.—(1) The court may make an order for security for costs under rule 20.6 if—

    (a) it is satisfied, having regard to all the circumstances of the case, that it is just to make such an order; and

    (b) either—

        (i) one or more of the conditions in paragraph (2) applies; or

        (ii) an enactment permits the court to require security for costs.

(2) The conditions are—

    (a) the applicant is—

        (i) resident out of the jurisdiction; but

        (ii) not resident in a Brussels Contracting State, a Lugano Contracting State or a Regulation State, as defined in section 1(3) of the Civil Jurisdiction and Judgments Act 1982 or a Member State bound by the Council Regulation;

    (b) the applicant has changed address since the application was started with a view to evading the consequences of the litigation;

    (c) the applicant failed to give an address in the application form, or gave an incorrect address in that form;

    (d) the applicant has taken steps in relation to the applicant's assets that would make it difficult to enforce an order for costs against the applicant.

(3) The court may not make an order for security for costs under rule 20.6 in relation to the costs of proceedings under the 1980 Hague Convention.

(Rule 4.4 allows the court to strike out^(GL) a statement of case.)

Security for costs of an appeal

20.8. The court may order security for costs of an appeal against—

    (a) an appellant;

    (b) a respondent who also appeals,

on the same grounds as it may order security for costs against an applicant under this Part.

PART 21

MISCELLANEOUS RULES ABOUT DISCLOSURE AND INSPECTION OF DOCUMENTS

Interpretation

21.1.—(1) A party discloses a document by stating that the document exists or has existed.

(2) Inspection of a document occurs when a party is permitted to inspect a document disclosed by another person.

(3) For the purposes of disclosure and inspection—

    (a) "document" means anything in which information of any description is recorded; and

    (b) "copy" in relation to a document, means anything onto which information recorded in the document has been copied, by whatever means and whether directly or indirectly.

Orders for disclosure against a person not a party

21.2.—(1) This rule applies where an application is made to the court under any Act for disclosure by a person who is not a party to the proceedings.

(2) The application—

    (a) may be made without notice; and

    (b) must be supported by evidence.

(3) The court may make an order under this rule only where disclosure is necessary in order to dispose fairly of the proceedings or to save costs.

(4) An order under this rule must—

    (a) specify the documents or the classes of documents which the respondent must disclose; and

    (b) require the respondent, when making disclosure, to specify any of those documents—

        (i) which are no longer in the respondent's control; or

        (ii) in respect of which the respondent claims a right or duty to withhold inspection.

(5) Such an order may—

    (a) require the respondent to indicate what has happened to any documents which are no longer in the respondent's control; and

    (b) specify the time and place for disclosure and inspection.

(6) An order under this rule must not compel a person to produce any document which that person could not be compelled to produce at the final hearing.

(7) This rule does not limit any other power which the court may have to order disclosure against a person who is not a party to proceedings.

(Rule 35.3 contains provisions in relation to the disclosure and inspection of evidence arising out of mediation of cross-border disputes.)

Claim to withhold inspection or disclosure of a document

21.3.—(1) A person may apply, without notice, for an order permitting that person to withhold disclosure of a document on the ground that disclosure would damage the public interest.

(2) Unless the court otherwise orders, an order of the court under paragraph (1)—

    (a) must not be served on any other person; and

    (b) must not be open to inspection by any other person.

(3) A person who wishes to claim a right or a duty to withhold inspection of a document, or part of a document, must state in writing—

(a) the right or duty claimed; and

(b) the grounds on which that right or duty is claimed.

(4) The statement referred to in paragraph (3) must be made to the person wishing to inspect the document.

(5) A party may apply to the court to decide whether a claim made under paragraph (3) should be upheld.

(6) Where the court is deciding an application under paragraph (1) or (5) it may—

(a) require the person seeking to withhold disclosure or inspection of a document to produce that document to the court; and

(b) invite any person, whether or not a party, to make representations.

(7) An application under paragraph (1) or (5) must be supported by evidence.

(8) This Part does not affect any rule of law which permits or requires a document to be withheld from disclosure or inspection on the ground that its disclosure or inspection would damage the public interest.

PART 22

EVIDENCE

CHAPTER 1

GENERAL RULES

Power of court to control evidence

22.1.—(1) The court may control the evidence by giving directions as to—

(a) the issues on which it requires evidence;

(b) the nature of the evidence which it requires to decide those issues; and

(c) the way in which the evidence is to be placed before the court.

(2) The court may use its power under this rule to exclude evidence that would otherwise be admissible.

(3) The court may permit a party to adduce evidence, or to seek to rely on a document, in respect of which that party has failed to comply with the requirements of this Part.

(4) The court may limit cross-examination$^{(GL)}$.

Evidence of witnesses – general rule

22.2.—(1) The general rule is that any fact which needs to be proved by the evidence of witnesses is to be proved—

(a) at the final hearing, by their oral evidence; and

(b) at any other hearing, by their evidence in writing.

(2) The general rule does not apply—

(a) to proceedings under Part 12 for secure accommodation orders, interim care orders or interim supervision orders; or

(b) where an enactment, any of these rules, a practice direction or a court order provides to the contrary.

(Section 45(7) of the Children Act 1989 (emergency protection orders) is an example of an enactment which makes provision relating to the evidence that a court may take into account when hearing an application.)

Evidence by video link or other means

22.3. The court may allow a witness to give evidence through a video link or by other means.

Witness statements

22.4.—(1) A witness statement is a written statement signed by a person which contains the evidence which that person would be allowed to give orally.

(2) A witness statement must comply with the requirements set out in the Practice Direction 22A.

(Part 17 requires a witness statement to be verified by a statement of truth.)

Service of witness statements for use at the final hearing

22.5.—(1) The court may give directions as to service on the other parties of any witness statement of the oral evidence on which a party intends to rely in relation to any issues of fact to be decided at the final hearing.

(2) The court may give directions as to—

    (a) the order in which witness statements are to be served; and

    (b) whether or not the witness statements are to be filed.

(3) Where the court directs that a court officer is to serve a witness statement on the other parties, any reference in this Chapter to a party serving a witness statement is to be read as including a reference to a court officer serving the statement.

Use at the final hearing of witness statements which have been served

22.6.—(1) If a party—

    (a) has served a witness statement; and

    (b) wishes to rely at the final hearing on the evidence of the witness who made the statement,

that party must call the witness to give oral evidence unless the court directs otherwise or the party puts the statement in as hearsay evidence.

(Part 23 (miscellaneous rules about evidence) contains provisions about hearsay evidence.)

(2) The witness statement of a witness called to give oral evidence under paragraph (1) is to stand as the evidence in chief$^{(GL)}$ of that witness unless the court directs otherwise.

(3) A witness giving oral evidence at the final hearing may with the permission of the court—

    (a) amplify his witness statement; and

    (b) give evidence in relation to new matters which have arisen since the witness statement was served on the other parties.

(4) The court will give permission under paragraph (3) only if it considers that there is good reason not to confine the evidence of the witness to the contents of the witness statement.

(5) If a party who has served a witness statement does not—

    (a) call the witness to give evidence at the final hearing; or

    (b) put the witness statement in as hearsay evidence,

any other party may put the witness statement in as hearsay evidence.

Evidence at hearings other than the final hearing

22.7.—(1) Subject to paragraph (2), the general rule is that evidence at hearings other than the final hearing is to be by witness statement unless the court, any other rule, a practice direction or any other enactment requires otherwise.

(2) At hearings other than the final hearing, a party may rely on the matters set out in that party's—

    (a) application form;

    (b) application notice; or

    (c) answer,

if the application form, application notice or answer, as the case may be, is verified by a statement of truth.

Order for cross-examination

22.8.—(1) Where, at a hearing other than the final hearing, evidence is given in writing, any party may apply to the court for permission to cross-examine$^{(GL)}$ the person giving the evidence.

(2) If the court gives permission under paragraph (1) but the person in question does not attend, that person's evidence may not be used unless the court directs otherwise.

(Rules 35.3 and 35.4 contain rules in relation to evidence arising out of mediation of cross-border disputes.)

Witness summaries

22.9.—(1) A party who—

    (a) is required to serve a witness statement for use at any hearing; but

    (b) is unable to obtain one,

may apply, without notice, for permission to serve a witness summary instead.

(2) A witness summary is a summary of—

    (a) the evidence, if known, which would otherwise be included in a witness statement; or

    (b) if the evidence is not known, the matters about which the party serving the witness summary proposes to question the witness.

(3) Unless the court directs otherwise, a witness summary must include the name and address of the intended witness.

(4) Unless the court directs otherwise, a witness summary must be served within the period in which a witness statement would have had to be served.

(5) Where a party serves a witness summary, so far as practicable rules 22.4(2)(form of witness statements), 22.5 (service of witness statements for use at the final hearing) and 22.6(3) (amplifying witness statements) apply to the summary.

Consequence of failure to serve witness statement

22.10. If a witness statement for use at the final hearing is not served in respect of an intended witness within the time specified by the court, then the witness may not be called to give oral evidence unless the court gives permission.

Cross-examination on a witness statement

22.11. A witness who is called to give evidence at the final hearing may be cross-examined$^{(GL)}$ on the witness statement, whether or not the statement or any part of it was referred to during the witness's evidence in chief$^{(GL)}$.

Affidavit evidence

22.12.—(1) Evidence must be given by affidavit$^{(GL)}$ instead of or in addition to a witness statement if this is required by the court, a provision contained in any other rule, a practice direction or any other enactment.

(2) In relation to proceedings which are pending or treated as pending in a divorce county court or civil partnership county court, section 58(1)(c) of the County Courts Act 1984, shall have effect as if after paragraph (c) there were inserted—,

"or

  (d) a district judge of the principal registry; or

  (e) any officer of the principal registry authorised by the President under section 2 of the Commissioner for Oaths Act 1889**(a)**; or

  (f) any clerk in the Central Office of the Royal Courts of Justice authorised to take affidavits(GL) for the purposes of proceedings in the Supreme Court.".

(Rule 7.3 sets out when proceedings are treated as pending in a divorce county court or civil partnership proceedings county court.)

Form of affidavit

22.13. An affidavit$^{(GL)}$ must comply with the requirements set out in the Practice Direction 22A.

Affidavit made outside the jurisdiction

22.14. A person may make an affidavit $^{(GL)}$ outside the jurisdiction in accordance with—

  (a) this Part; or

  (b) the law of the place where the affidavit$^{(GL)}$ is made.

Notice to admit facts

22.15.—(1) A party may serve notice on another party requiring the other party to admit the facts, or the part of the case of the serving party, specified in the notice.

(2) A notice to admit facts must be served no later than 21 days before the final hearing.

(3) Where the other party makes any admission in answer to the notice, the admission may be used against that party only—

  (a) in the proceedings in which the notice to admit is served; and

  (b) by the party who served the notice.

(4) The court may allow a party to amend or withdraw any admission made by that party on such terms as it thinks just.

Notice to admit or produce documents

22.16.—(1) A party to whom a document is disclosed is deemed to admit the authenticity of that document unless notice is served by that party that the party wishes the document to be proved at the final hearing.

(2) A notice to prove a document must be served—

  (a) by the latest date for serving witness statements; or

  (b) within 7 days beginning with the date of service of the document, whichever is later.

Notarial acts and instruments

22.17. A notarial act or instrument may be received in evidence without further proof as duly authenticated in accordance with the requirements of law unless the contrary is proved.

(**a**) 1889 c.10. Section 2 was amended by section 59(5) of and paragraphs 15(1) and (2) of Schedule 11 to the Constitutional Reform Act 2005.

CHAPTER 2

RULES APPLYING ONLY TO PARTICULAR PROCEEDINGS

Scope of this Chapter

22.18. This Chapter of this Part applies to affidavits[GL] and affirmations as it applies to witness statements.

Availability of witness statements for inspection during the final hearing

22.19.—(1) This rule applies to proceedings under Part 7 (matrimonial and civil partnership proceedings).

(2) A witness statement which stands as evidence in chief[GL] is open to inspection during the course of the final hearing unless the court directs otherwise.

(3) Any person may ask for a direction that a witness statement is not open to inspection.

(4) The court will not make a direction under paragraph (2) unless it is satisfied that a witness statement should not be open to inspection because of—

    (a) the interests of justice;

    (b) the public interest;

    (c) the nature of any expert medical evidence in the statement;

    (d) the nature of any confidential information (including information relating to personal financial matters) in the statement; or

    (e) the need to protect the interests of any child or protected party.

(5) The court may exclude from inspection words or passages in the witness statement.

Use of witness statements for other purposes

22.20.—(1) This rule applies to proceedings under Part 7 (matrimonial and civil partnership proceedings) or Part 9 (financial remedies).

(2) Except as provided by this rule, a witness statement may be used only for the purpose of the proceedings in which it is served.

(3) Paragraph (2) does not apply if and to the extent that—

    (a) the court gives permission for some other use; or

    (b) the witness statement has been put in evidence at a hearing held in public.

PART 23

MISCELLANEOUS RULES ABOUT EVIDENCE

Scope and interpretation of this Part

23.1. Rules 23.2 to 23.6 apply to evidence to which the Children (Admissibility of Hearsay Evidence) Order 1993(**a**) does not apply.

Notice of intention to rely on hearsay evidence

23.2.—(1) Where a party intends to rely on hearsay evidence at the final hearing and either—

    (a) that evidence is to be given by a witness giving oral evidence; or

---

(**a**) S.I. 1993/621.

    (b)   that evidence is contained in a witness statement of a person who is not being called to give oral evidence,

that party complies with section 2(1)(a) of the Civil Evidence Act 1995(**a**) by serving a witness statement on the other parties in accordance with the court's directions.

(2) Where paragraph (1)(b) applies, the party intending to rely on the hearsay evidence must, when serving the witness statement—

    (a)   inform the other parties that the witness is not being called to give oral evidence; and

    (b)   give the reason why the witness will not be called.

(3) In all other cases where a party intends to rely on hearsay evidence at the final hearing, that party complies with section 2(1)(a) of the Civil Evidence Act 1995 by serving a notice on the other parties which—

    (a)   identifies the hearsay evidence;

    (b)   states that the party serving the notice proposes to rely on the hearsay evidence at the final hearing; and

    (c)   gives the reason why the witness will not be called.

(4) The party proposing to rely on the hearsay evidence must—

    (a)   serve the notice no later than the latest date for serving witness statements; and

    (b)   if the hearsay evidence is to be in a document, supply a copy to any party who requests it.

Circumstances in which notice of intention to rely on hearsay evidence is not required

23.3. Section 2(1) of the Civil Evidence Act 1995 (duty to give notice of intention to rely on hearsay evidence) does not apply—

    (a)   to evidence at hearings other than final hearings;

    (b)   to an affidavit[(GL)] or witness statement which is to be used at the final hearing but which does not contain hearsay evidence; or

    (c)   where the requirement is excluded by a practice direction.

Power to call witness for cross-examination on hearsay evidence

23.4.—(1) Where a party—

    (a)   proposes to rely on hearsay evidence; and

    (b)   does not propose to call the person who made the original statement to give oral evidence,

the court may, on the application of any other party, permit that party to call the maker of the statement to be cross-examined[(GL)] on the contents of the statement.

(2) An application for permission to cross-examine[(GL)] under this rule must be made within 14 days beginning with the date on which a notice of intention to rely on the hearsay evidence was served on the applicant.

(Rules 35.3 and 35.4 contain rules in relation to evidence arising out of mediation of cross-border disputes.)

Credibility

23.5.—(1) Where a party proposes to rely on hearsay evidence, but—

    (a)   does not propose to call the person who made the original statement to give oral evidence; and

---

(**a**) 1995 c.38.

(b) another party wishes to call evidence to attack the credibility of the person who made the statement,

the party who so wishes must give notice of that intention to the party who proposes to give the hearsay statement in evidence.

(2) A party must give notice under paragraph (1) within 14 days after the date on which a hearsay notice relating to the hearsay evidence was served on that party.

Use of plans, photographs and models etc as evidence

23.6.—(1) This rule applies to—

(a) evidence (such as a plan, photograph or model) which is not—

(i) contained in a witness statement, affidavit$^{(GL)}$ or expert's report;

(ii) to be given orally at the final hearing; or

(iii) evidence of which prior notice must be given under rule 23.2; and

(b) documents which may be received in evidence without further proof under section 9 of the Civil Evidence Act 1995.

(2) Except as provided below, section 2(1)(a) of the Civil Evidence Act 1995 (notice of proposal to adduce hearsay evidence) does not apply to evidence falling within paragraph (1).

(3) Such evidence is not receivable at the final hearing unless the party intending to rely on it (in this rule, "the party") has—

(a) served it or, in the case of a model, a photograph of it with an invitation to inspect the original, on the other party in accordance with this rule; or

(b) complied with such directions as the court may give for serving the evidence on, or for giving notice under section 2(1)(a) of the Civil Evidence Act 1995 in respect of the evidence to, the other party.

(4) Where the party intends to use the evidence as evidence of any fact then, except where paragraph (6) applies, the party must serve the evidence not later than the latest date for serving witness statements.

(5) The party must serve the evidence at least 21 days before the hearing at which the party proposes to rely on it if—

(a) there are not to be witness statements; or

(b) the party intends to put in the evidence solely in order to disprove an allegation made in a witness statement.

(6) Where the evidence forms part of expert evidence, the party must serve the evidence when the expert's report is served on the other party.

(7) Where the evidence is being produced to the court for any reason other than as part of factual or expert evidence, the party must serve the evidence at least 21 days before the hearing at which the party proposes to rely on it.

(8) Where the court directs a party to give notice that the party intends to put in the evidence, the court may direct that every other party be given an opportunity to inspect it and to agree to its admission without further proof.

Evidence of finding on question of foreign law

23.7.—(1) This rule sets out the procedure which must be followed by a party (in this rule, "the party") who intends to put in evidence a finding on a question of foreign law by virtue of section 4(2) of the Civil Evidence Act 1972.

(2) The party must give any other party notice of that intention.

(3) The party must give the notice—

(a) if there are to be witness statements, not later than the latest date for serving them; or

(b) otherwise, not less than 21 days before the hearing at which the party proposes to put the finding in evidence.

(4) The notice must—

(a) specify the question on which the finding was made; and

(b) enclose a copy of a document where it is reported or recorded.

Evidence of consent of trustee to act

23.8. In proceedings to which Part 9 (financial remedies) applies, a document purporting to contain the written consent of a person to act as trustee and to bear that person's signature verified by some other person is evidence of such consent.

Note of oral evidence in magistrates' courts

23.9. In proceedings in a magistrates' court, the justices' clerk or the court shall keep a note of the substance of the oral evidence given at a directions appointment or at a hearing of any proceedings.

PART 24

WITNESSES, DEPOSITIONS GENERALLY AND TAKING OF EVIDENCE IN MEMBER STATES OF THE EUROPEAN UNION

CHAPTER 1

WITNESSES AND DEPOSITIONS

Scope of this Chapter

24.1.—(1) This Chapter provides—

(a) for the circumstances in which a person may be required to attend court to give evidence or to produce a document; and

(b) for a party to obtain evidence before a hearing to be used at the hearing.

(2) This Chapter, apart from rule 24.10(2) to (4), does not apply to proceedings in a magistrates' court.

(Rules 34.16 to 34.21 and 34.24 of the CPR apply to incoming requests for evidence.)

Witness summonses

24.2.—(1) A witness summons is a document issued by the court requiring a witness to—

(a) attend court to give evidence; or

(b) produce documents to the court.

(2) A witness summons must be in the form set out in Practice Direction 24A.

(3) There must be a separate witness summons for each witness.

(4) A witness summons may require a witness to produce documents to the court either—

(a) on the date fixed for a hearing; or

(b) on such date as the court may direct.

(5) The only documents that a summons under this rule can require a person to produce before a hearing are documents which that person could be required to produce at the hearing.

(Rules 35.3 and 35.4 contain rules in relation to evidence arising out of mediation of cross-border disputes.)

Issue of a witness summons

24.3.—(1) A witness summons is issued on the date entered on the summons by the court.

(2) A party must obtain permission from the court where that party wishes to—

    (a) have a summons issued less than 7 days before the date of the final hearing;

    (b) have a summons issued for a witness to attend court to give evidence or to produce documents on any date except the date fixed for the final hearing; or

    (c) have a summons issued for a witness to attend court to give evidence or to produce documents at any hearing except the final hearing.

(3) A witness summons must be issued by—

    (a) the court where the case is proceeding; or

    (b) the court where the hearing in question will be held.

(4) The court may set aside ^(GL)or vary a witness summons issued under this rule.

Time for serving a witness summons

24.4.—(1) The general rule is that a witness summons is binding if it is served at least 7 days before the date on which the witness is required to attend before the court.

(2) The court may direct that a witness summons is binding although it is served less than 7 days before the date on which the witness is required to attend before the court.

(3) A witness summons which is—

    (a) served in accordance with this rule; and

    (b) requires the witness to attend court to give evidence,

is binding until the conclusion of the hearing at which the attendance of the witness is required.

(Rules 35.3 and 35.4 contain rules in relation to evidence arising out of mediation of cross-border disputes.)

Who is to serve a witness summons

24.5.—(1) Subject to paragraph (2), a witness summons is to be served by the party on whose behalf it is issued unless that party indicates in writing, when asking the court to issue the summons, that that party wishes the court to serve it instead.

(2) In proceedings to which Part 14 (procedure for applications in adoption, placement and related proceedings) applies, a witness summons is to be served by the court unless the court directs otherwise.

(3) Where the court is to serve the witness summons, the party on whose behalf it is issued must deposit, in the court office, the money to be paid or offered to the witness under rule 24.6.

Right of witness to travelling expenses and compensation for loss of time

24.6. At the time of service of a witness summons the witness must be offered or paid—

    (a) a sum reasonably sufficient to cover the expenses of the witness in travelling to and from the court; and

    (b) such sum by way of compensation for loss of time as may be specified in Practice Direction 24A.

Evidence by deposition

24.7.—(1) A party may apply for an order for a person to be examined before the hearing takes place.

(2) A person from whom evidence is to be obtained following an order under this rule is referred to as a 'deponent' and the evidence is referred to as a 'deposition'.

(3) An order under this rule is for a deponent to be examined on oath before—

    (a) a judge;

    (b) an examiner of the court; or

    (c) such other person as the court appoints.

(Rule 24.14 makes provision for the appointment of examiners of the court.)

(4) The order may require the production of any document which the court considers is necessary for the purposes of the examination.

(5) The order must state the date, time and place of the examination.

(6) At the time of service of the order the deponent must be offered or paid—

    (a) a sum reasonably sufficient to cover the expenses of the deponent in travelling to and from the place of examination; and

    (b) such sum by way of compensation for loss of time as may be specified in Practice Direction 24A.

(7) Where the court makes an order for a deposition to be taken, it may also order the party who obtained the order to serve a witness statement or witness summary in relation to the evidence to be given by the person to be examined.

(Part 22 (evidence) contains the general rules about witness statements and witness summaries.)

(Rules 35.3 and 35.4 contain rules in relation to evidence arising out of mediation of cross-border disputes.)

Conduct of examination

24.8.—(1) Subject to any directions contained in the order for examination, the examination must be conducted in the same way as if the witness were giving evidence at a final hearing.

(2) If all the parties are present, the examiner may conduct the examination of a person not named in the order for examination if all the parties and the person to be examined consent.

(3) In defended proceedings under Part 7 (matrimonial and civil partnership proceedings), the examiner may conduct the examination in private if of the view that it is appropriate to do so.

(4) Save in proceedings to which paragraph (3) applies, the examiner will conduct the examination in private unless of the view that it is not appropriate to do so.

(5) The examiner must ensure that the evidence given by the witness is recorded in full.

(6) The examiner must send a copy of the deposition—

    (a) to the person who obtained the order for the examination of the witness; and

    (b) to the court where the case is proceeding.

(7) The court will give directions as to service of the deposition on the other party.

Enforcing attendance of witness

24.9.—(1) If a person served with an order to attend before an examiner—

    (a) fails to attend; or

    (b) refuses to be sworn for the purpose of the examination or to answer any lawful question or produce any document at the examination,

a certificate of that person's failure or refusal, signed by the examiner, must be filed by the party requiring the deposition.

(2) On the certificate being filed, the party requiring the deposition may apply to the court for an order requiring that person to attend or to be sworn or to answer any question or produce any document, as the case may be.

(3) An application for an order under this rule may be made without notice.

(4) The court may order the person against whom an order is made under this rule to pay any costs resulting from that person's failure or refusal.

(Rules 35.3 and 35.4 contain rules in relation to evidence arising out of mediation of cross-border disputes. Rule 35.4(1)(d) relates specifically to this rule.)

Use of deposition at a hearing

24.10.—(1) A deposition ordered under rule 24.7 may be given in evidence at a hearing unless the court orders otherwise.

(2) A party intending to put in evidence a deposition at a hearing must file notice of intention to do so on the court and the court will give directions about serving the notice on every other party.

(3) The party must file the notice at least 21 days before the day fixed for the hearing.

(4) The court may require a deponent to attend the hearing and give evidence orally.

(5) Where a deposition is given in evidence at the final hearing, it is treated as if it were a witness statement for the purposes of rule 22.19 (availability of witness statements for inspection).

(Rules 35.3 and 35.4 contain rules in relation to evidence arising out of mediation of cross-border disputes. Rule 35.4(1)(e) relates specifically to this rule.)

Restrictions on subsequent use of deposition taken for the purpose of any hearing except the final hearing

24.11.—(1) This rule applies to proceedings under Part 7 (matrimonial and civil partnership proceedings) or Part 9 (financial remedies).

(2) Where the court orders a party to be examined about that party's or any other assets for the purpose of any hearing except the final hearing, the deposition may be used only for the purpose of the proceedings in which the order was made.

(3) However it may be used for some other purpose—

    (a) by the party who was examined;

    (b) if the party who was examined agrees; or

    (c) if the court gives permission.

Where a person to be examined is out of the jurisdiction – letter of request

24.12.—(1) This rule applies where a party wishes to take a deposition from a person who is—

    (a) out of the jurisdiction; and

    (b) not in a Regulation State within the meaning of Chapter 2 of this Part.

(2) The High Court may order the issue of a letter of request to the judicial authorities of the country in which the proposed deponent is.

(3) A letter of request is a request to a judicial authority to take the evidence of that person, or arrange for it to be taken.

(4) The High Court may make an order under this rule in relation to county court proceedings.

(5) If the government of a country allows a person appointed by the High Court to examine a person in that country, the High Court may make an order appointing a special examiner for that purpose.

(6) A person may be examined under this rule on oath or affirmation or in accordance with any procedure permitted in the country in which the examination is to take place.

(7) If the High Court makes an order for the issue of a letter of request, the party who sought the order must file—

(a) the following documents and, except where paragraph (8) applies, a translation of them—

    (i) a draft letter of request;

    (ii) a statement of the issues relevant to the proceedings; and

    (iii) a list of questions or the subject matter of questions to be put to the person to be examined; and

(b) an undertaking to be responsible for the Secretary of State's expenses.

(8) There is no need to file a translation if—

(a) English is one of the official languages of the country where the examination is to take place; or

(b) a practice direction has specified that country as a country where no translation is necessary.

(Rules 35.3 and 35.4 contain rules in relation to evidence arising out of mediation of cross-border disputes. Rule 35.4(1)(f) relates specifically to this rule.)

Fees and expenses of examiner of the court

24.13.—(1) An examiner of the court may charge a fee for the examination.

(2) The examiner need not send the deposition to the court unless the fee is paid.

(3) The examiner's fees and expenses must be paid by the party who obtained the order for examination.

(4) If the fees and expenses due to an examiner are not paid within a reasonable time, the examiner may report that fact to the court.

(5) The court may order the party who obtained the order for examination to deposit in the court office a specified sum in respect of the examiner's fees and, where it does so, the examiner will not be asked to act until the sum has been deposited.

(6) An order under this rule does not affect any decision as to the party who is ultimately to bear the costs of the examination.

Examiners of the court

24.14.—(1) The Lord Chancellor will appoint persons to be examiners of the court.

(2) The persons appointed must be barristers or solicitor-advocates who have been practising for a period of not less than 3 years.

(3) The Lord Chancellor may revoke an appointment at any time.

CHAPTER 2

TAKING OF EVIDENCE – MEMBER STATES OF THE EUROPEAN UNION

Interpretation

24.15. In this Chapter—

"designated court" has the meaning given in Practice Direction 24A;

"Regulation State" has the same meaning as 'Member State' in the Taking of Evidence Regulation, that is all Member States except Denmark;

"the Taking of Evidence Regulation" means Council Regulation (EC) No. 1206/2001 of 28 May 2001 on co-operation between the courts of the Member States in the taking of evidence in civil or commercial matters.

Where a person to be examined is in another Regulation State

24.16.—(1) This rule applies where a party wishes to take a deposition from a person who is—

(a) outside the jurisdiction; and

(b) in a Regulation State.

(2) The court may order the issue of a request to a designated court ('the requested court') in the Regulation State in which the proposed deponent is.

(3) If the court makes an order for the issue of a request, the party who sought the order must file—

(a) a draft Form A as set out in the annex to the Taking of Evidence Regulation (request for the taking of evidence);

(b) except where paragraph (4) applies, a translation of the form;

(c) an undertaking to be responsible for costs sought by the requested court in relation to—

(i) fees paid to experts and interpreters; and

(ii) where requested by that party, the use of special procedures or communications technology; and

(d) an undertaking to be responsible for the court's expenses.

(4) There is no need to file a translation if—

(a) English is one of the official languages of the Regulation State where the examination is to take place; or

(b) the Regulation State has indicated, in accordance with the Taking of Evidence Regulation, that English is a language which it will accept.

(5) Where article 17 of the Taking of Evidence Regulation (direct taking of evidence by the requested court) allows evidence to be taken directly in another Regulation State, the court may make an order for the submission of a request in accordance with that article.

(6) If the court makes an order for the submission of a request under paragraph (5), the party who sought the order must file—

(a) a draft Form I as set out in the annex to the Taking of Evidence Regulation (request for direct taking of evidence);

(b) except where paragraph (4) applies, a translation of the form; and

(c) an undertaking to be responsible for the court's expenses.

PART 25

EXPERTS AND ASSESSORS

Duty to restrict expert evidence

25.1. Expert evidence will be restricted to that which is reasonably required to resolve the proceedings.

Interpretation

25.2.—(1) A reference to an "expert" in this Part—

(a) is a reference to a person who has been instructed to give or prepare expert evidence for the purpose of family proceedings; and

(b) does not include—

(i) a person who is within a prescribed description for the purposes of section 94(1) of the 2002 Act (persons who may prepare a report for any person about the suitability of a child for adoption or of a person to adopt a child or about the adoption, or placement for adoption, of a child); or

(ii) an officer of the Service or a Welsh family proceedings officer when acting in that capacity.

(Regulation 3 of the Restriction on the Preparation of Adoption Reports Regulations 2005 (S.I. 2005/1711) sets out which persons are within a prescribed description for the purposes of section 94(1) of the 2002 Act.)

(2) "Single joint expert" means an expert instructed to prepare a report for the court on behalf of two or more of the parties (including the applicant) to the proceedings.

Experts- overriding duty to the court

25.3.—(1) It is the duty of experts to help the court on matters within their expertise.

(2) This duty overrides any obligation to the person from whom experts have received instructions or by whom they are paid.

Court's power to restrict expert evidence

25.4.—(1) No party may call an expert or put in evidence an expert's report without the court's permission.

(2) When parties apply for permission they must identify—

(a) the field in which the expert evidence is required; and

(b) where practicable, the name of the proposed expert.

(3) If permission is granted it will be in relation only to the expert named or the field identified under paragraph (2).

(4) The court may limit the amount of a party's expert's fees and expenses that may be recovered from any other party.

General requirement for expert evidence to be given in a written report

25.5.—(1) Expert evidence is to be given in a written report unless the court directs otherwise.

(2) The court will not direct an expert to attend a hearing unless it is necessary to do so in the interests of justice.

Written questions to experts

25.6.—(1) A party may put written questions about an expert's report (which must be proportionate) to—

(a) an expert instructed by another party; or

(b) a single joint expert appointed under rule 25.7.

(2) Written questions under paragraph (1)—

(a) may be put once only;

(b) must be put within 10 days beginning with the date on which the expert's report was served; and

(c) must be for the purpose only of clarification of the report,

unless in any case—

(i) the court directs otherwise; or

(ii) a practice direction provides otherwise.

(3) An expert's answers to questions put in accordance with paragraph (1) are treated as part of the expert's report.

(4) Where—

    (a)   a party has put a written question to an expert instructed by another party; and

    (b)   the expert does not answer that question,

the court may make use of one or both of the following orders in relation to the party who instructed the expert—

    (i)   that the party may not rely on the evidence of that expert; or

    (ii)   that the party may not recover the fees and expenses of that expert from any other party.

Court's power to direct that evidence is to be given by a single joint expert

25.7.—(1) Where two or more parties wish to submit expert evidence on a particular issue, the court may direct that the evidence on that issue is to be given by a single joint expert.

(2) Where the parties who wish to submit the evidence ("the relevant parties") cannot agree who should be the single joint expert, the court may—

    (a)   select the expert from a list prepared or identified by the instructing parties; or

    (b)   direct that the expert be selected in such other manner as the court may direct.

Instructions to a single joint expert

25.8.—(1) Where the court gives a direction under rule 25.7(1) for a single joint expert to be used, the instructions are to be contained in a jointly agreed letter unless the court directs otherwise.

(2) Where the instructions are to be contained in a jointly agreed letter, in default of agreement the instructions may be determined by the court on the written request of any relevant party copied to the other relevant parties.

(3) Where the court permits the relevant parties to give separate instructions to a single joint expert, each instructing party must, when giving instructions to the expert, at the same time send a copy of the instructions to the other relevant parties.

(4) The court may give directions about—

    (a)   the payment of the expert's fees and expenses; and

    (b)   any inspection, examination or assessments which the expert wishes to carry out.

(5) The court may, before an expert is instructed, limit the amount that can be paid by way of fees and expenses to the expert.

(6) Unless the court directs otherwise, the relevant parties are jointly and severally liable for the payment of the expert's fees and expenses.

Power of court to direct a party to provide information

25.9.—(1) Subject to paragraph (2), where a party has access to information which is not reasonably available to another party, the court may direct the party who has access to the information to prepare, file and serve a document recording the information.

(2) In proceedings under Part 14 (procedure for applications in adoption, placement and related proceedings),—

    (a)   the court may direct the party with access to the information to prepare and file a document recording the information; and

    (b)   a court officer will send a copy of that document to the other party.

Contents of report

25.10.—(1) An expert's report must comply with the requirements set out in Practice Direction 25A.

(2) At the end of an expert's report there must be a statement that the expert understands and has complied with their duty to the court.

(3) The instructions to the expert are not privileged against disclosure.

(Rule 21.1 explains what is meant by disclosure.)

Use by one party of expert's report disclosed by another

25.11. Where a party has disclosed an expert's report, any party may use that expert's report as evidence at any relevant hearing.

Discussions between experts

25.12.—(1) The court may, at any stage, direct a discussion between experts for the purpose of requiring the experts to—

    (a) identify and discuss the expert issues in the proceedings; and

    (b) where possible, reach an agreed opinion on those issues.

(2) The court may specify the issues which the experts must discuss.

(3) The court may direct that following a discussion between the experts they must prepare a statement for the court setting out those issues on which—

    (a) they agree; and

    (b) they disagree,

with a summary of their reasons for disagreeing.

Expert's right to ask court for directions

25.13.—(1) Experts may file written requests for directions for the purpose of assisting them in carrying out their functions.

(2) Experts must, unless the court directs otherwise, provide copies of the proposed request for directions under paragraph (1)—

    (a) to the party instructing them, at least 7 days before they file the requests; and

    (b) to all other parties, at least 4 days before they file them.

(3) The court, when it gives directions, may also direct that a party be served with a copy of the directions.

Assessors

25.14.—(1) This rule applies where the court appoints one or more persons under section 70 of the Senior Courts Act 1981 or section 63 of the County Courts Act 1984(**a**) as an assessor

(2) An assessor will assist the court in dealing with a matter in which the assessor has skill and experience.

(3) The assessor will take such part in the proceedings as the court may direct and in particular the court may direct an assessor to—

    (a) prepare a report for the court on any matter at issue in the proceedings; and

    (b) attend the whole or any part of the hearing to advise the court on any such matter.

(**a**) Section 63 was amended by sections 14(2) and (3) and 125(7) of and Schedule 20 to the Courts and Legal Services Act 1990 and by articles 6(d)(i) to (iv) of the Civil Procedure (Modification of Enactments) Order 1998 (S.I. 1998/2940).

(4) If the assessor prepares a report for the court before the hearing has begun—

(a) the court will send a copy to each of the parties; and

(b) the parties may use it at the hearing.

(5) Unless the court directs otherwise, an assessor will be paid at the daily rate payable for the time being to a fee-paid deputy district judge of the principal registry and an assessor's fees will form part of the costs of the proceedings.

(6) The court may order any party to deposit in the court office a specified sum in respect of an assessor's fees and, where it does so, the assessor will not be asked to act until the sum has been deposited.

(7) Paragraphs (5) and (6) do not apply where the remuneration of the assessor is to be paid out of money provided by Parliament.

PART 26

CHANGE OF SOLICITOR

Solicitor acting for a party

26.1. Where the address for service of a party is the business address of that party's solicitor, the solicitor will be considered to be acting for that party until the provisions of this Part have been complied with.

(Part 6 contains provisions about the address for service.)

Change of solicitor – duty to give notice

26.2.—(1) This rule applies where—

(a) a party for whom a solicitor is acting wants to change solicitor;

(b) a party, after having conducted the application in person, appoints a solicitor to act for that party (except where the solicitor is appointed only to act as an advocate for a hearing); or

(c) a party, after having conducted the application by a solicitor, intends to act in person.

(2) Where this rule applies, the party or the party's solicitor (where one is acting) must—

(a) serve notice of the change on—

(i) every other party; and

(ii) where paragraph (1)(a) or (c) applies, the former solicitor; and

(b) file notice of the change.

(3) Except where a serial number has been assigned under rule 14.2 or the name or address of a party is not being revealed in accordance with rule 29.1, the notice must state the party's new address for service.

(4) The notice filed at court must state that notice has been served as required by paragraph (2)(a) or, where rule 2.4 applies, in accordance with the court's directions given under that rule.

(5) Subject to paragraph (6), where a party has changed solicitor or intends to act in person, the former solicitor will be considered to be the party's solicitor unless and until—

(a) notice is filed and served in accordance with paragraph (2)(a) or, where rule 2.4 applies, in accordance with the court's directions given under that rule; or

(b) the court makes an order under rule 26.3 and the order is served as required by paragraph (3) of that rule.

(6) Where the certificate of a LSC funded client or an assisted person (in this rule "C") is revoked or discharged –

(a) the solicitor who acted for C will cease to be the solicitor acting in the case as soon as the retainer is determined under regulation 4 of the Community Legal Service (Costs) Regulations 2000(**a**); and

(b) if C wishes to continue—

(i) where C appoints a solicitor to act on C's behalf, paragraph (2) will apply as if C had previously conducted the application in person; and

(ii) where C wants to act in person, C must give an address for service, in accordance with rule 6.26, unless the court directs otherwise.

(7) In this rule—

"assisted person" means an assisted person within the statutory provisions relating to legal aid;

"certificate" means a certificate issued under the Funding Code (approved under section 9 of the Access to Justice Act 1999(**b**)); and

"LSC funded client" means an individual who receives services funded by the Legal Services Commission as part of the Community Legal Service within the meaning of Part 1 of the Access to Justice Act 1999.

Order that a solicitor has ceased to act

26.3.—(1) A solicitor may apply for an order declaring that that solicitor has ceased to be the solicitor acting for—

(a) a party; or

(b) a children's guardian.

(2) Where an application is made under this rule—

(a) notice of the application must be given to the party, or children's guardian, for whom the solicitor is acting, unless the court directs otherwise; and

(b) the application must be supported by evidence.

(3) Where the court makes an order declaring that a solicitor has ceased to act, a court officer will serve a copy of the order on—

(a) every party to the proceedings; and

(b) where applicable, a children's guardian.

Removal of solicitor who has ceased to act on application of another party

26.4.—(1) Where—

(a) a solicitor who has acted for a party—

(i) has died;

(ii) has become bankrupt;

(iii) has ceased to practise; or

(iv) cannot be found; and

(b) the party has not given notice of a change of solicitor or notice of intention to act in person as required by rule 26.2(2),

any other party may apply for an order declaring that the solicitor has ceased to be the solicitor acting for the other party in the case.

(2) Where an application is made under this rule, notice of the application must be given to the party to whose solicitor the application relates unless the court directs otherwise.

(**a**) S.I. 2000/441.

(**b**) Section 9 was amended by article 8 of and paragraph 4(a) of the Schedule to the Transfer of Functions (Lord Chancellor and Secretary of State) Order 2005 (S.I. 2005/3429) and section 149(1) and (4) of the Coroners and Justice Act 2009 (c.25).

(3) Where the court makes an order made under this rule, a court officer will serve a copy of the order on every other party to the proceedings.

PART 27

HEARINGS AND DIRECTIONS APPOINTMENTS

Application of this Part

27.1. This Part is subject to any enactment, any provision in these rules or a practice direction.

(Rule 27.4(7) makes additional provision in relation to requirements to stay proceedings where the respondent does not appear and a relevant European regulation or international convention applies)

Reasons for a decision of the magistrates' courts

27.2.—(1) This rule applies to proceedings in a magistrates' court.

(2) After a hearing, the court will make its decision as soon as is practicable.

(3) The court must give written reasons for its decision.

(4) Paragraphs (5) and (6) apply where the functions of the court are being performed by—

(a) two or three lay justices; or

(b) by a single lay justice in accordance with these rules and Practice Direction 2A.

(5) The justices' clerk must, before the court makes an order or refuses an application or request, make notes of—

(a) the names of the justice or justices constituting the court by which the decision is made; and

(b) in consultation with the justice or justices, the reasons for the court's decision.

(6) The justices' clerk must make a written record of the reasons for the court's decision.

(7) When making an order or refusing an application, the court, or one of the justices constituting the court by which the decision is made, will announce its decision and—

(a) the reasons for that decision; or

(b) a short explanation of that decision.

(8) Subject to any other rule or practice direction, the court officer will supply a copy of the order and the reasons for the court's decision to the persons referred to in paragraph (9)—

(a) by close of business on the day when the court announces its decision; or

(b) where that time is not practicable and the proceedings are on notice, no later than 72 hours from the time when the court announced its decision.

(9) The persons referred to in paragraph (8) are—

(a) the parties (unless the court directs otherwise);

(b) any person who has actual care of a child who is the subject of proceedings, or who had such care immediately prior to the making of the order;

(c) in the case of an emergency protection order and a recovery order, the local authority in whose area the child lives or is found;

(d) in proceedings to which Part 14 applies—

(i) an adoption agency or local authority which has prepared a report on the suitability of the applicant to adopt a child;

(ii) a local authority which has prepared a report on the placement of the child for adoption;

(e) any other person who has requested a copy if the court is satisfied that it is required in connection with an appeal or possible appeal.

(10) In this rule, "lay justice" means a justice of the peace who is not a District Judge (Magistrates' Courts).

(Rule 12.16(5) provides for the applicant to serve a section 8 order and an order in emergency proceedings made without notice within 48 hours after the making of the order. Rule 10.6(1) provides for the applicant to serve the order in proceedings under Part 4 of the 1996 Act. Rule 4.1(3)(a) permits the court to extend or shorten the time limit for compliance with any rule. Rule 6.33 provides for other persons to be supplied with copy documents under paragraph (8).)

Attendance at hearing or directions appointment

27.3. Unless the court directs otherwise, a party shall attend a hearing or directions appointment of which that party has been given notice.

Proceedings in the absence of a party

27.4.—(1) Proceedings or any part of them shall take place in the absence of any party, including a party who is a child, if—

    (a) the court considers it in the interests of the party, having regard to the matters to be discussed or the evidence likely to be given; and

    (b) the party is represented by a children's guardian or solicitor,

and when considering the interests of a child under sub-paragraph (a) the court shall give the children's guardian, the solicitor for the child and, if of sufficient understanding and the court thinks it appropriate, the child, an opportunity to make representations.

(2) Subject to paragraph (3), where at the time and place appointed for a hearing or directions appointment the applicant appears but one or more of the respondents do not, the court may proceed with the hearing or appointment.

(3) The court shall not begin to hear an application in the absence of a respondent unless—

    (a) it is proved to the satisfaction of the court that the respondent received reasonable notice of the date of the hearing; or

    (b) the court is satisfied that the circumstances of the case justify proceeding with the hearing.

(4) Where, at the time and place appointed for a hearing or directions appointment, one or more of the respondents appear but the applicant does not, the court may refuse the application or, if sufficient evidence has previously been received, proceed in the absence of the applicant.

(5) Where, at the time and place appointed for a hearing or directions appointment, neither the applicant nor any respondent appears, the court may refuse the application.

(6) Paragraphs (2) to (5) do not apply to a hearing to which paragraphs (5) to (8) of rule 12.14 do not apply by virtue of paragraph (9) of that rule.

(7) Nothing in this rule affects any provision of a European regulation or international convention by which the United Kingdom is bound which requires a court to stay proceedings where a respondent in another State has not been adequately served with proceedings in accordance with the requirements of that regulation or convention.

Application to set aside judgment or order following failure to attend

27.5.—(1) Where a party does not attend a hearing or directions appointment and the court gives judgment or makes an order against him, the party who failed to attend may apply for the judgment or order to be set aside^(GL).

(2) An application under paragraph (1) must be supported by evidence.

(3) Where an application is made under paragraph (1), the court may grant the application only if the applicant—

(a) acted promptly on finding out that the court had exercised its power to enter judgment or make an order against the applicant;

(b) had a good reason for not attending the hearing or directions appointment; and

(c) has a reasonable prospect of success at the hearing or directions appointment.

(4) This rule does not apply to magistrates' courts.

Court bundles and place of filing of documents and bundles

27.6.—(1) The provisions of Practice Direction 27A must be followed for the preparation of court bundles and for other related matters in respect of hearings and directions appointments.

(2) Paragraph (3) applies where the file of any family proceedings has been sent from one designated county court or registry to another for the purpose of a hearing or for some other purpose.

(3) A document needed for the purpose for which the proceedings have been sent to the other court or registry must be filed in that court or registry.

(Practice Direction 27A (Family Proceedings: Court Bundles (Universal Practice to be applied in All Courts other than the Family Proceedings Courts)) does not apply to magistrates' courts.)

Representation of companies or other corporations

27.7. A company or other corporation may be represented at a hearing or directions appointment by an employee if—

(a) the employee has been authorised by the company or corporation to appear at the hearing or directions appointment on its behalf; and

(b) the court gives permission.

Impounded documents

27.8.—(1) Documents impounded by order of the court must not be released from the custody of the court except in compliance with—

(a) a court order; or

(b) a written request made by a Law Officer or the Director of Public Prosecutions.

(2) A document released from the custody of the court under paragraph (1)(b) must be released into the custody of the person who requested it.

(3) Documents impounded by order of the court, while in the custody of the court, may not be inspected except by a person authorised to do so by a court order.

Official shorthand note etc of proceedings

27.9.—(1) Unless the judge directs otherwise, an official shorthand note will be taken at the hearing in open court of proceedings pending in the High Court.

(2) An official shorthand note may be taken of any other proceedings before a judge if directions for the taking of such a note are given by the Lord Chancellor.

(3) The shorthand writer will sign the note and certify it to be a correct shorthand note of the proceedings and will retain the note unless directed by the district judge to forward it to the court.

(4) On being so directed, the shorthand writer will furnish the court with a transcript of the whole or such part of the shorthand note as may be directed.

(5) Any party, any person who has intervened in the proceedings, the Queen's Proctor or, where a declaration of parentage has been made under section 55A of the 1986 Act, the Registrar General is entitled to require from the shorthand writer a transcript of the shorthand note, and the shorthand writer will, at the request of any person so entitled, supply that person with a transcript of the whole

or any part of the note on payment of the shorthand writer's charges authorised by any scheme in force providing for the taking of official shorthand notes of legal proceedings.

(6) Save as permitted by this rule, the shorthand writer will not, without the permission of the court, furnish the shorthand note or a transcript of the whole or any part of it to anyone.

(7) In these rules, references to a shorthand note include references to a record of the proceedings made by mechanical means and in relation to such a record references to the shorthand writer include the person responsible for transcribing the record.

Hearings in private

27.10.—(1) Proceedings to which these rules apply will be held in private, except—

  (a) where these rules or any other enactment provide otherwise;

  (b) subject to any enactment, where the court directs otherwise.

(2) For the purposes of these rules, a reference to proceedings held "in private" means proceedings at which the general public have no right to be present.

Attendance at private hearings

27.11.—(1) This rule applies when proceedings are held in private, except in relation to —

  (a) hearings conducted for the purpose of judicially assisted conciliation or negotiation;

  (b) proceedings to which the following provisions apply—

    (i) Part 13 (proceedings under section 54 of the Human Fertilisation and Embryology Act 2008);

    (ii) Part 14 (procedure for applications in adoption, placement and related proceedings); and

    (iii) any proceedings identified in a practice direction as being excepted from this rule.

(2) When this rule applies, no person shall be present during any hearing other than—

  (a) an officer of the court;

  (b) a party to the proceedings;

  (c) a litigation friend for any party, or legal representative instructed to act on that party's behalf;

  (d) an officer of the service or Welsh family proceedings officer;

  (e) a witness;

  (f) duly accredited representatives of news gathering and reporting organisations; and

  (g) any other person whom the court permits to be present.

(3) At any stage of the proceedings the court may direct that persons within paragraph (2)(f) shall not attend the proceedings or any part of them, where satisfied that—

  (a) this is necessary—

    (i) in the interests of any child concerned in, or connected with, the proceedings;

    (ii) for the safety or protection of a party, a witness in the proceedings, or a person connected with such a party or witness; or

    (iii) for the orderly conduct of the proceedings; or

  (b) justice will otherwise be impeded or prejudiced.

(4) The court may exercise the power in paragraph (3) of its own initiative or pursuant to representations made by any of the persons listed in paragraph (5), and in either case having given to any person within paragraph (2)(f) who is in attendance an opportunity to make representations.

(5) At any stage of the proceedings, the following persons may make representations to the court regarding restricting the attendance of persons within paragraph (2)(f) in accordance with paragraph (3)—

(a) a party to the proceedings;

(b) any witness in the proceedings;

(c) where appointed, any children's guardian;

(d) where appointed, an officer of the service or Welsh family proceedings officer, on behalf of the child the subject of the proceedings;

(e) the child, if of sufficient age and understanding.

(6) This rule does not affect any power of the court to direct that witnesses shall be excluded until they are called for examination.

(7) In this rule "duly accredited" refers to accreditation in accordance with any administrative scheme for the time being approved for the purposes of this rule by the Lord Chancellor.

PART 28

COSTS

Costs

28.1. The court may at any time make such order as to costs as it thinks just.

Application of other rules

28.2.—(1) Subject to rule 28.3 and to paragraph (2), Parts 43, 44 (except rules 44.3(2) and (3), 44.9 to 44.12C, 44.13(1A) and (1B) and 44.18 to 20), 47 and 48 and rule 45.6 of the CPR apply to costs in proceedings, with the following modifications—

(a) in rule 43.2(1)(c)(ii), "district judge" includes a district judge of the principal registry;

(b) in rule 48.7(1) after "section 51(6) of the Senior Courts Act 1981" insert "or section 145A of the Magistrates' Courts Act 1980(**a**)";

(c) in accordance with any provisions in Practice Direction 28A; and

(d) any other necessary modifications.

(2) Part 47 and rules 44.3C and 45.6 of the CPR do not apply to proceedings in a magistrates' court.

Costs in financial remedy proceedings

28.3.—(1) This rule applies in relation to financial remedy proceedings.

(2) Rule 44.3(1), (4) and (5) of the CPR do not apply to financial remedy proceedings.

(3) Rule 44.3(6) to (9) of the CPR apply to an order made under this rule as they apply to an order made under rule 44.3 of the CPR.

(4) In this rule –

(a) "costs" has the same meaning as in rule 43.2(1)(a) of the CPR; and

(b) "financial remedy proceedings" means proceedings for—

(i) a financial order except an order for maintenance pending suit, an order for maintenance pending outcome of proceedings, an interim periodical payments order or any other form of interim order for the purposes of rule 9.7(1)(a), (b), (c) and (e);

(ii) an order under Part 3 of the 1984 Act;

(iii) an order under Schedule 7 to the 2004 Act;

(**a**) Section 145A was inserted by section 112 of the Courts and Legal Services Act 1990 and amended by section 24 of and paragraphs 15 and 19 of Schedule 4 to that Act.

(iv) an order under section 10(2) of the 1973 Act(**a**);

(v) an order under section 48(2) of the 2004 Act.

(5) Subject to paragraph (6), the general rule in financial remedy proceedings is that the court will not make an order requiring one party to pay the costs of another party.

(6) The court may make an order requiring one party to pay the costs of another party at any stage of the proceedings where it considers it appropriate to do so because of the conduct of a party in relation to the proceedings (whether before or during them).

(7) In deciding what order (if any) to make under paragraph (6), the court must have regard to—

(a) any failure by a party to comply with these rules, any order of the court or any practice direction which the court considers relevant;

(b) any open offer to settle made by a party;

(c) whether it was reasonable for a party to raise, pursue or contest a particular allegation or issue;

(d) the manner in which a party has pursued or responded to the application or a particular allegation or issue;

(e) any other aspect of a party's conduct in relation to proceedings which the court considers relevant; and

(f) the financial effect on the parties of any costs order.

(8) No offer to settle which is not an open offer to settle is admissible at any stage of the proceedings, except as provided by rule 9.17.

Wasted costs orders in the magistrates' court: appeals

28.4. A legal or other representative against whom a wasted costs order is made in the magistrates' court may appeal to the Crown Court.

PART 29

MISCELLANEOUS

Personal details

29.1.—(1) Unless the court directs otherwise, a party is not required to reveal—

(a) the party's home address or other contact details;

(b) the address or other contact details of any child;

(c) the name of a person with whom the child is living, if that person is not the applicant; or

(d) in relation to an application under section 28(2) of the 2002 Act (application for permission to change the child's surname), the proposed new surname of the child.

(2) Where a party does not wish to reveal any of the particulars in paragraph (1), that party must give notice of those particulars to the court and the particulars will not be revealed to any person unless the court directs otherwise.

(3) Where a party changes home address during the course of proceedings, that party must give notice of the change to the court.

(**a**) Section 10(2) has been prospectively repealed by section 66(3) of and Schedule 10 to the Family Law Act 1996.

Disclosure of information under the 1991 Act

29.2. Where the Commission requires a person mentioned in regulation 3(1), 4(2) or 6(2)(a) of the Child Support Information Regulations 2008(**a**) to furnish information or evidence for a purpose mentioned in regulation 4(1) of those Regulations, nothing in these rules will—

(a) prevent that person from furnishing the information or evidence sought; or

(b) require that person to seek permission of the court before doing so.

Method of giving notice

29.3.—(1) Unless directed otherwise, a notice which is required by these rules to be given to a person must be given—

(a) in writing; and

(b) in a manner in which service may be effected in accordance with Part 6.

(2) Rule 6.33 applies to a notice which is required by these rules to be given to a child as it applies to a document which is to be served on a child.

Withdrawal of applications in proceedings

29.4.—(1) This rule applies to applications in proceedings—

(a) under Part 7;

(b) under Parts 10 to 14 or under any other Part where the application relates to the welfare or upbringing of a child or;

(c) where either of the parties is a protected party.

(2) Where this rule applies, an application may only be withdrawn with the permission of the court.

(3) Subject to paragraph (4), a person seeking permission to withdraw an application must file a written request for permission setting out the reasons for the request.

(4) The request under paragraph (3) may be made orally to the court if the parties are present.

(5) A court officer will notify the other parties of a written request.

(6) The court may deal with a written request under paragraph (3) without a hearing if the other parties, and any other persons directed by the court, have had an opportunity to make written representations to the court about the request.

The Human Rights Act 1998

29.5.—(1) In this rule—

"the 1998 Act" means the Human Rights Act 1998;

"Convention right" has the same meaning as in the 1998 Act; and

"declaration of incompatibility" means a declaration of incompatibility under section 4 of the 1998 Act(**b**).

(2) A party who seeks to rely on any provision of or right arising under the 1998 Act or seeks a remedy available under that Act must inform the court in that party's application or otherwise in writing specifying—

(a) the Convention right which it is alleged has been infringed and details of the alleged infringement; and

---

(**a**) S.I. 2008/2551.
(**b**) Section 4 was amended by section 40(4) of and paragraphs 66(1) and (2) of Schedule 9 to the Constitutional Reform Act 2005 and section 378(1) and paragraph 156 of Schedule 16 to the Armed Forces Act 2006 and section 67(1) of and paragraph 43 of Schedule 6 to the Mental Capacity Act 2005.

(b) the relief sought and whether this includes a declaration of incompatibility.

(3) The High Court may not make a declaration of incompatibility unless 21 days' notice, or such other period of notice as the court directs, has been given to the Crown.

(4) Where notice has been given to the Crown, a Minister, or other person permitted by the 1998 Act, will be joined as a party on giving notice to the court.

(5) Where a claim is made under section 7(1) of the 1998 Act (claim that public authority acted unlawfully) in respect of a judicial act—

(a) that claim must be set out in the application form or the appeal notice; and

(b) notice must be given to the Crown.

(6) Where paragraph (4) applies and the appropriate person (as defined in section 9(5) of the 1998 Act) has not applied within 21 days, or such other period as the court directs, beginning with the date on which the notice to be joined as a party was served, the court may join the appropriate person as a party.

(7) On any application concerning a committal order, if the court ordering the release of the person concludes that that person's Convention rights have been infringed by the making of the order to which the application or appeal relates, the judgment or order should so state, but if the court does not do so, that failure will not prevent another court from deciding the matter.

(8) Where by reason of a rule, practice direction or court order the Crown is permitted or required—

(a) to make a witness statement;

(b) to swear an affidavit$^{(GL)}$;

(c) to verify a document by a statement of truth; or

(d) to discharge any other procedural obligation,

that function will be performed by an appropriate officer acting on behalf of the Crown, and the court may if necessary nominate an appropriate officer.

(Practice Direction 29A (Human Rights – Joining the Crown) makes provision for the notices mentioned in this rule.)

Documents in proceedings concerning gender recognition

29.6.—(1) This rule applies to all documents in proceedings brought under—

(a) section 12(g) or (h) of, or paragraph 11(1)(e) of Schedule 1 to, the 1973 Act(**a**); or

(b) the Gender Recognition Act 2004.

(2) Documents to which this rule applies must, while they are in the custody of the court, be kept in a place of special security.

Stamping or sealing court documents

29.7.—(1) A court officer must, when issuing the following documents, seal$^{(GL)}$, or otherwise authenticate them with the stamp of the court—

(a) the application form;

(b) an order; and

(c) any other document which a rule or practice direction requires the court officer to seal$^{(GL)}$ or stamp.

(2) The court officer may place the seal$^{(GL)}$ or the stamp on the document—

(a) by hand; or

(**a**) Section 12(g) was amended by section 148 of and paragraph 34 of Schedule 4 to the Mental Health Act 1983 and section 4(4) of and paragraphs 1 and 2 of Schedule 2 to the Gender Recognition Act 2004.

(b) by printing a facsimile of the seal$^{(GL)}$ on the document whether electronically or otherwise.

(3) A document purporting to bear the court's seal$^{(GL)}$ or stamp will be admissible in evidence without further proof.

Applications for relief which is precluded by the 1991 Act

29.8.—(1) This rule applies where an application is made for an order which, in the opinion of the court, it would be prevented from making under section 8 or 9 of the 1991 Act and in this rule, "the matter" means the question of whether or not the court would be so prevented.

(2) The court will consider the matter without holding a hearing.

(3) Where the court officer receives the opinion of the court, as mentioned in paragraph (1), the court officer must send a notice to the applicant of that opinion.

(4) Paragraphs (5) to (11) apply where the court officer sends a notice under paragraph (3).

(5) Subject to paragraph (6), no requirement of these rules apply except the requirements—

(a) of this rule;

(b) as to service of the application by the court officer; and

(c) as to any procedural step to be taken following the making of an application of the type in question.

(6) The court may direct that the requirements of these rules apply, or apply to such extent or with such modifications as are set out in the direction.

(7) If the applicant informs the court officer, within 14 days of the date of the notice, that the applicant wishes to persist with the application, the court will give appropriate directions for the matter to be heard and determined and may provide for the hearing to be without notice.

(8) Where directions are given in accordance with paragraph (7), the court officer must—

(a) inform the applicant of the directions;

(b) send a copy of the application to the other parties;

(c) if the hearing is to be without notice, inform the other parties briefly—

(i) of the nature and effect of the notice given to the applicant under paragraph (3);

(ii) that the matter is being resolved without a hearing on notice; and

(iii) that they will be notified of the result; and

(d) if the hearing is to be on notice, inform the other parties of—

(i) the circumstances which led to the directions being given; and

(ii) the directions.

(9) If the applicant does not inform the court officer as mentioned in paragraph (7), the application shall be treated as having been withdrawn.

(10) Where—

(a) the matter is heard in accordance with directions given under paragraph (7); and

(b) the court determines that it would be prevented, under section 8 or 9 of the 1991 Act, from making the order sought by the applicant,

the court will dismiss the application.

(11) Where the court dismisses the application—

(a) the court must give its reasons in writing; and

(b) the court officer must send a copy of the reasons to the parties.

Modification of rule 29.8 where the application is not freestanding

29.9.—(1) Where the court officer sends a notice under rule 29.8(3) in relation to an application which is contained in another document ("the document") which contains material extrinsic to the application—

    (a) subject to paragraph (2), the document will be treated as if it did not contain the application in respect of which the notice was served; and

    (b) the court officer, when sending copies of the documents to the respondents under any provision of these rules, must attach—

        (i) a copy of the notice under rule 29.8(3); and

       (ii) a notice informing the respondents of the effect of paragraph (1)(a).

(2) If the court determines that it is not prevented by section 8 or 9 of the 1991 Act from making the order sought by the application, the court—

    (a) must direct that the document shall be treated as if it contained the application; and

    (b) may give such directions as it considers appropriate for the subsequent conduct of the proceedings.

Standard requirements

29.10.—(1) Every judgment or order must state the name and judicial title of the person who made it.

(2) Every judgment or order must—

    (a) bear the date on which it is given or made; and

    (b) be sealed$^{(GL)}$ by the court.

Drawing up and filing of judgments and orders

29.11.—(1) Except as provided by a rule or a practice direction, every judgment or order will be drawn up by the court unless—

    (a) the court orders a party to draw it up;

    (b) a party, with the permission of the court, agrees to draw it up; or

    (c) the court dispenses with the need to draw it up.

(2) The court may direct that—

    (a) a judgment or an order drawn up by a party must be checked by the court before it is sealed$^{(GL)}$; or

    (b) before a judgment or an order is drawn up by the court, the parties must file an agreed statement of its terms.

(3) Where a judgment or an order is to be drawn up by a party—

    (a) that party must file it no later than 7 days after the date on which the court ordered or gave permission for the order to be drawn up so that it can be sealed by the court; and

    (b) if that party fails to file it within that period, any other party may draw it up and file it.

Copies of orders made in open court

29.12. A copy of an order made in open court will be issued to any person who requests it on payment of the prescribed fee.

Service of judgments and orders

29.13.—(1) The court officer must, unless the court directs otherwise, serve a copy of a judgment or an order made in family proceedings to every party affected by it.

(2) Where a judgment or an order has been drawn up by a party and is to be served by the court officer the party who drew it up must file a copy to be retained at court and sufficient copies for service on all the parties.

(3) A party in whose favour an order is made need not prove that a copy of the order has reached a party to whom it is required to be sent under this rule.

(4) This rule does not affect the operation of any rule or enactment which requires an order to be served in a particular way

Power to require judgment or order to be served on a party as well as the party's solicitor

29.14. Where the party on whom a judgment or order is served is acting by a solicitor, the court may order the judgment or order to be served on the party as well as on the party's solicitor.

When judgment or order takes effect

29.15. A judgment or order takes effect from the day when it is given or made, or such later date as the court may specify.

Correction of errors in judgments and orders

29.16.—(1) The court may at any time correct an accidental slip or omission in a judgment or order.

(2) A party may apply for a correction without notice.

PART 30

APPEALS

Scope and interpretation

30.1.—(1) The rules in this Part apply to appeals to—

  (a) the High Court; and

  (b) a county court.

(2) This Part does not apply to an appeal in detailed assessment proceedings against a decision of an authorised court officer.

(Rules 47.20 to 47.23 of the CPR deal with appeals against a decision of an authorised court officer in detailed assessment proceedings.)

(3) In this Part—

  "appeal court" means the court to which an appeal is made;

  "appeal notice" means an appellant's or respondent's notice;

  "appellant" means a person who brings or seeks to bring an appeal;

  "lower court" means the court from which, or the person from whom, the appeal lies; and

  "respondent" means—

  (a) a person other than the appellant who was a party to the proceedings in the lower court and who is affected by the appeal; and

  (b) a person who is permitted by the appeal court to be a party to the appeal.

(4) This Part is subject to any rule, enactment or practice direction which sets out special provisions with regard to any particular category of appeal.

Parties to comply with the practice direction

30.2. All parties to an appeal must comply with Practice Direction 30A.

Permission

30.3.—(1) An appellant or respondent requires permission to appeal—

(a) against a decision in proceedings where the decision appealed against was made by a district judge or a costs judge, unless paragraph (2) applies; or

(b) as provided by Practice Direction 30A.

(2) Permission to appeal is not required where the appeal is against—

(a) a committal order; or

(b) a secure accommodation order under section 25 of the 1989 Act.

(3) An application for permission to appeal may be made—

(a) to the lower court at the hearing at which the decision to be appealed was made; or

(b) to the appeal court in an appeal notice.

(Rule 30.4 sets out the time limits for filing an appellant's notice at the appeal court. Rule 30.5 sets out the time limits for filing a respondent's notice at the appeal court. Any application for permission to appeal to the appeal court must be made in the appeal notice (see rules 30.4(1) and 30.5(3).)

(4) Where the lower court refuses an application for permission to appeal, a further application for permission to appeal may be made to the appeal court.

(5) Where the appeal court, without a hearing, refuses permission to appeal, the person seeking permission may request the decision to be reconsidered at a hearing.

(6) A request under paragraph (5) must be filed within 7 days beginning with the date on which the notice that permission has been refused was served.

(7) Permission to appeal may be given only where—

(a) the court considers that the appeal would have a real prospect of success; or

(b) there is some other compelling reason why the appeal should be heard.

(8) An order giving permission may—

(a) limit the issues to be heard; and

(b) be made subject to conditions.

(9) In this rule "costs judge" means a taxing master of the Senior Courts.

Appellant's notice

30.4.—(1) Where the appellant seeks permission from the appeal court it must be requested in the appellant's notice.

(2) Subject to paragraph (3), the appellant must file the appellant's notice at the appeal court within —

(a) such period as may be directed by the lower court (which may be longer or shorter than the period referred to in sub-paragraph (b)); or

(b) where the court makes no such direction, 21 days after the date of the decision of the lower court against which the appellant wishes to appeal.

(3) Where the appeal is against an order under section 38(1) of the 1989 Act, the appellant must file the appellant's notice within 7 days beginning with the date of the decision of the lower court.

(4) Unless the appeal court orders otherwise, an appellant's notice must be served on each respondent and the persons referred to in paragraph (5)—

(a) as soon as practicable; and

(b) in any event not later than 7 days,

after it is filed.

(5) The persons referred to in paragraph (4) are—

(a) any children's guardian, welfare officer, or children and family reporter;

(b) a local authority who has prepared a report under section 14A(8) or (9) of the 1989 Act;

(c) an adoption agency or local authority which has prepared a report on the suitability of the applicant to adopt a child;

(d) a local authority which has prepared a report on the placement of the child for adoption; and

(e) where the appeal is from a magistrates' court, the court officer.

Respondent's notice

30.5.—(1) A respondent may file and serve a respondent's notice.

(2) A respondent who—

(a) is seeking permission to appeal from the appeal court; or

(b) wishes to ask the appeal court to uphold the order of the lower court for reasons different from or additional to those given by the lower court,

must file a respondent's notice.

(3) Where the respondent seeks permission from the appeal court it must be requested in the respondent's notice.

(4) A respondent's notice must be filed within—

(a) such period as may be directed by the lower court; or

(b) where the court makes no such direction, 14 days beginning with the date referred to in paragraph (5).

(5) The date referred to in paragraph (4) is—

(a) the date on which the respondent is served with the appellant's notice where—

(i) permission to appeal was given by the lower court; or

(ii) permission to appeal is not required;

(b) the date on which the respondent is served with notification that the appeal court has given the appellant permission to appeal; or

(c) the date on which the respondent is served with notification that the application for permission to appeal and the appeal itself are to be heard together.

(6) Unless the appeal court orders otherwise, a respondent's notice must be served on the appellant, any other respondent and the persons referred to in rule 30.4(5)—

(a) as soon as practicable; and

(b) in any event not later than 7 days,

after it is filed.

(7) Where there is an appeal against an order under section 38(1) of the 1989 Act—

(a) a respondent may not, in that appeal, bring an appeal from the order or ask the appeal court to uphold the order of the lower court for reasons different from or additional to those given by the lower court; and

(b) paragraphs (2) and (3) do not apply.

Grounds of appeal

30.6. The appeal notice must state the grounds of appeal.

Variation of time

30.7.—(1) An application to vary the time limit for filing an appeal notice must be made to the appeal court.

(2) The parties may not agree to extend any date or time limit set by—

    (a) these rules;

    (b) Practice Direction 30A; or

    (c) an order of the appeal court or the lower court.

(Rule 4.1(3)(a) provides that the court may extend or shorten the time for compliance with a rule, practice direction or court order (even if an application for extension is made after the time for compliance has expired).)

(Rule 4.1(3)(c) provides that the court may adjourn or bring forward a hearing.)

Stay

30.8. Unless the appeal court or the lower court orders otherwise, an appeal does not operate as a stay$^{(GL)}$ of any order or decision of the lower court.

Amendment of appeal notice

30.9. An appeal notice may not be amended without the permission of the appeal court.

Striking out appeal notices and setting aside or imposing conditions on permission to appeal

30.10.—(1) The appeal court may—

    (a) strike out$^{(GL)}$ the whole or part of an appeal notice;

    (b) set aside$^{(GL)}$ permission to appeal in whole or in part;

    (c) impose or vary conditions upon which an appeal may be brought.

(2) The court will only exercise its powers under paragraph (1) where there is a compelling reason for doing so.

(3) Where a party was present at the hearing at which permission was given that party may not subsequently apply for an order that the court exercise its powers under paragraphs (1)(b) or (1)(c).

Appeal court's powers

30.11.—(1) In relation to an appeal the appeal court has all the powers of the lower court.

(Rule 30.1(4) provides that this Part is subject to any enactment that sets out special provisions with regard to any particular category of appeal.)

(2) The appeal court has power to—

    (a) affirm, set aside$^{(GL)}$ or vary any order or judgment made or given by the lower court;

    (b) refer any application or issue for determination by the lower court;

    (c) order a new hearing;

    (d) make orders for the payment of interest;

    (e) make a costs order.

(3) The appeal court may exercise its powers in relation to the whole or part of an order of the lower court.

(Rule 4.1 contains general rules about the court's case management powers.)

(4) If the appeal court—

    (a) refuses an application for permission to appeal;

    (b) strikes out an appellant's notice; or

(c) dismisses an appeal,

and it considers that the application, the appellant's notice or the appeal is totally without merit, the provisions of paragraph (5) must be complied with.

(5) Where paragraph (4) applies—

(a) the court's order must record the fact that it considers the application, the appellant's notice or the appeal to be totally without merit; and

(b) the court must at the same time consider whether it is appropriate to make a civil restraint order.

Hearing of appeals

30.12.—(1) Every appeal will be limited to a review of the decision of the lower court unless—

(a) an enactment or practice direction makes different provision for a particular category of appeal; or

(b) the court considers that in the circumstances of an individual appeal it would be in the interests of justice to hold a re-hearing.

(2) Unless it orders otherwise, the appeal court will not receive—

(a) oral evidence; or

(b) evidence which was not before the lower court.

(3) The appeal court will allow an appeal where the decision of the lower court was—

(a) wrong; or

(b) unjust because of a serious procedural or other irregularity in the proceedings in the lower court.

(4) The appeal court may draw any inference of fact which it considers justified on the evidence.

(5) At the hearing of the appeal a party may not rely on a matter not contained in that party's appeal notice unless the appeal court gives permission.

Assignment of appeals to the Court of Appeal

30.13.—(1) Where the court from or to which an appeal is made or from which permission to appeal is sought ("the relevant court") considers that—

(a) an appeal which is to be heard by a county court or the High Court would raise an important point of principle or practice; or

(b) there is some other compelling reason for the Court of Appeal to hear it,

the relevant court may order the appeal to be transferred to the Court of Appeal.

(2) This rule does not apply to proceedings in a magistrates' court.

Reopening of final appeals

30.14.—(1) The High Court will not reopen a final determination of any appeal unless—

(a) it is necessary to do so in order to avoid real injustice;

(b) the circumstances are exceptional and make it appropriate to reopen the appeal; and

(c) there is no alternative effective remedy.

(2) In paragraphs (1), (3), (4) and (6), "appeal" includes an application for permission to appeal.

(3) This rule does not apply to appeals to a county court.

(4) Permission is needed to make an application under this rule to reopen a final determination of an appeal.

(5) There is no right to an oral hearing of an application for permission unless, exceptionally, the judge so directs.

(6) The judge will not grant permission without directing the application to be served on the other party to the original appeal and giving that party an opportunity to make representations.

(7) There is no right of appeal or review from the decision of the judge on the application for permission, which is final.

(8) The procedure for making an application for permission is set out in Practice Direction 30A.

PART 31

REGISTRATION OF ORDERS UNDER THE COUNCIL REGULATION, THE CIVIL PARTNERSHIP (JURISDICTION AND RECOGNITION OF JUDGMENTS) REGULATIONS 2005 AND UNDER THE HAGUE CONVENTION 1996

Scope

31.1. This Part applies to proceedings for the recognition, non-recognition and registration of—

(a) judgments to which the Council Regulation applies;

(b) measures to which the 1996 Hague Convention applies; and

(c) judgments to which the Jurisdiction and Recognition of Judgments Regulations apply, and which relate to dissolution or annulment of overseas relationships entitled to be treated as a civil partnership, or legal separation of the same.

Interpretation

31.2.—(1) In this Part —

(a) "judgment" is to be construed —

  (i) in accordance with the definition in Article 2(4) of the Council Regulation where it applies;

  (ii) in accordance with regulation 6 of the Jurisdiction and Recognition of Judgments Regulations where those Regulations apply; or

  (iii) as meaning any measure taken by an authority with jurisdiction under Chapter II of the 1996 Hague Convention where that Convention applies;

(b) "the Jurisdiction and Recognition of Judgments Regulations" means the Civil Partnership (Jurisdiction and Recognition of Judgments) Regulations 2005(**a**);

(c) "Member State" means —

  (i) where registration, recognition or non-recognition is sought of a judgment under the Council Regulation, a Member State of the European Union which is bound by that Regulation or a country which has subsequently adopted it;

  (ii) where recognition is sought of a judgment to which the Jurisdiction and Recognition of Judgments Regulations apply, a Member State of the European Union to which Part II of those Regulations applies;

(d) "Contracting State" means a State, other than a Member State within the meaning of (c) above, in relation to which the 1996 Hague Convention is in force as between that State and the United Kingdom; and

(e) "parental responsibility" —

  (i) where the Council Regulation applies, has the meaning given in Article 2(7) of that Regulation; and

---

(**a**) S.I. 2005/3334.

(ii) where the 1996 Hague Convention applies, has the meaning given in Article 1(2) of that Convention.

(2) References in this Part to registration are to the registration of a judgment in accordance with the provisions of this Part.

Where to start proceedings

31.3.—(1) Every application under this Part, except for an application under rule 31.18 for a certified copy of a judgment, or under rule 31.20 for rectification of a certificate issued under Articles 41 or 42, must be made to the principal registry.

(2) Nothing in this rule prevents the determination of an issue of recognition as an incidental question by any court in proceedings, in accordance with Article 21(4) of the Council Regulation.

(3) Notwithstanding paragraph (1), where recognition of a judgment is raised as an incidental question in proceedings under the 1996 Hague Convention or the Jurisdiction and Recognition of Judgments Regulations the court hearing those proceedings may determine the question of recognition.

Application for registration, recognition or non-recognition of a judgment

31.4.—(1) Any interested person may apply to the court for an order that the judgment be registered, recognised or not recognised.

(2) Except for an application under rule 31.7, an application for registration, recognition or non-recognition must be —

(a) made to a district judge of the principal registry; and

(b) in the form, and supported by the documents and the information required by a practice direction.

Documents – supplementary

31.5.—(1) Except as regards a copy of a judgment required by Article 37(1)(a) of the Council Regulation, where the person making an application under this Part does not produce the documents required by rule 31.4(2)(b) the court may —

(a) fix a time within which the documents are to be produced;

(b) accept equivalent documents; or

(c) dispense with production of the documents if the court considers it has sufficient information.

(2) This rule does not apply to applications under rule 31.7.

Directions

31.6.—(1) As soon as practicable after an application under this Part has been made, the court may (subject to the requirements of the Council Regulation) give such directions as it considers appropriate, including as regards the following matters —

(a) whether service of the application may be dispensed with;

(b) expedition of the proceedings or any part of the proceedings (and any direction for expedition may specify a date by which the court must give its decision);

(c) the steps to be taken in the proceedings and the time by which each step is to be taken;

(d) the service of documents; and

(e) the filing of evidence.

(2) The court or court officer will —

(a) record the giving, variation or revocation of directions under this rule; and

(b)   as soon as practicable serve a copy of the directions order on every party.

Recognition and enforcement under the Council Regulation of a judgment given in another Member State relating to rights of access or under Article 11(8) for the return of the child to that State

31.7.—(1) This rule applies where a judgment has been given in another Member State —

(a)   relating to rights of access: or

(b)   under Article 11(8) of the Council Regulation for the return of a child to that State,

which has been certified, in accordance with Article 41(2) or 42(2) as the case may be, by the judge in the court of origin.

(2) An application for recognition or enforcement of the judgment must be —

(a)   made in writing to a district judge of the principal registry; and

(b)   accompanied by a copy of the certificate issued by the judge in the court of origin.

(3) The application may be made without notice.

(4) Rules 31.5 and 31.8 to 31.17 do not apply to an application made under this rule.

(5) Nothing in this rule shall prevent a holder of parental responsibility from seeking recognition and enforcement of a judgment in accordance with the provisions of rules 31.8 to 31.17.

Registration for enforcement or order for non-recognition of a judgment

31.8.—(1) This rule applies where an application is made for an order that a judgment given in another Member State, or a Contracting State, should be registered, or should not be recognised, except where rule 31.7 applies.

(2) where the application is made for an order that the judgment should be registered —

(a)   upon receipt of the application, and subject to any direction given by the court under rule 31.6, the court officer will serve the application on the person against whom registration is sought;

(b)   the court will not accept submissions from either the person against whom registration is sought or any child in relation to whom the judgment was given.

(3) Where the application is for an order that the judgment should not be recognised —

(a)   upon receipt of the application, and subject to any direction given by the court under rule 31.6, the court officer will serve the application on the person in whose favour judgment was given;

(b)   the person in whose favour the judgment was given must file an answer to the application and serve it on the applicant —

(i)   within 1 month of service of the application; or

(ii)   if the applicant is habitually resident in another Member State, within two months of service of the application.

(4) In cases to which the 1996 Hague Convention applies and the Council Regulation does not apply, the court may extend the time set out in subparagraph (3)(b)(ii) on account of distance.

(5) The person in whose favour the judgment was given may request recognition or registration of the judgment in their answer, and in that event must comply with 31.4(2)(b), to the extent that such documents, information and evidence are not already contained in the application for non-recognition.

(6) If, in a case to which the Council Regulation applies, the person in whose favour the judgment was given fails to file an answer as required by paragraph (3), the court will act in accordance with the provisions of Article 18 of the Council Regulation.

(7) If, in a case to which the 1996 Hague Convention applies and the Service Regulation does not, the person in whose favour the judgment was given fails to file a answer as required by paragraph (3) —

(a) where the Hague Convention of 15th November 1965 on the service abroad of judicial and extrajudicial documents in civil or commercial matters applies, the court shall apply Article 15 of that Convention; and

(b) in all other cases, the court will not consider the application unless —

(i) it is proved to the satisfaction of the court that the person in whose favour judgment was given was served with the application within a reasonable period of time to arrange his or her response; or

(ii) the court is satisfied that the circumstances of the case justify proceeding with consideration of the application.

(8) In a case to which the Jurisdiction and Recognition of Judgments Regulations apply, if the person in whose favour judgment was given fails to file an answer as required by paragraph (3), the court will apply the Service Regulation where that regulation applies, and if it does not —

(a) where the Hague Convention of 15th November 1965 on the service abroad of judicial and extrajudicial documents in civil or commercial matters applies, the court shall apply Article 15 of that Convention; and

(b) in all other cases, the court will apply the provisions of paragraph (7)(b).

Stay of recognition proceedings by reason of an appeal

31.9. Where recognition or non-recognition of a judgment given in another Member State or Contracting State is sought, or is raised as an incidental question in other proceedings, the court may stay the proceedings —

(a) if an ordinary appeal against the judgment has been lodged; or

(b) if the judgment was given in the Republic of Ireland, if enforcement of the judgment is suspended there by reason of an appeal.

Effect of refusal of application for a decision that a judgment should not be recognised

31.10. Where the court refuses an application for a decision that a judgment should not be recognised, the court may —

(a) direct that the decision to refuse the application is to be treated as a decision that the judgment be recognised; or

(b) treat the answer under paragraph (3)(b) of rule 31.8 as an application that the judgment be registered for enforcement if paragraph (5) of that rule is complied with and order that the judgment be registered for enforcement in accordance with rule 31.11.

Notification of the court's decision on an application for registration or non-recognition

31.11.—(1) Where the court has —

(a) made an order on an application for an order that a judgment should be registered for enforcement; or

(b) refused an application that a judgment should not be recognised and ordered under rule 31.10 that the judgment be registered for enforcement,

the court officer will as soon as practicable take the appropriate action under paragraph (2) or (3).

(2) If the court refuses the application for the judgment to be registered for enforcement, the court officer will serve the order on the applicant and the person against whom judgment was given in the state of origin.

(3) If the court orders that the judgment should be registered for enforcement, the court officer will —

(a) register the judgment in the central index of judgments kept by the principal registry;

(b) confirm on the order that the judgment has been registered; and

(c) serve on the parties the court's order endorsed with the court officer's confirmation that the judgment has been registered.

(4) A sealed order of the court endorsed in accordance with paragraph (3)(b) will constitute notification that the judgment has been registered under Article 28(2) of the Council Regulation or under Article 26 of the 1996 Hague Convention, as the case may be, and in this Part "notice of registration" means a sealed order so endorsed.

(5) The notice of registration must state —

(a) full particulars of the judgment registered and the order for registration;

(b) the name of the party making the application and his address for service within the jurisdiction;

(c) the right of the person against whom judgment was given to appeal against the order for registration; and

(d) the period within which an appeal against the order for registration may be made.

Effect of registration under rule 31.11

31.12. Registration of a judgment under rule 31.11 will serve for the purpose of Article 21(3) of the Council Regulation, Article 24 of the 1996 Hague Convention, or regulation 7 of the Jurisdiction and Recognition of Judgments Regulations (as the case may be) as a decision that the judgment is recognised.

The central index of judgments registered under rule 31.11

31.13. The central index of judgments registered under rule 31.11will be kept by the principal registry.

Decision on recognition of a judgment only

31.14.—(1) Where an application is made seeking recognition of a judgment only, the provisions of rules 31.8 and 31.9 apply to that application as they do to an application for registration for enforcement.

(2) Where the court orders that the judgment should be recognised, the court officer will serve a copy of the order on each party as soon as practicable.

(3) A sealed order of the court will constitute notification that the judgment has been recognised under Article 21(3) of the Council Regulation, Article 24 of the 1996 Hague convention or regulation 7 of the Jurisdiction and Recognition of Judgments Regulations, as the case may be.

(4) The sealed order shall indicate —

(a) full particulars of the judgment recognised;

(b) the name of the party making the application and his address for service within the jurisdiction;

(c) the right of the person against whom judgment was given to appeal against the order for recognition; and

(d) the period within which an appeal against the order for recognition may be made.

Appeal against the court's decision under rules 31.10, 31.11 or 31.14

31.15.—(1) An appeal against the court's decision under rules 31.10, 31.11 or 31.14 must be made to a judge of the High Court —

(a) within one month of the date of service of the notice of registration; or

(b) if the party bringing the appeal is habitually resident in another Member State, or a Contracting State, within two months of the date of service.

(2) The court may not extend time for an appeal on account of distance unless the matter is one to which the 1996 Hague Convention applies and the Council Regulation does not apply.

(3) If, in a case to which the 1996 Hague Convention applies and the Service Regulation does not, the appeal is brought by the applicant for a declaration of enforceability or registration and the respondent fails to appear —

(a) where the Hague Convention of 15th November 1965 on the service abroad of judicial and extrajudicial documents in civil or commercial matters applies, the court shall apply Article 15 of that Convention; and

(b) in all other cases, the court will not consider the appeal unless —

(i) it is proved to the satisfaction of the court that the respondent was served with notice of the appeal within a reasonable period of time to arrange his or her response; or

(ii) the court is satisfied that the circumstances of the case justify proceeding with consideration of the appeal.

(4) This rule is subject to rule 31.16.

(The procedure for applications under rule 31.15 is set out in Practice Direction 30A (Appeals).)

Stay of enforcement where appeal pending in state of origin

31.16.—(1) A party against whom enforcement is sought of a judgment which has been registered under rule 31.11 may apply to the court with which an appeal is lodged under rule 31.15 for the proceedings to be stayed where —

(a) that party has lodged an ordinary appeal in the Member State or Contracting State of origin; or

(b) the time for such an appeal has not yet expired.

(2) Where an application for a stay is filed in the circumstances described in paragraph (1)(b), the court may specify the time within which an appeal must be lodged.

Enforcement of judgments registered under rule 31.11

31.17.—(1) The court will not enforce a judgment registered under rule 31.11 until after —

(a) the expiration of any applicable period under rules 31.15 or 31.16; or

(b) if that period has been extended by the court, the expiration of the period so extended.

(2) A party applying to the court for the enforcement of a registered judgment must produce to the court a certificate of service of —

(a) the notice of registration of the judgment; and

(b) any order made by the court in relation to the judgment.

(Service out of the jurisdiction, including service in accordance with the Service Regulation, is dealt with in chapter 4 of Part 6 and in Practice Direction 6B.)

Request for a certificate or a certified copy of a judgment

31.18.—(1) An application for a certified copy of a judgment, or for a certificate under Articles 39, 41 or 42 of the Council Regulation, must be made to the court which made the order or judgment in respect of which certification is sought and without giving notice to any other party.

(2) The application must be made in the form, and supported by the documents and information required by a practice direction.

(3) The certified copy of the judgment will be an office copy sealed with the seal of the court and signed by the district judge, or by the court where the application is made to the Magistrates' Court.

It will be issued with a certified copy of any order which has varied any of the terms of the original order.

(4) Where the application is made for the purposes of applying for recognition or recognition and enforcement of the order in another Contracting State, the court must indicate on the certified copy of the judgment the grounds on which it based its jurisdiction to make the order, for the purposes of Article 23(2)(a) of the 1996 Hague Convention.

Certificates issued in England and Wales under Articles 41 and 42 of the Council Regulation

31.19. The court officer will serve —

    (a)   a certificate issued under Article 41 or 42; or

    (b)   a certificate rectified under rule 31.20,

on all parties and will transmit a copy to the Central Authority for England and Wales.

Rectification of certificate issued under Article 41 or 42 of the Council Regulation

31.20.—(1) Where there is an error in a certificate issued under Article 41 or 42, an application to rectify that error must be made to the court which issued the certificate.

(2) A rectification under paragraph (1) may be made —

    (a)   by the court of its own initiative; or

    (b)   on application by —

        (i)   any party to the proceedings; or

        (ii)   the court or Central Authority of another Member State.

(3) An application under paragraph (2)(b) may be made without notice being served on any other party.

Authentic instruments and agreements under Article 46 of the Council Regulation

31.21. This Chapter applies to an authentic instrument and an agreement to which Article 46 of the Council Regulation applies as it applies to a judgment.

Application for provisional, including protective measures.

31.22. An application for provisional, including protective, measures under Article 20 of the Council Regulation or Articles 11 or 12 of the 1996 Hague Convention may be made notwithstanding that the time for appealing against an order for registration of a judgment has not expired or that a final determination of any issue relating to enforcement of the judgment is pending.

PART 32

REGISTRATION AND ENFORCEMENT OF ORDERS

CHAPTER 1

SCOPE AND INTERPRETATION OF THIS PART

Scope and interpretation

32.1.—(1) This Part contains rules about the registration and enforcement of maintenance orders and custody orders.

(2) In this Part—

"the 1950 Act" means the Maintenance Orders Act 1950(**a**);

"the 1958 Act" means the Maintenance Orders Act 1958(**b**).

(3) Chapter 2 of this Part relates to—

    (a) the registration of a maintenance order, made in the High Court or a county court, in a court in Scotland or Northern Ireland in accordance with the 1950 Act; and

    (b) the registration of a maintenance order, made in Scotland or Northern Ireland, in the High Court in accordance with the 1950 Act.

(Provision in respect of proceedings in the magistrates' court under the 1950 Act is in rules made under section 144 of the Magistrates' Courts Act 1980).

(4) Chapter 3 of this Part contains rules to be applied in the High Court or a county court in relation—

    (a) The registration of a maintenance order, made in the Hight Court or a county court, in a magistrates' court in accordance with the 1958 Act; and

    (b) The registration of a maintenance order, made in a magistrates' court, in the High Court in accordance with the 1958 Act.

(Provision in respect of proceedings in the magistrates' court under the 1958 Act is in rules made under section 144 of the Magistrates' Courts Act 1980).

(5) Chapter 4 of this Part relates to the registration and enforcement of custody orders in accordance with the 1986 Act.

CHAPTER 2

REGISTRATION ETC. OF ORDERS UNDER THE 1950 ACT

SECTION 1

Interpretation of this Chapter

Interpretation

32.2. In this Chapter—

"the clerk of the Court of Session" means the deputy principal clerk in charge of the petition department of the Court of Session;

"county court order" means a maintenance order made in a county court;

"High Court order" means a maintenance order made in the High Court;

"maintenance order" means a maintenance order to which section 16 of the 1950 Act applies;

"Northern Irish order" means a maintenance order made by the Court of Judicature of Northern Ireland;

"the register" means the register kept for the purposes of the 1950 Act;

"the registrar in Northern Ireland" means the chief registrar of the Queen's Bench Division (Matrimonial) of the High Court of Justice in Northern Ireland;

"registration" means registration under Part 2 of the 1950 Act and "registered" is to be construed accordingly; and

"Scottish Order" means a maintenance order made by the Court of Session.

(**a**) 1950 c.37.
(**b**) 1958 c.39.

Registration etc of High Court and county court orders

Registration of a High Court order

32.3.—(1) An application for the registration of a High Court order may be made by sending to a court officer at the court which made the order—

    (a) a certified copy of the order; and

    (b) a statement which—

        (i) contains the address in the United Kingdom, and the occupation, of the person liable to make payments under the order;

        (ii) contains the date on which the order was served on the person liable to make payments, or, if the order has not been served, the reason why service has not been effected;

        (iii) contains the reason why it is convenient for the order to be enforced in Scotland or Northern Ireland, as the case may be;

        (iv) contains the amount of any arrears due to the applicant under the order;

        (v) confirms that the order is not already registered; and

        (vi) is verified by a statement of truth.

(2) If it appears to the court that—

    (a) the person liable to make payments under the order resides in Scotland or Northern Ireland; and

    (b) it is convenient for the order to be enforced there,

the court officer will send the documents filed under paragraph (1) to the clerk of the Court of Session or to the registrar in Northern Ireland, as the case may be.

(3) On receipt of a notice of the registration of a High Court order in the Court of Session or the Court of Judicature of Northern Ireland, the court officer (who is the prescribed officer for the purposes of section 17(4) of the 1950 Act) will—

    (a) enter particulars of the notice of registration in the register;

    (b) note the fact of registration in the court records; and

    (c) send particulars of the notice to the principal registry.

Notice of Variation etc. of a High Court order

32.4.—(1) This rule applies where a High Court order, which is registered in the Court of Session or the Court of Judicature of Northern Ireland, is discharged or varied.

(2) A court officer in the court where the order was discharged or varied will send a certified copy of that order to the clerk of the Court of Session or the registrar in Northern Ireland, as the case may be.

Cancellation of registration of a High Court order

32.5.—(1) This rule applies where—

    (a) the registration of a High Court order registered in the Court of Session or the Court of Judicature of Northern Ireland is cancelled under section 24(1) of the 1950 Act; and

(b) notice of the cancellation is given to a court officer in the court in which the order was made (who is the prescribed officer for the purposes of section 24(3)(a) of the 1950 Act(**a**)).

(2) On receipt of a notice of cancellation of registration, the court officer will enter particulars of the notice in Part 1 of the register.

Application of this Chapter to a county court order

32.6. Rules 32.3 to 32.5 apply to an application to register a county court order as if—

(a) references to a High Court order were references to a county court order;

(b) where the order is to be registered in Scotland, references to the Court of Session and the clerk of the Court of Session were references to the sheriff court and the sheriff-clerk of the sheriff court respectively; and

(c) where the order is to be registered in Northern Ireland, references to the Court of Judicature of Northern Ireland and the registrar of Northern Ireland were references to the court of summary jurisdiction and the clerk of the court of summary jurisdiction respectively.

SECTION 3

Registration etc. of Scottish and Northern Irish orders

Registration of Scottish and Northern Irish orders

32.7. On receipt of a certified copy of a Scottish order or a Northern Irish order for registration, a court officer in the principal registry (who is the prescribed officer for the purposes of section 17(2) of the 1950 Act) will—

(a) enter particulars of the order in Part 2 of the register;

(b) notify the clerk of the Court of Session or the registrar in Northern Ireland, as the case may be, that the order has been registered; and

(c) file the certified copy of the order and any statutory declaration, affidavit$^{(GL)}$ or statement as to the amount of any arrears due under the order.

Application to adduce evidence before High Court

32.8. The Part 18 procedure applies to an application by a person liable to make payments under a Scottish order registered in the High Court to adduce before that court any evidence on which that person would be entitled to rely in any proceedings brought before the court by which the order was made for the variation or discharge of the order.

Notice of variation etc. of Scottish and Northern Irish orders

32.9.—(1) This rule applies where—

(a) a Scottish order or a Northern Irish order, which is registered in the High Court, is discharged or varied; and

(b) notice of the discharge or variation is given to a court officer in the High Court (who is the prescribed officer for the purposes of section 23(1)(a) of the 1950 Act(**b**)).

(2) On receipt of a notice of discharge or variation, the court officer will enter particulars of the notice in Part 2 of the register.

(**a**) Section 24(3)(a) was amended by section 3 of and paragraph 9 of Schedule 3 to the Administration of Justice Act 1977 (c.38).

(**b**) Section 23(1)(a) was amended by section 3 of and paragraph 8 of Schedule 3 to the Administration of Justice Act 1977.

Cancellation of registration of Scottish and Northern Irish orders

32.10.—(1) The Part 18 procedure applies to an application for the cancellation of the registration of a Scottish order or a Northern Irish order in the High Court.

(2) The application must be made without notice to the person liable to make payments under the order.

(3) If the registration of the order is cancelled, the court officer will—

    (a) note the cancellation in Part II of the register; and

    (b) send written notice of the cancellation to—

        (i) the clerk of the Court of Session or the registrar in Northern Ireland, as the case may be; and

        (ii) the court officer in any magistrates' court in which the order has been registered in accordance with section 2(5) of the 1958 Act.

Enforcement

32.11.—(1) The Part 18 procedure applies to an application for or with respect to the enforcement of a Scottish order or a Northern Irish order registered in the High Court.

(2) The application may be made without notice to the person liable to make payments under the order.

Inspection of register and copies of order

32.12. Any person—

    (a) who is entitled to receive, or liable to make, payments under a maintenance order made by the High Court, the Court of Session or the Court of Judicature of Northern Ireland; or

    (b) with the permission of the court,

may—

        (i) inspect the register; or

        (ii) request a copy of any order registered in the High Court under Part 2 of the 1950 Act and any statutory declaration, affidavit$^{(GL)}$ or statement filed with the order.

CHAPTER 3

REGISTRATION OF MAINTENANCE ORDERS UNDER THE 1958 ACT

Interpretation

32.13. In this Chapter "the register" means the register kept for the purposes of the 1958 Act.

Registration of orders – prescribed period

32.14. The prescribed period for the purpose of section 2(2) of the 1958 Act is 14 days.

(Section 2(2) sets out the period during which an order, which is to be registered in a magistrates' court, may not be enforced)

Application for registration of a maintenance order in a magistrates' court

32.15.—(1) An application under section 2(1) of the 1958 Act may be made by sending to the court officer at the court which made the order—

    (a) a certified copy of the maintenance order; and

(b) two copies of the application.

(2) When, on the grant of an application, the court officer sends the certified copy of the maintenance order to the magistrates' court in accordance with section 2(2), the court officer must—

(a) note on the order that the application for registration has been granted; and

(b) send to the magistrates' court a copy of the application for registration of the order.

(3) On receiving notice that the magistrates' court has registered the order, the court officer must enter particulars of the registration in the court records.

Registration in a magistrates' court of an order registered in the High Court

32.16.—(1) This rule applies where—

(a) a maintenance order is registered in the High Court in accordance with section 17(4) of the 1950 Act; and

(b) the court officer receives notice that the magistrates' court has registered the order in accordance with section 2(5) of the 1958 Act.

(2) The court officer must enter particulars of the registration in Part II of the register.

Registration in the High Court of a magistrates' court order

32.17.—(1) This rule applies where a court officer receives a certified copy of a magistrates' court order for registration in accordance with section 2(4)(c) of the 1958 Act.

(2) The court officer must register the order in the High Court by—

(a) filing the copy of the order; and

(b) entering particulars in—

(i) the register; or

(ii) if the order is received in a district registry, the cause book or cause card.

(3) The court officer must notify the magistrates' court that the order has been registered.

Registration in the High Court of an order registered in a magistrates' court

32.18.—(1) This rule applies where—

(a) an order has been registered in the magistrates' court in accordance with section 17(4) of the 1950 Act; and

(b) a sheriff court in Scotland or a magistrates' court in Northern Ireland has—

(i) made an order for the registration of that order in the High Court; and

(ii) sent a certified copy of the maintenance order to the court officer of the High Court in accordance with section 2(4)(c) of the 1958 Act.

(2) The court officer must register the order in the High Court by—

(a) filing the copy of the order; and

(b) entering particulars in the register.

(3) The court officer must notify—

(a) the court which made the order; and

(b) the magistrates' court in which the order was registered in accordance with section 17(4) of the 1950 Act,

that the order has been registered in the High Court.

Variation or discharge of an order registered in a magistrates' court

32.19.—(1) This rule applies where a maintenance order is registered in a magistrates' court under Part 1 of the 1958 Act.

(2) If the court which made the order makes an order varying or discharging that order the court officer must send a certified copy of the order of variation or discharge to the magistrates' court.

(3) If the court officer receives from the magistrates' court a certified copy of an order varying the maintenance order the court officer must—

    (a) file the copy of the order; and

    (b) enter the particulars of the variation in the place where the details required by rule 32.15(3) were entered.

Variation or discharge of an order registered in the High Court

32.20.—(1) This rule applies where a maintenance order is registered in the High Court under Part 1 of the 1958 Act.

(2) If the court officer receives from the magistrates' court a certified copy of an order varying or discharging the maintenance order the court officer must—

    (a) file the copy of the order;

    (b) enter the particulars of the variation or discharge in—

        (i) the register; or

        (ii) if the order is received in a district registry, the cause book or cause card; and

    (c) send notice of the variation or discharge to the court officer of a county court—

        (i) who has notified the court officer of enforcement proceedings in that court relating to the maintenance order; or

        (ii) to whom a payment is to be made under an attachment of earnings order made by the High Court for the enforcement of the registered order.

Cancellation of registration – orders registered in the High Court

32.21.—(1) This rule applies where an order is registered in the High Court.

(2) A person giving notice under section 5(1) of the 1958 Act must give the notice to the court officer.

(3) The court officer must take the steps mentioned in paragraph (4) if—

    (a) notice is given under section 5 of the 1958 Act; and

    (b) the court officer is satisfied, by a witness statement by the person entitled to receive payments under the order that no enforcement proceedings in relation to the order, that were started before the giving of the notice, remain in force.

(4) The court officer must, if satisfied as mentioned in paragraph (3)—

    (a) cancel the registration by entering particulars of the notice in the register or cause book (or cause card) as the case may be; and

    (b) send notice of the cancellation to—

        (i) the court which made the order; and

        (ii) where applicable, to the magistrates' court in which the order was registered in accordance with section 17(4) of the 1950 Act.

(5) Where the cancellation results from a notice given under section 5(1) of the 1958 Act, the court officer must state that fact in the notice of cancellation sent in accordance with paragraph (4)(b).

(6) If notice is received from a magistrates' court that the registration in that court under the 1958 Act of an order registered in the High Court in accordance with section 17(4) of the 1950 Act has been cancelled, the court officer must note the cancellation in Part II of the register.

Cancellation of registration – orders registered in a magistrates' court

32.22.—(1) Where the court gives notice under section 5(2) of the 1958 Act, the court officer must endorse the notice on the certified copy of the order of variation or discharge sent to the magistrates' court in accordance with rule 32.19(2).

(2) Where notice is received from a magistrates' court that registration of an order made by the High Court or a county court under Part 1 of the 1958 Act has been cancelled, the court officer must enter particulars of the cancellation in the place where the details required by rule 32.15(3) were entered.

CHAPTER 4

REGISTRATION AND ENFORCEMENT OF CUSTODY ORDERS UNDER THE 1986 ACT

Interpretation

32.23. In this Chapter—

"appropriate court" means, in relation to—

(a) Scotland, the Court of Session;

(b) Northern Ireland, the High Court in Northern Ireland; and

(c) a specified dependent territory, the corresponding court in that territory;

"appropriate officer" means, in relation to—

(a) the Court of Session, the Deputy Principal Clerk of Session;

(b) the High Court in Northern Ireland, the Master (Care and Protection) of that court; and

(c) the appropriate court in a specified dependent territory, the corresponding officer of that court;

"Part 1 order" means an order under Part 1 of the 1986 Act;

"the register" means the register kept for the purposes of Part 1 of the 1986 Act; and

"specified dependent territory" means a dependent territory specified in column 1 of Schedule 1 to the Family Law Act 1986 (Specified Dependent Territories) Order 1991(**a**).

Prescribed officer and functions of the court

32.24.—(1) The prescribed officer for the purposes of sections 27(4) and 28(1) of the 1986 Act(**b**) is the family proceedings department manager of the principal registry.

(2) The function of the court under sections 27(3) and 28(1) of the 1986 Act(**c**) shall be performed by a court officer.

Application for the registration of an order made by the High Court or a county court

32.25.—(1) An application under section 27 of the 1986 Act for the registration of an order made in the High Court or a county court may be made by sending to a court officer at the court which made the order—

(a) a certified copy of the order;

(b) a copy of any order which has varied the terms of the original order;

(**a**) S.I. 1991/1723.

(**b**) Section 27(4) was amended by section 108(5) of and paragraph 62 of Schedule 13 to the Children Act 1989.

(**c**) Section 27(3) was amended by section 108(5) of and paragraph 62 of Schedule 13 to the Children Act 1989.

(c) a statement which—

    (i) contains the name and address of the applicant and the applicant's interest under the order;

    (ii) contains—

        (aa) the name and date of birth of the child in respect of whom the order was made;

        (bb) the whereabouts or suspected whereabouts of the child; and

        (cc) the name of any person with whom the child is alleged to be;

    (iii) contains the name and address of any other person who has an interest under the order and states whether the order has been served on that person;

    (iv) states in which of the jurisdictions of Scotland, Northern Ireland or a specified dependent territory the order is to be registered;

    (v) states that to the best of the applicant's information and belief, the order is in force;

    (vi) states whether, and if so where, the order is already registered;

    (vii) gives details of any order known to the applicant which affects the child and is in force in the jurisdiction in which the order is to be registered;

    (viii) annexes any document relevant to the application; and

    (ix) is verified by a statement of truth; and

(d) a copy of the statement referred to in paragraph (c).

(2) On receipt of the documents referred to in paragraph (1), the court officer will, subject to paragraph (4)—

    (a) keep the original statement and send the other documents to the appropriate officer;

    (b) record in the court records the fact that the documents have been sent to the appropriate officer; and

    (c) file a copy of the documents.

(3) On receipt of a notice that the document has been registered in the appropriate court the court officer will record that fact in the court records.

(4) The court officer will not send the documents to the appropriate officer if it appears to the court officer that—

    (a) the order is no longer in force; or

    (b) the child has reached the age of 16.

(5) Where paragraph (4) applies—

    (a) the court officer must, within 14 days of the decision, notify the applicant of the decision of the court officer in paragraph (4) and the reasons for it; and

    (b) the applicant may apply to a judge, but not a district judge, in private for an order that the documents be sent to the appropriate court.

Registration of orders made in Scotland, Northern Ireland or a specified dependent territory

32.26.—(1) This rule applies where the prescribed officer receives, for registration, a certified copy of an order made in Scotland, Northern Ireland or a specified dependent territory.

(2) The prescribed officer will—

    (a) enter in the register—

        (i) the name and address of the applicant and the applicant's interest under the order;

        (ii) the name and date of birth of the child and the date the child will attain the age of 16;

        (iii) the whereabouts or suspected whereabouts of the child; and

        (iv) the terms of the order, its date and the court which made it;

(b) file the certified copy and accompanying documents; and

(c) notify—

    (i) the court which sent the order; and

    (ii) the applicant,

that the order has been registered.

Revocation and variation of an order made in the High Court or a county court

32.27.—(1) Where a Part 1 order, registered in an appropriate court, is varied or revoked, the court officer of the court making the order of variation or revocation will—

(a) send a certified copy of the order of variation or revocation to—

    (i) the appropriate officer; and

    (ii) if a different court, the court which made the Part 1 order;

(b) record in the court records the fact that a copy of the order has been sent; and

(c) file a copy of the order.

(2) On receipt of notice from the appropriate court that its register has been amended, this fact will be recorded by the court officer of—

(a) the court which made the order of variation or revocation; and

(b) if different, the court which made the Part 1 order.

Registration of varied, revoked or recalled orders made in Scotland, Northern Ireland or a specified dependent territory

32.28.—(1) This rule applies where the prescribed officer receives a certified copy of an order made in Scotland, Northern Ireland or a specified dependent territory which varies, revokes or recalls a registered Part 1 order.

(2) The prescribed officer shall enter particulars of the variation, revocation or recall in the register and give notice of the entry to—

(a) the court which sent the certified copy;

(b) if different, the court which made the Part 1 order;

(c) the applicant for registration; and

(d) if different, the applicant for the variation, revocation of recall of the order.

(3) An application under section 28(2) of the 1986 Act must be made in accordance with the Part 19 procedure.

(4) The applicant for the Part 1 order, if not the applicant under section 28(2) of the 1986 Act, must be made a defendant to the application.

(5) Where the court cancels a registration under section 28(2) of the 1986 Act, the court officer will amend the register and give notice of the amendment to the court which made the Part 1 order.

Interim directions

32.29. The following persons will be made parties to an application for interim directions under section 29 of the 1986 Act(**a**)—

(a) the parties to the proceedings for enforcement; and

(b) if not a party to those proceedings, the applicant for the Part 1 order.

(**a**)   Section 29 was amended by section 108(5) of and paragraphs 62(1) and (2)(a) of Schedule 13 to the Children Act 1989 and by section 15(1) of and paragraphs 2 and 4 of Schedule 2 to the Children and Adoption Act 2006.

Staying and dismissal of enforcement proceedings

32.30.—(1) The following persons will be made parties to an application under section 30(1) or 31(1) of the 1986 Act—

    (a) the parties to the proceedings for enforcement which are sought to be stayed^(GL); and

    (b) if not a party to those proceedings, the applicant for the Part 1 order.

(2) Where the court makes an order under section 30(2) or (3) or section 31(3) of the 1986 Act, the court officer will amend the register and give notice of the amendment to—

    (a) the court which made the Part 1 order; and

    (b) the applicants for—

        (i) registration;

      (ii) enforcement; and

     (iii) stay^(GL)or dismissal of the enforcement proceedings.

Particulars of other proceedings

32.31. A party to proceedings for or relating to a Part 1 order who knows of other proceedings which relate to the child concerned (including proceedings out of the jurisdiction and concluded proceedings) must file a witness statement which—

    (a) states in which jurisdiction and court the other proceedings were begun;

    (b) states the nature and current state of the proceedings and the relief claimed or granted;

    (c) sets out the names of the parties to the proceedings and their relationship to the child;

    (d) if applicable and if known, states the reasons why relief claimed in the proceedings for or relating to the Part 1 order was not claimed in the other proceedings; and

    (e) is verified by a statement of truth.

Inspection of register

32.32. The following persons may inspect any entry in the register relating to a Part 1 order and may request copies of the order any document relating to it—

    (a) the applicant for registration of the Part 1 order;

    (b) a person who, to the satisfaction of a district judge, has an interest under the Part 1 order; and

    (c) a person who obtains the permission of a district judge.

PART 33

ENFORCEMENT

CHAPTER 1

GENERAL RULES

Application

33.1.—(1) The rules in this Part apply to an application made in the High Court and a county court to enforce an order made in family proceedings.

(2) Part 50 of, and Schedules 1 and 2 to, the CPR apply, as far as they are relevant and with necessary modification (including the modifications referred to in rule 33.7), to an application made in the High Court and a county court to enforce an order made in family proceedings.

SECTION 1

Enforcement of orders for the payment of money

Application of the Civil Procedure Rules

33.2. Part 70 of the CPR applies to proceedings under this Section as if—

(a) in rule 70.1, in paragraph (2)(d), "but does not include a judgment or order for the payment of money into court" is omitted; and

(b) rule 70.5 is omitted.

How to apply

33.3.—(1) Except where a rule or practice direction otherwise requires, an application for an order to enforce an order for the payment of money must be made in a notice of application accompanied by a statement which must—

(a) state the amount due under the order, showing how that amount is arrived at; and

(b) be verified by a statement of truth.

(2) The notice of application may either—

(a) apply for an order specifying the method of enforcement; or

(b) apply for an order for such method of enforcement as the court may consider appropriate.

(3) If an application is made under paragraph (2)(b), an order to attend court will be issued and rule 71.2 (6) and (7) of the CPR will apply as if the application had been made under that rule.

Transfer of orders

33.4.—(1) This rule applies to an application for the transfer—

(a) to the High Court of an order made in a designated county court; and

(b) to a designated county court of an order made in the High Court.

(2) The application must be—

(a) made without notice; and

(b) accompanied by a statement which complies with rule 33.3(1).

(3) The transfer will have effect upon the filing of the application.

(4) Where an order is transferred from a designated county court to the High Court—

(a) it will have the same force and effect; and

(b) the same proceedings may be taken on it,

as if it were an order of the High Court.

(5) This rule does not apply to the transfer of orders for periodical payments or for the recovery of arrears of periodical payments.

SECTION 2

Committal and injunction

General rule - committal hearings to be in public

33.5.—(1) The general rule is that proceedings in the High Court for an order of committal will be heard in public.

(2) An order of committal may be heard in private where this is permitted by rule 6 of Order 52 of the RSC (cases in which a court may sit in private).

Proceedings in the principal registry treated as pending in a designated county court

33.6.—(1) This rule applies where an order for the warrant of committal of any person to prison has been made or issued in proceedings which are—

(a) in the principal registry; and

(b) treated as pending in a designated county court or a county court.

(2) The person subject to the order will, wherever located, be treated for the purposes of section 122 of the County Courts Act 1984(**a**) as being out of the jurisdiction of the principal registry.

(3) Where—

(a) a committal is for failure to comply with the terms of an injunction^(GL); or

(b) an order or warrant for the arrest or committal of any person is made or issued in proceedings under Part 4 of the 1996 Act in the principal registry which are treated as pending in a county court,

the order or warrant may, if the court so directs, be executed by the tipstaff within any county court.

Specific modifications of the CCR

33.7.—(1) CCR Order 29, rule 1 (committal for breach of an order or undertaking) applies to—

(a) section 8 orders, except those referred to in paragraph (2)(a); and

(b) orders under the following sections of the 1989 Act(**b**)—

(i) section 14A (special guardianship orders);

(ii) section 14B(2)(b) (granting of permission on making a special guardianship order to remove a child from the United Kingdom);

(iii) section 14C(3)(b) (granting of permission to remove from the United Kingdom a child who is subject to a special guardianship order); and

(iv) section 14D (variation or discharge of a special guardianship order),

as if paragraph (3) of that rule were substituted by the following paragraph—

"(3) In the case of a section 8 order (within the meaning of section 8(2) of the Children Act 1989) or an order under section 14A, 14B(2)(b), 14C(3)(b) or 14D of the Children Act 1989 enforceable by committal order under paragraph (1), the judge or the district judge may, on the application of the person entitled to enforce the order, direct that the proper officer issue a copy of the order, endorsed with or incorporating a notice as to the consequences of disobedience, for service in accordance with paragraph (2), and no copy of the order shall be issued with any such notice endorsed or incorporated save in accordance with such a direction.".

(2) CCR Order 29, rule 1 applies to—

(a) contact orders to which a notice has been attached under section 11I of the 1989 Act(**c**) or under section 8(2) of the Children and Adoption Act 2006;

(b) orders under section 11J of the 1989 Act (enforcement orders); and

(c) orders under paragraph 9 of Schedule A1 to the 1989 Act (orders following breach of enforcement orders),

as if paragraph (3) were omitted.

(**a**) Section 122 was amended by section 10 of and paragraph 2(2) of Schedule 2 to the Civil Procedure Act 1997 and sections 74(1) and (3) of the Courts and Legal Services Act 1990.
(**b**) Sections 14A, 14B, 14C and 14D were inserted by section 115(1) of the Adoption and Children Act 2002 and amended by section 38 of the Children and Young Persons Act 2008.
(**c**) Section 11I was inserted by section 3 of the Children and Adoption Act 2006.

Section 118 County Courts Act 1984 and the tipstaff

33.8. For the purposes of section 118 of the County Courts Act 1984(**a**) in its application to the hearing of family proceedings at the Royal Courts of Justice or the principal registry, the tipstaff is deemed to be an officer of the court.

CHAPTER 2

COMMITTAL BY WAY OF JUDGMENT SUMMONS

Interpretation

33.9. In this Chapter, unless the context requires otherwise—

"order" means an order made in family proceedings for the payment of money;

"judgment creditor" means a person entitled to enforce an order under section 5 of the Debtors Act 1869;

"debtor" means a person liable under an order; and

"judgment summons" means a summons under section 5 of the Debtor's Act 1869(**b**) requiring a debtor to attend court.

Application

33.10.—(1) An application for the issue of a judgment summons may be made—

   (a) in the case of an order of the High Court—

      (i) where the order was made in matrimonial proceedings, to the principal registry, a district registry or a divorce county court, whichever in the opinion of the judgment creditor is most convenient;

      (ii) where the order was made in civil partnership proceedings, to the principal registry, a district registry or a civil partnership proceedings county court, whichever in the opinion of the judgment creditor is the most convenient; and

      (iii) in any other case, to the principal registry, a district registry or a designated county court, whichever in the opinion of the judgment creditor is most convenient;

   (b) in the case of an order of a divorce county court, to whichever divorce county court is in the opinion of the judgment creditor most convenient; and

   (c) in the case of an order of a civil partnership proceedings county court, to whichever civil partnership proceedings county court is in the opinion of the judgment creditor most convenient,

having regard (in any case) to the place where the debtor resides or carries on business and irrespective of the court or registry in which the order was made.

(2) An application must be accompanied by a statement which—

   (a) complies with rule 33.3(1);

   (b) contains all the evidence on which the judgment creditor intends to rely; and

   (c) has exhibited to it a copy of the order.

(**a**) Section 118 was amended by the Statute Law (Repeals) Act 1986 and sections 17(3) and 101(1) of and paragraph 6 of Schedule 12 to the Criminal Justice Act 1991 and section 74(6) of the Courts and Legal Services Act 1990.

(**b**) 1869 c.62. Section 5 was amended by articles 2 and 3 of the Civil Procedure (Modification of Enactments) Order 2002 (S.I. 2002/439) and the Statute Law (Repeals) Act 2004 (c.14).

Judgment summons

33.11.—(1) If the debtor is in default under an order of committal made on a previous judgment summons in respect of the same order, a judgment summons must not be issued without the court's permission.

(2) A judgment summons must—

(a) be accompanied by the statement referred to in rule 33.10(2) and

(b) be served on the debtor personally not less than 14 days before the hearing.

(3) A debtor served with the judgment summons under paragraph (2)(b) must be paid or offered a sum reasonably sufficient to cover the expenses of travelling to and from the court at which the debtor is summoned to appear.

Successive judgment summonses

33.12. Subject to rule 33.11(1), successive judgment summonses may be issued even if the debtor has ceased to reside or carry on business at the address stated in the application for the issue of a judgment summons since the issue of the original judgment summons.

Requirement for personal service

33.13. In proceedings for committal by way of judgment summons, the following documents must be served personally on the debtor—

(a) where the court has summonsed the debtor to attend and the debtor has failed to do so, the notice of the date and time fixed for the adjourned hearing; and

(b) copies of the judgment summons and the documents mentioned in rule 33.10(2).

Committal on application for judgment summons

33.14.—(1) No person may be committed on an application for a judgment summons unless—

(a) where the proceedings are in the High Court, the debtor has failed to attend both the hearing that the debtor was summonsed to attend and the adjourned hearing;

(b) where the proceedings are in a county court, an order is made under section 110(2) of the County Courts Act 1984(**a**); or

(c) the judgment creditor proves that the debtor—

(i) has, or has had, since the date of the order the means to pay the sum in respect of which the debtor has made default; and

(ii) has refused or neglected, or refuses or neglects, to pay that sum.

(2) The debtor may not be compelled to give evidence.

Orders for the benefit of different persons

33.15. Where an applicant has obtained one or more orders in the same application but for the benefit of different persons—

(a) where the judgment creditor is a child, the applicant may apply for the issue of a judgment summons in respect of those orders on behalf of the judgment creditor without seeking permission to act as the child's litigation friend; and

(b) only one judgment summons need be issued in respect of those orders.

(**a**)   Section 110(2) was amended by articles 2 and 8 of the Civil Procedure (Modification of Enactments) Order 2002.

Hearing of judgment summons

33.16.—(1) On the hearing of the judgment summons the court may—

    (a) where the order is for lump sum provision or costs; or

    (b) where the order is an order for maintenance pending suit, an order for maintenance pending outcome of proceedings or an order for other periodical payments and it appears to the court that the order would have been varied or suspended if the debtor had made an application for that purpose,

make a new order for payment of the amount due under the original order, together with the costs of the judgment summons, either at a specified time or by instalments.

(2) If the court makes an order of committal, it may direct its execution to be suspended on terms that the debtor pays to the judgment creditor—

    (a) the amount due;

    (b) the costs of the judgment summons; and

    (c) any sums accruing due under the original order,

either at a specified time or by instalments.

(3) All payments under a new order or an order of committal must be made to the judgment creditor unless the court directs otherwise.

(4) Where an order of committal is suspended on such terms as are mentioned in paragraph (2)—

    (a) all payments made under the suspended order will be deemed to be made—

        (i) first, in or towards the discharge of any sums from time to time accruing due under the original order; and

        (ii) secondly, in or towards the discharge of a debt in respect of which the judgment summons was issued and the costs of the summons; and

    (b) the suspended order must not be executed until the judgment creditor has filed a statement of default on the part of the debtor.

Special provisions as to judgment summonses in the High Court

33.17.—(1) The court may summons witnesses to give evidence to prove the means of the debtor and may issue a witness summons for that purpose.

(2) Where the debtor appears at the hearing, the court may direct that the travelling expenses paid to the debtor be allowed as expenses of a witness.

(3) Where the debtor appears at the hearing and no order of committal is made, the court may allow the debtor's proper costs including compensation for any loss of earnings.

(4) When the court makes—

    (a) a new order; or

    (b) an order of committal,

a court officer must send notice of the order to the debtor and, if the original order was made in another court, to that court.

(5) An order of committal must be directed—

    (a) where the order is to be executed by the tipstaff, to the tipstaff; or

    (b) where the order is to be executed by a deputy tipstaff, to the county court within the district of which the debtor is to be found.

Special provisions as to judgment summonses in designated county courts

33.18.—(1) Rules 1, 2, 3(2), 5, 7(3) and 9(2) of Order 28 of the CCR (which deal with the issue of a judgment summons in a county court and the subsequent procedure) do not apply to judgment summons issued in a designated county court.

(2) Rule 9(1) of Order 28 of the CCR (notification of order on judgment of High Court) applies to such a summons as if for the words "the High Court" there were substituted the words—

(a) "any other court" where they first appear; and

(b) "that other court" where they next appear.

(3) Rule 7(1) and (2) of Order 28 of the CCR (suspension of a committal order) apply to such a summons subject to rule 33.16(2) and (3).

CHAPTER 3

ATTACHMENT OF EARNINGS

Proceedings in the Principal Registry

33.19. The Attachment of Earnings Act 1971(**a**) and Order 27 of the CCR (attachment of earnings) apply to the enforcement of an order made in family proceedings in the principal registry which are treated as pending in a designated county court as if they were an order made by such a court.

CHAPTER 4

WARRANT OF EXECUTION

Applications to vary existing orders

33.20. Where an application is pending for a variation of—

(a) a financial order;

(b) an order under section 27 of the 1973 Act; or

(c) an order under Part 9 of Schedule 5 to the 2004 Act,

no warrant of execution may be issued to enforce payment of any sum due under those orders, except with the permission of the district judge.

Section 103 County Courts Act 1984

33.21. Where a warrant of execution has been issued to enforce an order made in family proceedings pending in the principal registry which are treated as pending in a designated county court, the goods and chattels against which the warrant has been issued must, wherever they are located, be treated for the purposes of section 103 of the County Courts Act 1984(**b**) as being out of the jurisdiction of the principal registry.

CHAPTER 5

COURT'S POWER TO APPOINT A RECEIVER

Application of the CPR

33.22. Part 69 of the CPR applies to proceedings under this Part.

CHAPTER 6

ORDERS TO OBTAIN INFORMATION FROM JUDGMENT DEBTORS

Application of the CPR

33.23. Part 71 of the CPR applies to proceedings under this Part.

(**a**) 1971 c.32.
(**b**) Section 103 has been amended by section 74(1) and (3) and 125(2) and paragraph 16 of Schedule 17 to the Courts and Legal Services Act 1990 and section 10 of and paragraph 2(2) of Schedule 2 to the Civil Procedure Act 1997.

CHAPTER 7

THIRD PARTY DEBT ORDERS

Application of the CPR

33.24.—(1) Part 72 of the CPR applies to proceedings under this Part with the following modifications.

(2) In rule 72.4—

    (a) in paragraph (1), for "a judge" there is substituted "the court"; and

    (b) in paragraph (2), for "judge" there is substituted "court".

(3) In rule 72.7, in paragraph (2)(a), after "the Royal Courts of Justice" insert ", or the principal registry".

(4) Rule 72.10 is omitted.

CHAPTER 8

CHARGING ORDER, STOP ORDER, STOP NOTICE

Application of the CPR

33.25.—(1) Part 73 of the CPR applies to proceedings under this Part with the following modifications.

(2) In rule 73.1, paragraph (2), sub-paragraphs (b) and (c) are omitted.

(3) For rule 73.2, there is substituted "This Section applies to an application by a judgment creditor for a charging order under section 1 of the 1979 Act(**a**).".

(4) In rule 73.3, paragraph (2), sub-paragraphs (b) and (c) are omitted.

(5) In rule 73.4—

    (a) in paragraph (1), for "a judge" there is substituted "the court,"; and

    (b) in paragraph (2), for "judge" there is substituted "court".

(6) In rule 73.9, in the parenthesis after paragraph (1)—

    (a) "and regulation 51.4 of the 1992 Regulations" is omitted;

    (b) for "provides" there is substituted "provide", and

    (c) ", or (where the 1992 Regulations apply) of the authority," is omitted.

(7) In rule 73.10—

    (a) in paragraph (1), for "a claim" there is substituted "an application";

    (b) in paragraph (2) and the parenthesis following it, for "A claim" each time it appears there is substituted "An application";

    (c) in paragraph (3), for "claimant" there is substituted "applicant";

    (d) in paragraph (4), for "claim form" there is substituted "application"; and

    (e) in paragraph (5), for "claimant's" there is substituted "applicant's".

(8) In rule 73.11, "funds in court or" is omitted.

(9) In rule 73.12—

    (a) paragraph (1)(a) is omitted;

    (b) in paragraph (1)(b) "other than securities held in court" is omitted;

(**a**) 1979 c. 53. Section 1 was amended by sections 34 and 37 of and paragraphs 2, 3 and 6 of Schedule 3 to the Administration of Justice Act 1982 (c.53) and section 148(1) of and paragraph 71 of Schedule 2 to the County Courts Act 1984. Subsections (6) to (8) of that section were inserted by section 93(1) and (2) of the Tribunals, Courts and Enforcement Act 2007 (c.15).

(c) in paragraph (2), in sub-paragraph (b), for "claim form" there is substituted "application notice"; and

(d) in paragraph (3)—

(i) "or claim form" is omitted; and

(ii) for sub-paragraph (b) there is substituted "the person specified in rule 73.5(1)(d)".

(10) Rule 73.13 is omitted.

(11) In rule 73.14, in paragraph (1), "other than securities held in court" is omitted.

(12) In rule 73.16—

(a) in paragraph (a) for "; and" there is substituted "."; and

(b) paragraph (b) is omitted.

PART 34

RECIPROCAL ENFORCEMENT OF MAINTENANCE ORDERS

Scope and interpretation of this Part

34.1.—(1) This Part contains rules about the reciprocal enforcement of maintenance orders.

(2) In this Part—

"the 1920 Act" means the Maintenance Orders (Facilities for Enforcement) Act 1920(**a**);

"the 1972 Act" means the Maintenance Orders (Reciprocal Enforcement) Act 1972;

"the 1982 Act" means the Civil Jurisdiction and Judgments Act 1982;

"the 1988 Convention" means the Convention on jurisdiction and the enforcement of judgments in civil and commercial matters done at Lugano on 16th September 1988;

"the Judgments Regulation" means Council Regulation (EC) No. 44/2001 of 22nd December 2000 on jurisdiction and the recognition and enforcement of judgments in civil and commercial matters; and

"the Lugano Convention" means the Convention on jurisdiction and the recognition and enforcement of judgments in civil and commercial matters, between the European Community and the Republic of Iceland, the Kingdom of Norway, the Swiss Confederation and the Kingdom of Denmark signed on behalf of the European Community on 30th October 2007.

(3) Chapter 1 of this Part relates to the enforcement of maintenance orders in accordance with the 1920 Act.

(4) Chapter 2 of this Part relates to the enforcement of maintenance orders in accordance with Part 1 of the 1972 Act.

(5) Chapter 3 of this Part relates to the enforcement of maintenance orders in accordance with—

(a) the 1982 Act;

(b) the Judgments Regulation; and

(c) the Lugano Convention.

Meaning of prescribed officer in a magistrates' court

34.2.—(1) For the purposes of the 1920 Act, the prescribed officer in relation to a magistrates' court is the designated officer for that court.

(**a**) 1920 c.33.

(2) For the purposes of Part 1 of the 1972 Act and section 5(2) of the 1982 Act, the prescribed officer in relation to a magistrates' court is the justices' clerk for the local justice area in which the court is situated.

Registration of maintenance orders in magistrates' courts in England and Wales

34.3. Where a magistrates' court is required by any of the enactments referred to in rule 34.1(2) to register a foreign order the court officer must—

(a) enter and sign a memorandum of the order in the register kept in accordance with rules made under section 144 of the Magistrates' Courts Act 1980; and

(b) state on the memorandum the statutory provision under which the order is registered.

CHAPTER 1

ENFORCEMENT OF MAINTENANCE ORDERS UNDER THE MAINTENANCE ORDERS (FACILITIES FOR ENFORCEMENT) ACT 1920

Interpretation

34.4.—(1) In this Chapter—

"payer", in relation to a maintenance order, means the person liable to make the payments for which the order provides; and

"reciprocating country" means a country or territory to which the 1920 Act extends.

(2) In this Chapter, an expression defined in the 1920 Act has the meaning given to it in that Act.

Confirmation of provisional orders made in a reciprocating country

34.5.—(1) This rule applies where, in accordance with section 4(1) of the 1920 Act(**a**), the court officer receives a provisional maintenance order.

(2) The court must fix the date, time and place for a hearing.

(3) The court officer must register the order in accordance with rule 34.3.

(4) The court officer must serve on the payer—

(a) certified copies of the provisional order and accompanying documents; and

(b) a notice—

(i) specifying the time and date fixed for the hearing; and

(ii) stating that the payer may attend to show cause why the order should not be confirmed.

(5) The court officer must inform—

(a) the court which made the provisional order; and

(b) the Lord Chancellor,

whether the court confirms, with or without modification, or decides not to confirm, the order.

Payment of sums due under registered orders

34.6. Where an order made by a reciprocating country is registered in a magistrates' court, the court must order payments due to be made to the court officer.

(Practice Direction 34A contains further provisions relating to the payment of sums due under registered orders.)

(**a**) Section 4(1) was amended by article 4(1) and (2) of the Transfer of Functions (Magistrates' Courts and Family Law) Order 1992 (S.I.1992/709) and section 1(1) of and paragraph 2(2) of Schedule 1 to the Maintenance Orders (Reciprocal Enforcement) Act 1992 (c.56).

Enforcement of sums due under registered orders

34.7.—(1) This rule applies to—

    (a) an order made in a reciprocating country which is registered in a magistrates' court; and

    (b) a provisional order made in a reciprocating country which has been confirmed by a magistrates' court.

(2) The court officer must—

    (a) collect the monies due under the order in the same way as for a magistrates' court maintenance order; and

    (b) send the monies collected to—

        (i) the court in the reciprocating country which made the order; or

        (ii) such other person or authority as that court or the Lord Chancellor may from time to time direct.

(3) The court officer may take proceedings in that officer's own name for enforcing payment of monies due under the order.

Prescribed notice for the taking of further evidence

34.8.—(1) This rule applies where a court in a reciprocating country has sent a provisional order to a magistrates' court for the purpose of taking further evidence.

(2) The court officer must send a notice to the person who applied for the provisional order specifying—

    (a) the further evidence required; and

    (b) the time and place fixed for taking the evidence.

Transmission of maintenance orders made in a reciprocating country to the High Court

34.9. A maintenance order to be sent by the Lord Chancellor to the High Court in accordance with section 1(1) of the 1920 Act(**a**) will be—

    (a) sent to the senior district judge who will register it in the register kept for the purpose of the 1920 Act; and

    (b) filed in the principal registry.

Transmission of maintenance orders made in the High Court to a reciprocating country

34.10.—(1) This rule applies to maintenance orders made in the High Court.

(2) An application for a maintenance order to be sent to a reciprocating country under section 2 of the 1920 Act(**b**) must be made in accordance with this rule.

(3) The application must be made to a district judge in the principal registry unless paragraph (4) applies.

(4) If the order was made in the course of proceedings in a district registry, the application may be made to a district judge in that district registry.

(5) The application must be—

    (a) accompanied by a certified copy of the order; and

    (b) supported by a record of the sworn written evidence.

(6) The written evidence must give—

(**a**) Section 1(1) was amended by article 4(1) and (2) of the Transfer of Functions (Magistrates' Courts and Family Law) Order 1992.

(**b**) Section 2 was amended by article 4(1) and (2) of the Transfer of Functions (Magistrates' Courts and Family Law) Order 1992.

(a) the applicant's reason for believing that the payer resides in the reciprocating country;

(b) such information as the applicant has as to the whereabouts of the payer; and

(c) such other information as may be set out in Practice Direction 34A.

Inspection of the register in the High Court

34.11.—(1) A person may inspect the register and request copies of a registered order and any document filed with it if the district judge is satisfied that that person is entitled to, or liable to make, payments under a maintenance order made in—

(a) the High Court; or

(b) a court in a reciprocating country.

(2) The right to inspect the register referred to in paragraph (1) may be exercised by—

(a) a solicitor acting on behalf of the person entitled to, or liable to make, the payments referred to in that paragraph; or

(b) with the permission of the district judge, any other person.

CHAPTER 2

ENFORCEMENT OF MAINTENANCE ORDERS UNDER PART 1 OF THE 1972 ACT

Interpretation

34.12.—(1) In this Chapter—

(a) "reciprocating country" means a country to which Part 1 of the 1972 Act extends; and

(b) 'relevant court in the reciprocating country' means, as the case may be—

    (i) the court which made the order which has been sent to England and Wales for confirmation;

    (ii) the court which made the order which has been registered in a court in England and Wales;

    (iii) the court to which an order made in England and Wales has been sent for registration; or

    (iv) the court to which a provisional order made in England and Wales has been sent for confirmation.

(2) In this Chapter, an expression defined in the 1972 Act has the meaning given to it in that Act.

(3) In this Chapter, "Hague Convention Countries" means the countries listed in Schedule 1 to the Reciprocal Enforcement of Maintenance Orders (Hague Convention Countries) Order 1973.

Scope

34.13.—(1) Section 1 of this Chapter contains rules relating to the reciprocal enforcement of maintenance orders under Part 1 of the 1972 Act.

(2) Section 2 of this Chapter modifies the rules contained in Section 1 of this Chapter in their application to—

(a) the Republic of Ireland;

(b) the Hague Convention Countries; and

(c) the United States of America.

(Practice Direction 34A sets out in full the rules for the Republic of Ireland, the Hague Convention Countries and the United States of America as modified by Section 2 of this Chapter.)

Reciprocal enforcement of maintenance orders under Part 1 of the 1972 Act

Application for transmission of maintenance order to reciprocating country

34.14. An application for a maintenance order to be sent to a reciprocating country under section 2 of the 1972 Act must be made in accordance with Practice Direction 34A.

Certification of evidence given on provisional orders

34.15. A document setting out or summarising evidence is authenticated by a court in England and Wales by a certificate signed, as the case may be, by—

(a) one of the justices; or

(b) the District Judge (Magistrates' Courts),

before whom that evidence was given.

(Section 3(5)(b), 5(4) and 9(5) of the 1972 Act require a document to be authenticated by the court.)

Confirmation of a provisional order made in a reciprocating country

34.16.—(1) This rule applies to proceedings for the confirmation of a provisional order made in a reciprocating country.

(2) Paragraph (3) applies on receipt by the court of—

(a) a certified copy of the order; and

(b) the documents required by the 1972 Act to accompany the order.

(3) On receipt of the documents referred to in paragraph (2)—

(a) the court must fix the date, time and place for a hearing or a directions appointment; and

(b) the court officer must send to the payer notice of the date, time and place fixed together with a copy of the order and accompanying documents.

(4) The date fixed for the hearing must be not less than 21 days beginning with the date on which the court officer sent the documents to the payer in accordance with paragraph (2).

(5) The court officer will send to the relevant court in the reciprocating country a certified copy of any order confirming or refusing to confirm the provisional order.

(6) This rule does not apply to the confirmation of a provisional order made in a reciprocating country varying a maintenance order to which sections 5(5) or 9(6) of the 1972 Act applies.

(Section 5(5) and 7 of the 1972 Act provide for proceedings for the confirmation of a provisional order.)

(Provision in respect of confirmation of a provisional order varying a maintenance order under the 1972 Act is in rules made under section 144 of the Magistrates' Courts Act 1980).

(Rule 34.22 provides for the transmission of documents to a court in a reciprocating country.)

Consideration of revocation of a provisional order made by a magistrates' court

34.17.—(1) This rule applies where—

(a) a magistrates' court has made a provisional order by virtue of section 3 of the 1972 Act;

(b) before the order is confirmed, evidence is taken by the court or received by it as set out in section 5(9) of the 1972 Act; and

(c) on consideration of the evidence the court considers that the order ought not to have been made.

(Section 5(9) of the 1972 Act provides that a magistrates' court may revoke a provisional order made by it, before the order has been confirmed in a reciprocating country, if it receives new evidence.)

(2) The court officer must serve on the person who applied for the provisional order ("the applicant") a notice which must—

(a) set out the evidence taken or received by the court;

(b) inform the applicant that the court considers that the order ought not to have been made; and

(c) inform the applicant that the applicant may—

(i) make representations in relation to that evidence either orally or in writing; and

(ii) adduce further evidence.

(3) If an applicant wishes to adduce further evidence—

(a) the applicant must notify the court officer at the court which made the order;

(b) the court will fix a date for the hearing of the evidence; and

(c) the court officer will notify the applicant in writing of the date fixed.

Notification of variation or revocation of a maintenance order by the High Court or a county court

34.18.—(1) This rule applies where—

(a) a maintenance order has been sent to a reciprocating country in pursuance of section 2 of the 1972 Act; and

(b) the court makes an order, not being a provisional order, varying or revoking that order.

(2) The court officer must send a certified copy of the order of variation or revocation to the relevant court in the reciprocating country.

(Rule 34.22 provides for the transmission of documents to a court in a reciprocating country.)

Notification of confirmation or revocation of a maintenance order by a magistrates' court

34.19.—(1) This rule applies where a magistrates' court makes an order—

(a) not being a provisional order, revoking a maintenance order to which section 5 of the 1972 Act(**a**) applies;

(b) under section 9 of the 1972 Act, revoking a registered order; or

(c) under section 7(2) of the 1972 Act(**b**), confirming an order to which section 7 of that Act applies.

(2) The court officer must send written notice of the making, revocation or confirmation of the order, as appropriate, to the relevant court in the reciprocating country.

(3) This rule does not apply to a provisional order varying a maintenance order to which sections 5 or 9 of the 1972 Act apply.

(Section 5 of the 1972 Act applies to a provisional order made by a magistrates' court in accordance with section 3 of that Act which has been confirmed by a court in a reciprocating country.)

(**a**) Section 5 was amended by section 1 (2) of and paragraph 7 of Schedule 1 to the Maintenance Orders (Reciprocal Enforcement) Act 1992 and article 185(1) of and paragraph 67 of Schedule 9 to the Children (Northern Ireland) Order 1995 (S.I. 1995/755) and section 54(a) and (b) of the Domestic Proceedings and Magistrates' Courts Act 1978.

(**b**) Section 7(2) was amended by section 1(2) of and paragraphs 8(2) to (5) of Schedule 1 to the Maintenance Orders (Reciprocal Enforcement) Act 1992.

(Provision in respect of notification of variation of a maintenance order by a magistrates' court under the 1972 Act is made in rules made under section 144 of the Magistrates' Courts Act 1980.)

(Rule 34.22 provides for the transmission of documents to a court in a reciprocating country.)

Taking of evidence for court in reciprocating country

34.20.—(1) This rule applies where a request is made by or on behalf of a court in a reciprocating country for the taking of evidence for the purpose of proceedings relating to a maintenance order to which Part 1 of the 1972 Act applies.

(Section 14 of the 1972(**a**) Act makes provision for the taking of evidence needed for the purpose of certain proceedings.)

(2) The High Court has power to take the evidence where—

    (a) the request for evidence relates to a maintenance order made by a superior court in the United Kingdom; and

    (b) the witness resides in England and Wales.

(3) The county court has power to take the evidence where—

    (a) the request for evidence relates to a maintenance order made by a county court; and

    (b) the maintenance order has not been registered in a magistrates' court under the 1958 Act.

(4) The following magistrates' courts have power to take the evidence, that is—

    (a) where the proceedings in the reciprocating country relate to a maintenance order made by a magistrates' court, the court which made the order;

    (b) where the proceedings relate to an order which is registered in a magistrates' court, the court in which the order is registered; and

    (c) a magistrates' court to which the Secretary of State sends the request to take evidence.

(5) A magistrates' court not mentioned in paragraph (4) has power to take the evidence if the magistrates' court which would otherwise have that power consents because the evidence could be taken more conveniently.

(6) The evidence is to be taken in accordance with Part 22.

Request for the taking of evidence by a court in a reciprocating country

34.21.—(1) This rule applies where a request is made by a magistrates' court for the taking of evidence in a reciprocating country in accordance with section 14(5) of the 1972 Act.

(2) The request must be made in writing to the court in the reciprocating country.

(Rule 34.22 provides for the transmission of documents to a court in a reciprocating country.)

Transmission of documents

34.22.—(1) This rule applies to any document, including a notice or request, which is required to be sent to a court in a reciprocating country by—

    (a) Part 1 of the 1972 Act; or

    (b) Section 1 of Chapter 2 of this Part of these rules.

(2) The document must be sent to the Lord Chancellor for transmission to the court in the reciprocating country.

(**a**) Section 14 was amended by article 14(1) of and paragraph 22 of Schedule 5 to the Northern Ireland (Modification of Enactments – No 1) Order 1973 (S.I. 1973/2163) and section 154 of and paragraph 105 of Schedule 7 to the Magistrates' Courts Act 1980 and article 170(2) of and paragraph 21 of Schedule 6 to the Magistrates' Courts (Northern Ireland) Order 1981.

Method of payment under registered orders

34.23.—(1) Where an order is registered in a magistrates' court in accordance with section 6(3) of the 1972 Act, the court must order that the payment of sums due under the order be made—

    (a) to the court officer for the registering court; and

    (b) at such time and place as the court officer directs.

(Section 6(3) of the 1972 Act makes provision for the registration of maintenance orders made in a reciprocating country.)

(2) Where the court orders payments to be made to the court officer, whether in accordance with paragraph (1) or otherwise, the court officer must send the payments—

    (a) by post to either—

        (i) the court which made the order; or

        (ii) such other person or authority as that court, or the Lord Chancellor, directs; or

    (b) if the court which made the order is a country or territory specified in the Practice Direction 34A—

        (i) to the Crown Agents for Overseas Governments and Administrations for transmission to the person to whom they are due; or

        (ii) as the Lord Chancellor directs.

(Practice Direction 34A contains further provisions relating to the payment of sums due under registered orders.)

Enforcement of payments under registered orders

34.24.—(1) This rule applies where a court has ordered periodical payments under a registered maintenance order to be made to the court officer.

(2) The court officer must take reasonable steps to notify the payee of the means of enforcement available.

(3) Paragraph (4) applies where periodical payments due under a registered order are in arrears.

(4) The court officer, on that officer's own initiative—

    (a) may; or

    (b) if the sums due are more than 4 weeks in arrears, must,

proceed in that officer's own name for the recovery of the sums due unless of the view that it is unreasonable to do so.

Notification of registration and cancellation

34.25.—(1) The court officer must send written notice to the Lord Chancellor of the due registration of orders registered in accordance with section 6(3), 7(5), or 10(4) of the 1972 Act.

(2) The court officer must, when registering an order in accordance with section 6(3), 7(5), 9(10), 10(4) or (5) or 23(3) of the 1972 Act(**a**), send written notice to the payer stating—

    (a) that the order has been registered;

    (b) that payments under the order should be made to the court officer; and

    (c) the hours during which and the place at which the payments should be made.

(3) The court officer must, when cancelling the registration of an order in accordance with section 10(1) of the 1972 Act, send written notice of the cancellation to the payer.

(**a**) Section 23(3) was amended by section 90(1) of and paragraphs 71 and 75(1) and (2) of Schedule 13 to the Access to Justice Act 1999.

SECTION 2

Modification of rules in Section 1 of this Chapter

SUB-SECTION 1

Republic of Ireland

Application of Section 1 of this Chapter to the Republic of Ireland

34.26.—(1) In relation to the Republic of Ireland, Section 1 of this Chapter has effect as modified by this rule.

(2) A reference in this rule and in any rule which has effect in relation to the Republic of Ireland by virtue of this rule to—

(a) the 1972 Act is a reference to the 1972 Act as modified by Schedule 2 to the Reciprocal Enforcement of Maintenance Orders (Republic of Ireland) Order 1993(**a**); and

(b) a section under the 1972 Act is a reference to the section so numbered in the 1972 Act as so modified.

(3) A reference to a reciprocating country in rule 34.12(1) and Section 1 of this Chapter is a reference to the Republic of Ireland.

(4) In the words in brackets at the end of rule 34.15 (certification of evidence given on provisional orders), for the sections mentioned substitute "section 3(5)(b) or 5(3)".

(5) Rules 34.16 (confirmation of provisional orders) and 34.21 (request for the taking of evidence by a court in a reciprocating country) do not apply.

(6) For rule 34.17 (consideration of revocation of a provisional order made by a magistrates' court) substitute—

"Consideration of confirmation of a provisional order made by a magistrates' court

34.17.—(1) This rule applies where—

(a) a magistrates' court has made a provisional order by virtue of section 3 of the 1972 Act;

(b) the payer has made representations or adduced evidence to the court; and

(c) the court has fixed a date for the hearing at which it will consider confirmation of the order.

(2) The court officer must serve on the applicant for the provisional order—

(a) a copy of the representations or evidence; and

(b) written notice of the date fixed for the hearing.".

(7) For rules 34.18 and 34.19 (notification of variation or revocation) substitute—

"Notification of variation or revocation of a maintenance order by the High Court

34.18. Where the High Court makes an order varying or revoking an order to which section 5 of the 1972 Act applies the court officer must send—

(a) a certified copy of the order of variation or revocation; and

(b) a statement as to the service on the payer of the documents mentioned in section 5(3) of the 1972 Act,

to the court in the Republic of Ireland.

(Rule 34.22 provides for the transmission of documents to a court in a reciprocating country.)

(**a**)   S.I. 1993/594.

Notification of revocation of a maintenance order by a magistrates' court

34.19. Where a magistrates' court makes an order revoking an order to which section 5 of the 1972 Act applies, the court officer must send written notice of the making of the order to the Lord Chancellor.

(Section 5 of the 1972 Act applies to a maintenance order sent to the Republic of Ireland in accordance with section 2 of that Act and a provisional order made by a magistrates' court in accordance with section 3 of that Act which has been confirmed by such a court.)

(Provision in respect of notification of variation of a maintenance order by magistrates' court under the 1972 Act is made in rules made under section 144 of the Magistrates' Courts Act 1980.)".

(8) For rule 34.23(2) (method of payment under registered orders), substitute—

"(2) Where the court orders payment to be made to the court officer, the court officer must send the payments by post—

    (a) to the payee under the order; or

    (b) where a public authority has been authorised by the payee to receive the payments, to that public authority.".

(9) For rule 34.24 (enforcement of payments under registered orders), substitute—

"Enforcement of payments under registered orders

34.24.—(1) This rule applies where periodical payments under a registered order are in arrears.

(2) The court officer must, on the written request of the payee, proceed in that officer's own name for the recovery of the sums due unless of the view that it is unreasonable to do so.

(3) If the sums due are more than 4 weeks in arrears the court officer must give the payee notice in writing of that fact stating the particulars of the arrears.".

(10) For rule 34.25 (notification of registration and cancellation) substitute—

"Notification of registration and cancellation

34.25. The court officer must send written notice to—

    (a) the Lord Chancellor, on the due registration of an order under section 6(3) or 10(4) of the 1972 Act; and

    (b) to the payer under the order, on—

        (i) the registration of an order under section 10(4) of the 1972 Act; or

        (ii) the cancellation of the registration of an order under section 10(1) of that Act. ".

(11) After rule 34.25 insert—

"Other notices under section 6 of the 1972 Act(a)

34.25A.—(1) A notice required under section 6(6) or (10) of the 1972 Act must be in the form referred to in a practice direction.

(2) Where a magistrates' court sets aside the registration of an order following an appeal under section 6(7) of the 1972 Act, the court officer must send written notice of the court's decision to the payee.

(a)   Section 6 was amended by section 37 of and Schedule 11 to the Civil Jurisdiction and Judgments Act 1982 (c.27).

(Section 6(6) of the 1972 Act provides for notice of registration in a United Kingdom court of a maintenance order made in the Republic of Ireland, and section 6(10) of that Act for notice that a maintenance order made in the Republic of Ireland has not been registered in a United Kingdom court.)"

SUB-SECTION 2

Hague Convention Countries

Application of Section 1 of this Chapter to the Hague Convention Countries

34.27.—(1) In relation to the Hague Convention Countries, Section 1 of this Chapter has effect as modified by this rule.

(2) A reference in this rule, and in any rule which has effect in relation to the Hague Convention Countries by virtue of this rule to—

(a) the 1972 Act is a reference to the 1972 Act as modified by Schedule 2 to the Reciprocal Enforcement of Maintenance Orders (Hague Convention Countries) Order 1993(**a**); and

(b) a section under the 1972 Act is a reference to the section so numbered in the 1972 Act as so modified.

(3) A reference to a reciprocating country in rule 34.12(1) and Section 1 of this Chapter is a reference to a Hague Convention Country.

(4) Rules 34.15 (certification of evidence given on provisional orders), 34.16 (confirmation of provisional orders), 34.19 (notification of confirmation or revocation of a maintenance order by a magistrates' court) and 34.21 (request for the taking of evidence by a court in a reciprocating country) do not apply.

(5) For rule 34.17 (consideration of revocation of a provisional order made by a magistrates' court) substitute—

"Consideration of revocation of a maintenance order made by a magistrates' court

34.17.—(1) This rule applies where—

(a) an application has been made to a magistrates' court by a payee for the revocation of an order to which section 5 of the 1972 Act applies; and

(b) the payer resides in a Hague Convention Country.

(2) The court officer must serve on the payee, by post, a copy of any representations or evidence adduced by or on behalf of the payer.

(Provision relating to consideration of variation of a maintenance order made by a magistrates' court to which section 5 of the 1972 Act applies is made in rules made under section 144 of the Magistrates' Courts Act 1980.)".

(6) For rule 34.18 (notification of variation or revocation of a maintenance order by the High Court or county court) substitute—

"Notification of variation or revocation of a maintenance order by the High Court or a county court

34.18.—(1) This rule applies if the High Court or a county court makes an order varying or revoking a maintenance order to which section 5 of the 1972 Act applies.

(2) If the time for appealing has expired without an appeal having been entered, the court officer will send to the Lord Chancellor—

(a) the documents required by section 5(8) of the 1972 Act; and

---

(**a**) S.I. 1993/593.

(b) a certificate signed by the district judge stating that the order of variation or revocation is enforceable and no longer subject to the ordinary forms of review.

(3) A party who enters an appeal against the order of variation or revocation must, at the same time, give written notice to the court officer.".

(7) For rule 34.23(2) (method of payment under registered orders) substitute—

"(2) Where the court orders payment to be made to the court officer, the court officer must send the payments by post to the payee under the order.".

(8) For rule 34.25 (notification of registration and cancellation) substitute—

"Notification of registration and cancellation

34.25. The court officer must send written notice to—

(a) the Lord Chancellor, on the due registration of an order under section 10(4) of the 1972 Act; and

(b) the payer under the order, on—

(i) the registration of an order under section 10(4) of the 1972 Act; or

(ii) the cancellation of the registration of an order under section 10(1) of the 1972 Act.".

(9) After rule 34.25 insert—

"General provisions as to notices

34.25A.—(1) A notice to a payer of the registration of an order in a magistrates' court in accordance with section 6(3) of the 1972 Act must be in the form referred to in a practice direction.

(Section 6(8) of the 1972 Act requires notice of registration to be given to the payer.)

(2) If the court sets aside the registration of a maintenance order following an appeal under section 6(9) of the 1972 Act, the court officer must send written notice of the decision to the Lord Chancellor.

(3) A notice to a payee that the court officer has refused to register an order must be in the form referred to in a practice direction.

(Section 6(11) of the 1972 Act requires notice of refusal of registration to be given to the payee.)

(4) Where, under any provision of Part 1 of the 1972 Act, a court officer serves a notice on a payer who resides in a Hague Convention Country, the court officer must send to the Lord Chancellor a certificate of service.".

SUB-SECTION 3

United States of America

Application of Section 1 of this Chapter to the United States of America

34.28.—(1) In relation to the United States of America, Section 1 of this Chapter has effect as modified by this rule.

(2) A reference in this rule and in any rule which has effect in relation to the United States of America by virtue of this rule to—

(a) the 1972 Act is a reference to the 1972 Act as modified by Schedule 1 to the Reciprocal Enforcement of Maintenance Orders (United States of America) Order 2007(**a**); and

---

(**a**) S.I. 2007/2006.

(b) a section under the 1972 Act is a reference to the section so numbered in the 1972 Act as so modified.

(3) A reference to a reciprocating country in rule 34.12(1) and Section 1 of this Chapter is a reference to the United States of America.

(4) Rules 34.15 (certification of evidence given on provisional orders), 34.16 (confirmation of provisional orders), 34.19 (notification of confirmation or revocation of a maintenance order made by a magistrates' court) and 34.21 (request for the taking of evidence in a reciprocating country) do not apply.

(5) For rule 34.17 (consideration of revocation of a provisional order made by a magistrates' court) substitute—

"Consideration of revocation of a maintenance order made by a magistrates' court

34.17.—(1) This rule applies where—

    (a) an application has been made to a magistrates' court by a payee for the revocation of an order to which section 5 of the 1972 Act applies; and

    (b) the payer resides in the United States of America.

(2) The court officer must serve on the payee by post a copy of any representations or evidence adduced by or on behalf of the payer.

(Provision relating to consideration of variation of a maintenance order made by a magistrates' court to which section 5 of the 1972 Act applies is made in rules made under section 144 of the Magistrates' Courts Act 1980.)".

(6) For rule 34.18 (notification of variation or revocation), substitute—

"Notification of variation or revocation

34.18. If the High Court or a county court makes an order varying or revoking a maintenance order to which section 5 of the 1972 Act applies, the court officer will send to the Lord Chancellor the documents required by section 5(7) of that Act.".

(7) For rule 34.23(2)(method of payment under registered orders) substitute—

"(2) Where the court orders payment to be made to the court officer, the court officer must send the payments by post to the payee under the order.".

(8) For rule 34.25 (notification of registration and cancellation) substitute—

"Notification of registration and cancellation

34.25. The court officer must send written notice to—

    (a) the Lord Chancellor, on the due registration of an order under section 10(4) of the 1972 Act; or

    (b) the payer under the order, on—

        (i) the registration of an order under section 10(4) of the 1972 Act; or

        (ii) the cancellation of the registration of an order under section 10(1) of that Act.
"

CHAPTER 3

ENFORCEMENT OF MAINTENANCE ORDERS UNDER THE CIVIL JURISDICTION AND JUDGMENTS ACT 1982, THE JUDGMENTS REGULATION AND THE LUGANO CONVENTION

SECTION 1

Registration and Enforcement in a Magistrates' Court of Maintenance Orders made in a Contracting State to the 1968 Convention, a Contracting State to the 1988 Convention, a Regulation State or a State bound by the Lugano Convention

Interpretation

34.29. In this Section—

    (a) an expression defined in the 1982 Act has the meaning given to it in that Act; and

    (b) "the 1958 Act" means the Maintenance Orders Act 1958.

Registration of maintenance orders

34.30.—(1) In this rule, "assets to which the 1958 Act applies" means assets against which, after registration in the High Court, the maintenance order could be enforced under Part 1 of the 1958 Act.

(2) This rule applies where the court officer for a magistrates' court receives—

    (a) an application under Article 31 of the 1968 Convention for the enforcement of a maintenance order made in a Contracting State other than the United Kingdom;

    (b) an application under Article 31 of the 1988 Convention for the enforcement of a maintenance order made in a State bound by the 1988 Convention other than a Member State of the European Union;

    (c) an application under Article 38 of the Judgments Regulation for the enforcement of a maintenance order made in a Regulation State other than the United Kingdom; or

    (d) an application under Article 38 of the Lugano Convention for the enforcement of a maintenance order made in a State bound by the Lugano Convention other than a Member State of the European Union.

(3) The court officer must—

    (a) take such steps as appear appropriate for ascertaining whether the payer resides within the local justice area for which the court acts; and

    (b) consider any available information as to the nature and location of the payer's assets.

(4) If the court officer is satisfied that the payer—

    (a) does not reside within the local justice area for which the court acts; and

    (b) does not have assets to which the 1958 Act applies,

the court officer must refuse the application and return the application to the Lord Chancellor stating the information the court officer has as to the whereabouts of the payer and the nature and location of the payer's assets.

(5) If the court officer is satisfied that the payer—

    (a) does not reside within the local justice area for which the court acts; but

    (b) has assets to which the 1958 Act applies,

then either—

        (i) the court officer must register the order; or

        (ii) if the court officer believes that the payer is residing within the local justice area in which another magistrates' court acts, the court officer may refuse the application and return the documents to the Lord Chancellor with the information referred to in paragraph (4) above.

(6) Except where paragraphs (4) or (5) apply, the court officer must register the order unless—

(a) in the case of an application under Article 31 of the 1968 Convention, Articles 27 or 28 of that Convention apply; and

(b) in the case of an application under Article 31 of the 1988 Convention, Articles 27 or 28 of that Convention apply.

(7) If the court officer refuses to register an order to which this rule relates the court officer must notify the applicant.

(8) If the court officer registers an order the court officer must send written notice of that fact to—

(a) the Lord Chancellor;

(b) the payer; and

(c) the applicant.

(9) If the court officer considers that it would be appropriate for all or part of a registered order to be enforced in the High Court the court officer must notify the applicant—

(a) that the court officer so considers it appropriate; and

(b) that the applicant may apply under the 1958 Act for the order to be registered in the High Court.

Appeal from a decision relating to registration

34.31.—(1) This rule applies to an appeal under—

(a) Article 36 or Article 40 of the 1968 Convention;

(b) Article 36 or Article 40 of the 1988 Convention;

(c) Article 43 of the Judgments Regulation; or

(d) Article 43 of the Lugano Convention.

(2) The appeal must be to the magistrates' court—

(a) in which the order is registered; or

(b) in which the application for registration has been refused,

as the case may be.

Payment of sums due under a registered order

34.32.—(1) Where an order is registered in accordance with section 5(3) of the 1982 Act or Article 38 of the Judgments Regulation or Article 38 of the Lugano Convention, the court must order that payment of sums due under the order be made—

(a) to the court officer for the registering court; and

(b) at such time and place as the court officer directs.

(2) Where the court orders payments to be made to the court officer, whether in accordance with paragraph (1) or otherwise, the court officer must send the payments by post either—

(a) to the court which made the order; or

(b) to such other person or authority as that court, or the Lord Chancellor, directs.

(Practice Direction 34A contains further provisions relating to the payment of sums due under registered orders.)

Enforcement of payments under registered orders

34.33.—(1) This rule applies where a court has ordered periodical payments under a registered maintenance order to be made to the court officer for a magistrates' court.

(2) The court officer must take reasonable steps to notify the payee of the means of enforcement available.

(3) Paragraph (4) applies where periodical payments due under a registered order are in arrears.

(4) The court officer, on that officer's own initiative—

    (a) may; or

    (b) if the sums due are more than 4 weeks in arrears, must,

proceed in that officer's own name for the recovery of the sums due unless of the view that it is unreasonable to do so.

Variation and revocation of registered orders

34.34.—(1) This rule applies where the court officer for a registering court receives notice that a registered maintenance order has been varied or revoked by a competent court in a Contracting State to the 1968 Convention, a Contracting State to the 1988 Convention (other than a Member State of the European Union), a Regulation State or a State bound by the Lugano Convention, other than a Member State of the European Union.

(2) The court officer for the registering court must—

    (a) register the order of variation or revocation; and

    (b) send notice of the registration by post to the payer and payee under the order.

Transfer of registered order

34.35.—(1) This rule applies where the court officer for the court where an order is registered considers that the payer is residing within the local justice area in England and Wales for which another magistrates' court acts.

(2) Subject to paragraph (4), the court officer must transfer the order to the other court by sending to that court—

    (a) the information and documents relating to the registration;

    (b) a certificate of arrears, if applicable, signed by the court officer;

    (c) a statement giving such information as the court officer possesses as to the whereabouts of the payer and the nature and location of the payer's assets; and

    (d) any other relevant documents which the court officer has relating to the case.

(3) The information and documents referred to in paragraph (2)(a) are those required, as appropriate, under—

    (a) Articles 46 and 47 of the 1968 Convention;

    (b) Articles 46 and 47 of the 1988 Convention;

    (c) Article 53 of the Judgments Regulation; or

    (d) Article 53 of the Lugano Convention.

(4) If an application is pending in the registering court for the registration of the whole or part of the order in the High Court under Part 1 of the 1958 Act, the court officer must not transfer the order, or the part to which the application relates, under paragraph (2).

(5) The court officer must give notice of the transfer of an order to—

    (a) the payee; and

    (b) the Lord Chancellor.

(6) If an order is transferred, the court officer for the court to which it is transferred must register the order.

Cancellation of registered orders

34.36.—(1) Where the court officer for the registering court—

    (a) has no reason to transfer a registered order under rule 34.35; and

(b) considers that the payer under the registered order is not residing within the local justice area for which the court acts and has no assets to which the 1958 Act applies,

the court officer must cancel the registration of the order.

(2) The court officer must—

    (a) give notice of cancellation to the payee; and

    (b) send the information and documents relating to the registration and the other documents referred to in rule 34.35(2) to the Lord Chancellor.

SECTION 2

Reciprocal enforcement in a Contracting State or Regulation State of Orders of a court in England and Wales

Application in a magistrates' court for a maintenance order, or revocation of a maintenance order, to which the 1982 Act, the Judgments Regulations or the Lugano Convention applies

34.37.—(1) This rule applies where a person applies to a magistrates' court for a maintenance order, or for the revocation of a maintenance order, in relation to which the court has jurisdiction by virtue of the 1982 Act, the Judgments Regulation or the Lugano Convention, and the respondent is outside the United Kingdom.

(2) On the making of the application the court officer shall send the following documents to the Lord Chancellor—

    (a) notice of the proceedings, including a statement of the grounds of the application;

    (b) a statement signed by the court officer giving such information as he has regarding the whereabouts of, and information to assist in identifying, the respondent; and

    (c) where available, a photograph of the respondent.

(3) In considering whether or not to make a maintenance order pursuant to an application to which paragraph (1) applies, where the respondent does not appear and is not represented at the hearing the court shall take into account any written representations made and any evidence given by the respondent under these rules.

(Part 27 makes provision relating to attendance at hearings and directions appointments.)

(Part 9 makes provision for applications relating to financial remedies including those under Schedule 1 to the 1989 Act, Part 1 of the 1978 Act, and Schedule 6 to the 2004 Act.)

(Rules made under section 144 of the Magistrates' Courts Act 1980 make provision for applications to vary maintenance orders made in magistrates' courts.)

Admissibility of Documents

34.38.—(1) This rule applies to a document, referred to in paragraph (2) and authenticated in accordance with paragraph (3), which comprises, records or summarises evidence given in, or information relating to, proceedings in a court in another part of the UK , another Contracting State to the 1968 Convention or the 1988 Convention, Regulation State or State bound by the Lugano Convention, and any reference in this rule to "the court", without more, is a reference to that court.

(2) The documents referred to at paragraph (1) are documents which purport to—

    (a) set out or summarise evidence given in the court;

    (b) have been received in evidence the court;

    (c) set out or summarise evidence taken in the court for the purpose of proceedings in a court in England and Wales to which the 1982 Act applies; or

    (d) record information relating to payments made under an order of the court.

(3) A document to which paragraph (1) applies shall, in any proceedings in a magistrates' court in England and Wales relating to a maintenance order to which the 1982 Act applies, be admissible as

evidence of any fact stated in it to the same extent as oral evidence of that fact is admissible in those proceedings.

(4) A document to which paragraph (1) applies shall be deemed to be authenticated—

  (a) in relation to the documents listed at paragraph 2(a) or (c), if the document purports to be—

    (i) certified by the judge or official before whom the evidence was given or taken; or

    (ii) the original document recording or summarising the evidence, or a true copy of that document;

  (b) in relation to a document listed at paragraph (2)(b), if the document purports to be certified by a judge or official of the court to be, or to be a true copy of, the document received in evidence; and

  (c) in relation to the document listed at paragraph (2)(d), if the document purports to be certified by a judge or official of the court as a true record of the payments made under the order.

(5) It shall not be necessary in any proceedings in which evidence is to be received under this rule to prove the signature or official position of the person appearing to have given the certificate referred to in paragraph (4).

(6) Nothing in this rule shall prejudice the admission in evidence of any document which is admissible in evidence apart from this rule.

(7) Any request by a magistrates' court in England and Wales for the taking or providing of evidence by a court in another part of the United Kingdom or in another Contracting State to the 1968 Convention or the 1988 Convention or the Lugano Convention (other than a Member State of the European Union) for the purpose of proceedings to which the 1982 Act applies shall be communicated in writing to the court in question.

(Chapter 2 of Part 24 makes provision for taking of evidence by a court in another Regulation State).

Enforcement of orders of a magistrates' court

  34.39.—(1) This rule applies to applications to a magistrates' court under—

  (a) section 12 of the 1982 Act(**a**);

  (b) article 54 of the Judgments Regulation; or

  (c) article 54 of the Lugano Convention.

(2) A person who wishes to enforce in a Contracting State to the 1968 Convention, a Contracting State to the 1988 Convention (other than a Member State of the European Union), a Regulation State or a State bound by the Lugano Convention (other than a Member State of the European Union) a maintenance order obtained in a magistrates' court must apply for a certified copy of the order.

(3) An application under this rule must be made in writing to the court officer and must specify—

  (a) the names of the parties to the proceedings;

  (b) the date, or approximate date, of the proceedings in which the maintenance order was made and the nature of those proceedings;

  (c) the Contracting State or Regulation State in which the application for recognition or enforcement has been made or is to be made; and

  (d) the postal address of the applicant.

(4) The court officer must, on receipt of the application, send a copy of the order to the applicant certified in accordance with a practice direction.

(**a**) Section 12 was amended by section 3 of and paragraph 7 of Schedule 2 to the Civil Jurisdiction and Judgments Act 1991 (c.12).

(5) Paragraph (6) applies where—

    (a)   a maintenance order is registered in a magistrates' court in England and Wales; and

    (b)   a person wishes to obtain a certificate giving details of any payments made or arrears accrued under the order while it has been registered, for the purposes of an application made or to be made in connection with that order in—

        (i)   another Contracting State to the 1968 Convention;

        (ii)   another Contracting State to the 1988 Convention (other than a Member State of the European Union);

        (iii)   another Regulation State;

        (iv)   another State bound by the Lugano Convention (other than a Member State of the European Union); or

        (v)   another part of the United Kingdom.

(6) The person wishing to obtain the certificate referred to in paragraph (5) may make a written application to the court officer for the registering court.

(7) On receipt of an application under paragraph (6) the court officer must send to the applicant a certificate giving the information requested.

(Rule 74.12 (application for certified copy of a judgment) and 74.13 (evidence in support) of the CPR apply in relation to the application for a certified copy of a judgment obtained in the High Court or a county court.)

PART 35

MEDIATION DIRECTIVE

Scope and Interpretation

35.1.—(1) This Part applies to mediated cross-border disputes that are subject to Directive 2008/52/EC of the European Parliament and of the Council of 21 May 2008 on certain aspects of mediation in civil and commercial matters ("the Mediation Directive").

(2) In this Part—

"cross-border dispute" has the meaning given by article 2 of the Mediation Directive;

"mediation" has the meaning given by article 3(a) of the Mediation Directive;

"mediation administrator" means a person involved in the administration of the mediation process;

"mediation evidence" means evidence regarding information arising out of or in connection with a mediation process;

"mediator" has the meaning given by article 3(b) of the Mediation Directive; and

"relevant dispute" means a cross-border dispute that is subject to the Mediation Directive.

Relevant disputes: applications for consent orders in respect of financial remedies

35.2.—(1) This rule applies in relation to proceedings for a financial remedy where the applicant, with the explicit consent of the respondent, wishes to make an application that the content of a written agreement resulting from mediation of a relevant dispute be made enforceable by being made the subject of a consent order.

(2) The court will not include in a consent order any matter which is contrary to the law of England and Wales or which is not enforceable under that law.

(3) The applicant must file two copies of a draft of the order in the terms sought.

(4) Subject to paragraph (5), the application must be supported by evidence of the explicit consent of the respondent.

(5) Where the respondent has written to the court consenting to the making of the order sought, the respondent is deemed to have given explicit consent to the order and paragraph (4) does not apply.

(6) Paragraphs (1)(b) and (2) to (6) of rule 9.26 apply to an application to which this rule applies.

Mediation evidence: disclosure and inspection

35.3.—(1) Where a party to proceedings seeks disclosure or inspection of mediation evidence that is in the control of a mediator or mediation administrator, that party must first obtain the court's permission to seek the disclosure or inspection, by an application made in accordance with Part 18.

(2) The mediator or mediation administrator who has control of the mediation evidence must be named as a respondent to the application and must be served with a copy of the application notice.

(3) Evidence in support of the application must include evidence that—

    (a) all parties to the mediation agree to the disclosure or inspection of the mediation evidence;

    (b) disclosure or inspection of the mediation evidence is necessary for overriding considerations of public policy, in accordance with article 7(1)(a) of the Mediation Directive; or

    (c) the disclosure of the content of an agreement resulting from mediation is necessary to implement or enforce that agreement.

(4) Where this rule applies, Parts 21 to 24 apply to the extent they are consistent with this rule.

Mediation evidence: witnesses and depositions

35.4.—(1) This rule applies where a party wishes to obtain mediation evidence from a mediator or mediation administrator by–

    (a) a witness summons;

    (b) cross-examination with permission of the court under rule 22.8 or 23.4;

    (c) an order under rule 24.7 (evidence by deposition);

    (d) an order under rule 24.9 (enforcing attendance of witness);

    (e) an order under rule 24.10(4) (deponent's evidence to be given orally); or

    (f) an order under rule 24.12 (order for the issue of a letter of request).

(2) When applying for a witness summons, permission under rule 22.8 or 23.4 or order under rule 24.7, 24.9, 24.10(4) or 24.12, the party must provide the court with evidence that-

    (a) all parties to the mediation agree to the obtaining of the mediation evidence;

    (b) obtaining the mediation evidence is necessary for overriding considerations of public policy in accordance with article 7(1)(a) of the Mediation Directive; or

    (c) the disclosure of the content of an agreement resulting from mediation is necessary to implement or enforce that agreement.

(3) When considering a request for a witness summons, permission under rule 22.8 or 23.4 or order under rule 24.7, 24.9, 24.10(4) or 24.12, the court may invite any person, whether or not a party, to make representations.

(4) Where this rule applies, Parts 21 to 24 apply to the extent they are consistent with this rule.

PART 36

TRANSITIONAL ARRANGEMENTS AND PILOT SCHEMES

Transitional provisions

36.1. Practice Direction 36A shall make provision for the extent to which these rules shall apply to proceedings started before the day on which they come into force.

Pilot schemes

36.2. Practice directions may modify or disapply any provision of these rules—

    (a) for specified periods; and

    (b) in relation to proceedings in specified courts,

during the operation of pilot schemes for assessing the use of new practices and procedures in connection with proceedings.

GLOSSARY

Scope

This glossary is a guide to the meaning of certain legal expressions as used in these rules, but it does not give the expressions any meaning in the rules which they do not otherwise have in the law.

Expression	*Meaning*
Affidavit	A written, sworn, statement of evidence.
Cross-examination	Questioning of a witness by a party other than the party who called the witness.
Evidence in chief	The evidence given by a witness for the party who called him.
Injunction	A court order prohibiting a person from doing something or requiring a person to do something.
Official copy	A copy of an official document, supplied and marked as such by the office which issued the original.
Pre-action protocol	Statements of best practice about pre-action conduct which have been approved by the President of the Family Division and which are annexed to a Practice Direction.
Privilege	The right of a party to refuse to disclose a document or produce a document or to refuse to answer questions on the ground of some special interest recognised by law.
Seal	A seal is a mark which the court puts on document to indicate that the document has been issued by the court.
Service	Steps required by rules of court to bring documents used in court proceedings to a person's attention.
Set aside	Cancelling a judgment or order or a step taken by a party in the proceedings.

Stay	A stay imposes a halt on proceedings, apart from the taking of any steps allowed by the rules or the terms of the stay. Proceedings can be continued if a stay is lifted.
Strike out	Striking out means the court ordering written material to be deleted so that it may no longer be relied upon.
Without prejudice	Negotiations with a view to settlement are usually conducted "without prejudice" which means that the circumstances in which the content of those negotiations may be revealed to the court are very restricted.

Nicholas Wall, P
Philip Waller
Duncan Adam
John Baker
Timothy Becker
Paul Carr
Martyn Cook
Bruce Edgington
Angela Finnerty
Mike Hinchliffe
Ruth Lindley-Glover
David Salter
John Wilson

I allow these Rules
Signed by authority of the Lord Chancellor
13th December 2010

J Djanogly
Parliamentary Under Secretary of State
Ministry of Justice

EXPLANATORY NOTE

(This note is not part of the Order)

These rules provide a new code of procedure for family proceedings in the High Court, county courts and magistrates' courts, and replace existing rules of court for family proceedings. The principal rules being replaced are the Family Proceedings Rules 1991, the Family Procedure (Adoption) Rules 2005 and, in so far as they relate to family proceedings, the Family Proceedings Courts (Children Act 1989) Rules 1991, the Family Proceedings (Matrimonial Proceedings etc) Rules 1991, and rules relating to the reciprocal enforcement of maintenance orders, in particular the Magistrates' Courts (Reciprocal Enforcement of Maintenance Orders) Rules 1974.

The rules adopt a similar structure to the Civil Procedure Rules 1998. The introductory Parts provide for fundamental matters of general application and various preliminary matters, opening in Part 1 with the overriding objective of the rules, to enable the court to deal with cases justly, having regard to any welfare issues involved. Part 2 contains the provisions for interpreting and applying the rules including provision about the delegation of certain functions of a magistrates' court to a single justice. Part 3 contains the court's powers to encourage the use of alternative dispute resolution; Part 4 contains provision for case management powers; Part 5 provides for the forms which are to be used in family proceedings and how family proceedings are started; and Part 6 makes provision for service of documents in family proceedings (including service abroad).

The rules then make provision for procedure for the key types of family proceedings in separate Parts as follows—

— Part 7 (Procedure for applications in matrimonial and civil partnership proceedings);

— Part 8 (Procedure for miscellaneous applications such as applications for a gender recognition certificate, declarations and orders preventing avoidance under section 32L of the Child Support Act 1991(c.48));

— Part 9 (Applications for a financial remedy);

— Part 10 (Applications under Part 4 of the Family Law Act 1996 (c.27) (domestic violence));

— Part 11 (Applications under Part 4A of the Family Law Act 1996 (forced marriage));

— Part 12 (Proceedings relating to children, except parental order proceedings and proceedings for applications in adoption, placement and related proceedings);

— Part 13 (Proceedings under section 54 of the Human Fertilisation and Embryology Act 2008(c.22) (parental orders)); and

— Part 14 (Adoption, placement and related proceedings).

Parts 15 and 16 contain rules relating to representation of protected parties and children respectively, and Part 17 for when statements of truth are required to verify documents. Part 18 relates to the procedure for other applications in proceedings which, for example, will be used for applications for the court's permission to bring proceedings and Part 19 to the alternative procedure for applications which will be used for matters such as proceedings for an order to prevent disclosure of information to an adopted person under section 60(3) of the Adoption and Children Act 2002(c.38).

The remaining Parts of the rules are of general application and contain procedural provisions mirroring, with modifications for family proceedings, the general procedural parts of the Civil Procedure Rules 1998, as follows—

— Part 20 makes provision for applications for interim injunctions;

— Part 21 contains miscellaneous rules about disclosure and inspection of documents;

— Parts 22 to 24 contain rules about evidence;

— Part 25 deals with experts and assessors;

— Part 26 deals with change of solicitor;

— Part 27 relates to hearings and directions appointments and includes provision relating to the giving of reasons in a magistrates' court;

— Part 28 relates to costs across all three levels of court;

— Part 29 contains miscellaneous provisions including provision for protection of personal details in proceedings and provision for Human Rights Act 1998 (c.42) questions being raised in family proceedings;

— Part 30 deals with appeals;

— Parts 31 and 32 deal with registration and enforcement of foreign or Scottish or Northern Irish orders of different sorts, and Part 34 with reciprocal enforcement of maintenance orders;

— Part 33 provides for enforcement generally;

— Part 35 relates to the Mediation Directive; and

— Part 36 contains transitional provisions.

Detailed supplementary provisions supporting many parts of the rules such as the transitional provisions in Part 36 and appeals in Part 30 are, where indicated in the rules, contained in practice directions, which do not form part of the rules.

Printed and published in the UK by The Stationery Office Limited under the authority and superintendence of Carol Tullo, Controller of Her Majesty's Stationery Office and Queen's Printer of Acts of Parliament.